China and Globalization 2.0

Series Editor
Bai Gao
Department of Sociology
Duke University
Chapel Hill, NC, USA

China is now at the forefront of globalization, particularly with the One Belt, One Road policy. What does a Chinese globalization look like, though? This series will explore the distinct legacies and evolutions of China's worldview, even as China exports its development model to countries around the world.

More information about this series at
http://www.palgrave.com/gp/series/15881

Zeqi Qiu

When Friendship Comes First

A Case Study of Chinese Development Aid for Health in Uganda

palgrave
macmillan

Zeqi Qiu
Peking University
Beijing, China

ISSN 2523-7209 ISSN 2523-7217 (electronic)
China and Globalization 2.0
ISBN 978-981-32-9307-6 ISBN 978-981-32-9308-3 (eBook)
https://doi.org/10.1007/978-981-32-9308-3

This book is the result of a co-publication agreement between Social Sciences Academic Press and Palgrave Macmillan based on a translation from the Chinese language edition: 朋友在先: 中国对乌干达卫生发展援助案例研究 © Social Sciences Academic Press, 2017

This Palgrave Macmillan imprint is published by the registered company Springer Nature Singapore Pte Ltd.
The registered company address is: 152 Beach Road, #21-01/04 Gateway East, Singapore 189721, Singapore

Introduction

I believe: If you relate to each other based on power, when the power fades off, so does the relationship. If you relate to each other based on benefits, when the benefits are gone, the relationship is gone. Relationship of this sort is what a man of virtue is strongly against.

Wang Tong, *Chapter of Ritual and Music*, *Analects of Wang Tong*

If you relate to each other based on benefits, when the benefits are gone, the relationship is gone. If you relate to each other based on power, when the power fades off, so does the relationship. Only when you relate to each other with heart, can the relationship last long. The development of international relations depends on heart-to-heart communications.

Xi Jinping, 2014[1]

In the last sixty years, no country has made as big an impact on the political, economic, and social fabric of Africa as China has since the turn of the millennium. It's not the first time China has been there.

Dambisa Moyo, 2009: 153

[1]Xi Jinping drew upon Wang Tong's *Chapter of Ritual and Music, Analects of Wang Tong* on many occasions, including at the enlarged session of the Standing Committee of the CPC Lankao County Committee in Henan Province on March 8, 2014, in the speech entitled "Jointly Create a Beautiful Future of China-ROK Cooperation and Accomplish the Great Cause of Asia's Revitalization and Prosperity" in Seoul National University on July 4, 2014, and in the article entitled "A Lasting True Friend of the People of Pacific Island Countries" on *The Fiji Times* and *Fiji Sun* on November 21, 2014. Slight differences of the quotations arise from different occasions. Here is a quotation from the speech in Seoul National University.

In her book *Dead Aid: Why Aid Is Not Working and How There Is Another Way for Africa* (Moyo 2009), Dambisa Moyo spoke highly of China's influence over Africa and her remarks carried weight. Dambisa Moyo worked as an economist for Goldman Sachs and the World Bank, as well as a consultant for a number of investment companies. Her work footprint has covered over 70 countries and regions around the world. Her remarks have great influence in this field. What's more, this book is a bestseller recommended by *New York Times*, which showcases her observation resonates around the English-speaking world.

Two points in her remarks are of particular significance to our research. First, it's about China's influence over Africa. After the Second World War ended and the colonial system crumbled, Western countries started to offer aid to African countries (including but not limited to former colonies). Great efforts were made over those 60 years. According to the statistics released by OECD Development Assistance Committee (OECD-DAC), the total amount they offered in aid exceeded USD 2 trillion.

In theory, Western countries should have exerted greater influence over Africa than China. When we met with senior officials from Uganda's Ministry of Health, they told us the US had a huge sway over their country. If this is the case, why would Moyo believe after the twenty-first century, China's influence is unparalleled? Has Western foreign aid crumbled? If so, we need to get to the bottom of this: How did it happen? Moyo's words reminded us to take a closer look at China's and the Western world's influence in Africa respectively.

Second, it's what's behind the building up of China's influence over Africa. What Dambisa Moyo hinted is that China's presence in Africa was not established overnight. Being an economist, Dambisa Moyo may be more concerned with "investment and returns." She enumerated the 1860-kilometer-long Tanzania-Zambia Railway which cost China USD 5 million in the 1970s to demonstrate China's long-existing yet overlooked-by-Western-countries presence in Africa. In fact, China's presence in Africa dates back further beyond when the work on Tanzania-Zambia Railway started. It was in the 1960s when Western countries began to aid their former colonies that China started to engage in helping African countries in its power, such as sending medical teams to Africa. What we want to point out here is that the rapid economic growth China has witnessed over the past four decades is not a feat achieved overnight but a result of generations' hard work. China's soaring influence of its aid in Africa doesn't come easily and derives from 60 years' devotion to Africa.

Back then, as far as deep-pocketed Western countries were concerned, China's foreign aid was arguably almost nothing. They failed to comprehend the significance of "a useless move" in the game of Go or the importance of an "acupuncture point" to the overall health. Judging from the current situation, we will find the aid China offered then is similar to making "a useless move" in Go or stimulating "an acupuncture point," which maybe paves the way for China to exercise its influence over Africa in the twenty-first century. To put it another way, China's influence over Africa is related to the long-term aid China has provided in its power to Africa.

What are the characteristics of China's foreign aid? What were those early deployments of aid like? What was the focus of the aid back then? How was it correlated with the current foreign aid which puts people's lives at the center? These are what we are trying to figure out through the research of development aid for health from China to Uganda, or DAHCU for short.

The provision of DAHCU for more than three decades is part of China's long-term engagement with Africa. The scale of aid provided by DAHCU is minimal compared to the overall sum China has offered and the total amount Uganda has received in aid. However, just as an old Chinese saying goes, even a small gift can make a big difference. DAHCU means more than aid. It is a bridge connecting people of both sides. The influence of DAHCU is like the friendship, subtle but significant.

In China's diplomatic wisdom, two real friends have influences over each other and the influences go well beyond the political, economic and social spheres. The case is not what was claimed in literature that China offered aid to Africa for its resources as well as a further expansion of China's products and services into the market in Africa. "A man of virtue values justice and friendship, while a man of meanness only bears benefits in mind," Confucius was quoted as saying (*Virtues, Analects*). China–Africa relations and China–Uganda relations go beyond common interests and attach great importance to the value of justice and friendship, which are the cornerstones of relations, just as Wang Tong said in *Chapter of Ritual and Music, Analects of Wang Tong:* I believe: For relationships based on power, when the power wears off, so does the relationship. If a relationship is based on benefits, when the benefits are gone, the relationship is gone, too. These kinds of relationships are what a man of virtue is strongly against.

In 1964, China initiated the five principles guiding China's relations with the Arab and African countries, also known as the Five Principles of Peaceful Coexistence, and the Eight Principles for Economic Aid and Technical Assistance to Other Countries,[2] both of which reflected the norms of international relations China has learned from its experiences and lessons. In the course of China's history, it had risen to the challenges posed by relations among countries. Over the past 2000 years, China has not only learned its lessons in a hard way but also accumulated a wealth of experience and wisdom.

[2]For the readers' reference and a better understanding, we quote the Five Principles of Peaceful Coexistence and the Eight Principles for Economic Aid and Technical Assistance to Other Countries as follows:

Five Principles of Peaceful Coexistence: (a) China supports the Arab and African peoples in their struggle to oppose imperialism and old and new colonialism and to win and safeguard national independence. (b) It supports the pursuance of a policy of peace, neutrality, and nonalignment by the Governments of Arab and African countries. (c) It supports the desire of the Arab and African peoples to achieve unity and solidarity in the manner of their own choice. (d) It supports the Arab and African countries in their efforts to settle their disputes through peaceful consultations. (e) It holds that the sovereignty of the Arab and African countries should be respected by all other countries and that encroachment and interference from any quarter should be opposed.

Eight Principles for Economic Aid and Technical Assistance to Other Countries: (a) The Chinese Government always bases itself on the principle of equality and mutual benefit in providing aid to other countries. It never regards such aid as a kind of unilateral alms but as something mutual. (b) In providing aid to other countries, the Chinese Government strictly respects the sovereignty of the recipient countries, and never attaches any conditions or asks for any privileges. (c) China provides economic aid in the form of interest-free or low-interest loans and extends the time limit for repayment when necessary so as to lighten the burden of the recipient countries as far as possible. (d) In providing aid to other countries, the purpose of the Chinese Government is not to make the recipient countries dependent on China but to help them embark step by step on the road of self-reliance and independent economic development. (e) The Chinese Government tries its best to help the recipient countries build projects which require less investment while yielding quicker results, so that the recipient governments may increase their income and accumulate capital. (f) The Chinese Government provides the best-quality equipment and material of its own manufacture at international market prices. If the equipment and material provided by the Chinese Government are not up to the agreed specifications and quality, the Chinese Government undertakes to replace them. (g) In providing any technical assistance, the Chinese Government will see to it that the personnel of the recipient country fully master such technique. (h) The experts dispatched by China to help in construction in the recipient countries will have the same standard of living as the experts of the recipient country. The Chinese experts are not allowed to make any special demands or enjoy any special amenities.

On many occasions Chinese President Xi Jinping has reiterated the values of friendship, justice, and shared interests, which are rooted in China's cultural heritage. China has applied its principles for international relations and foreign aid to its development throughout the history. This practice helps us understand why China and Uganda are friends. The friendship matters more than the resources and markets when it comes to China's aid to Uganda.

According to China's diplomatic orthodoxy, not only is [access to] resources and markets the logical outcome of genuine friendship based on mutual respect and trust, it also creates opportunities for mutually beneficial cooperation and joint development.

Reference

Moyo, Dambisa. 2009. *Dead Aid: Why Aid Is Not Working and How There Is Another Way for Africa*. London: Allen Lane.

Contents

List of Tables

CHAPTER 1

Background to This Study: Motivation and Timing

1.1 About China-UK Global Health Support Program-Output

This book focuses on the development aid for health from China to Uganda (DAHCU). The research into DAHCU was inspired by the evaluation of the effectiveness of DAHCU run by the School of Public Health, Peking University within the framework of the China-UK Global Health Support Program-Output2 (GSHP-OP2).

The evaluation of social programs has been our expertise. We have teamed up with experts in public health to work on this project. That said, we do not specialize in international aid research, related practice or international issues. Before taking on this project, we had never been engaged with research of such nature. Despite all the hesitations, we decided to come on board at the invitation of the OP2 research group for the following reasons.

First, after preliminary exploration, we found that DAHCU did not fall into the category of large-scale aid programs. Therefore, adopting regular project evaluation methods employed by international organizations, OECD, the USA, and China for large-scale aid programs doesn't necessarily work the best. Besides, the OP2 research group is in favor of applying evaluation methods used in sociology and anthropology, in which we specialize and have a wealth of experience.

Second, the evaluation of aid for health in Uganda is a multidisciplinary area covering health, international aid, international relations, and

Z. Qiu, *When Friendship Comes First*, China and Globalization 2.0,
https://doi.org/10.1007/978-981-32-9308-3_1

related assessment and research. No discipline alone has the absolute advantage or authority. This means experts from any related discipline are at the same starting line. Evaluation research is a hard capacity that requires long-term training. We have an edge in this regard.

The evaluation of policies or programs is essentially about their goals. That is to use the goals as the evaluation criterion (known as the gold standard). We have compared policies, measures, process or impact of programs[1] with the gold standard to evaluate DAHCU.

Regrettably, difficulty arose from the onset of the research. Through two exploratory in-depth interviews, we learned that two ministries are in charge of DAHCU on the government level. The National Health and Family Planning Commission is responsible for technical support, while the Ministry of Commerce is in charge of aid-related programs, which means in order to get access to basic data of DAHCU, we needed to carry a survey in the Ministry of Commerce.

To press ahead with our project, we pulled some strings. However, we failed to get firsthand basic data. Furthermore, we were accused by officials of collecting intelligence for foreign countries. We were stuck in the obstacles. The only agency that had basic data wouldn't provide data, while those agencies that were ready to help did not have access to first-hand data.

Therefore, we turned to the basic method of gathering data applied in sociology and anthropology, i.e., field research, in the hope that we could get data in Uganda. As planned, the research group traveled twice to Uganda for field research, visiting the medical teams sent by China to Uganda, Jinja Hospital and China-Uganda Friendship Hospital where Chinese medical teams were stationed, the Economic and Commercial Counsellor's Office of the Embassy of the People's Republic of China in the Republic of Uganda, the Ministry of Health in Uganda and other government agencies and interviewing staff working there. We also hired Rehema Bavuma, a doctoral candidate from Makerere University, as an assistant to the research responsible for interviewing staff working in Uganda.

Unfortunately, we failed to get data as expected for reasons as follows. First, though the medical teams from Yunnan province were very supportive of our research, as the conditions were very harsh during their

[1] Process evaluation and impact evaluation are the two most common types of evaluation.

stay in Uganda, the documents and data of each medical team had not been kept systematically. Some documents were lost when they transferred from Jinja hospital to China-Uganda Friendship Hospital in Kampala in 2012, making the unsystematic database worse. Second, the Economic and Commercial Counsellor's Office also supported us in our research, but it did not have systematic data, DAHCU data from non-medical-team sources in particular. Third, agencies of the Ministry of Health of Uganda did not have DAHCU data.

For assessment and research, the absence of the gold standard in itself was a huge impediment, with the lack of data making the situation worse. Without basic data necessary for the setting of the gold standard, we could not carry the research with a regular assessment method. Without supportive data, it was impossible for us to use regular assessment and research models to compare data with the gold standard. This the biggest obstacle we encountered during our assessment of the effectiveness of DAHCU, which was also a big headache for peer who hoped to do research on China's aid to Africa.

1.2 "Aid": Some Preliminary Conceptual Clarifications

As this book touches on international aid, there will be terminology. Given that we do not have a clear picture of how much the readers know about this multidisciplinary area, in order to guarantee the optimal readability, concepts and background knowledge are listed in this section. Readers who have been familiar with the information may skip them.

1.2.1 Aid and Official Development Assistance

Assistance or aid is a concept that has been around for ages. Even based on the available legal evidence, such as the UK's *Colonial Loans Act 1889*, it dates back to over 100 years ago (Zhang and Sun 2014). However, aid in its modern sense has a shorter history, starting from the period after WWII when defeated countries and impoverished ones began to receive aid. As aid of the old days took place between countries, the term of overseas or foreign aid was used, meaning one country offering aid to another.[2]

[2]Aid offered at the time was mainly funds, equipment, technology, etc. such as the aid China provided for the Soviet Union in the 1950s.

Aid was officially intended to propel development in the recipient countries. As driving development may take different forms, in the practice of aid, different kinds of aid have come into existence, such as development aid or aid, technical aid, international aid or overseas aid, and so on.

Around 80–85% of the aid funds before the twenty-first century came from official organizations. Therefore, another term came into use, that is, official development assistance (ODA), which is quite commonly used by member states of OECD-DAC.

Aid programs run by OECD-DAC cover the following sectors: (1) social infrastructure and services, such as education, health, population policies, water and sanitation, etc.; (2) economic infrastructure and services, such as transport and storage, communications, energy generation, distribution and efficiency, banking and financial services, and business and other services; (3) production sectors, including agriculture, industry, trade policy and regulations and trade-related adjustment, tourism, etc.; (4) cross-cutting sectors, such as general environmental protection; (5) commodity aid and general program assistance such as general budget support, developmental food aid and other commodity assistance; (6) humanitarian aid, such as emergency response, reconstruction relief and rehabilitation, disaster prevention and preparedness; and (7) other sectors. The aid can also be classified into social infrastructure, production, and humanitarian aid.

What should be noted is that different categories of aid aforementioned are variations of aid in different contexts. In this book, we have adopted the regular method used in aid and program evaluation, without making distinctions between aid, foreign aid, development aid and ODA. The use of terminology varies according to contexts. However, in essence, all the variations refer to the aid donors offer to recipients.

1.2.2 Development Aid for Health

Development aid for health (DAH) is a health group of aid. In the classification of OECD-DAC, it falls into the category of social infrastructure and services.

DAH can be further classified into general health and basic health, including aid programs targeted at improving healthcare systems, provision of healthcare services, and health level and treating HIV/AIDS, malaria, tuberculosis, and other diseases in recipient countries. We had tried to set the scope of DAH but failed to find literature on further classification of DAH.

In this book, we have identified aid intended to improve health in recipient countries as DAH.

1.2.3 *Effectiveness of Aid and Development*

We need to figure out the origins of concepts with an emphasis on the differences in effectiveness from the perspectives of recipients and donors, respectively. Research methods will touch on the meaning of effectiveness.

Effective aid is a concept developed by OECD-DAC. In 2002, bilateral and multilateral institutions reached a consensus on enhancing the effectiveness of aid and scaling up aid at the first UN Forum on Financing for Development in Monterrey, Mexico. This concept was further enhanced at the first High-level Forum on Aid Effectiveness in 2003. In 2005 at the second High-level Forum on Aid Effectiveness, 61 bilateral and multilateral donors of foreign aid, 56 recipients and 14 civil society organizations made "effective aid" a policy in the cosigned *Paris Declaration on Aid Effectiveness* (hereinafter *Paris Declaration*).

The core of the *Paris Declaration* is to ensure the aid can meet the needs of recipient countries so that the strategies and plans formulated by recipient countries will be implemented with financial support. The aid modalities, therefore, should allow the aid to be integrated into recipient countries' financial budget, lift the restrictions on aid, and strengthen aid coordination to make aid accommodate recipient countries' needs and be effective.

In 2008, at the third High-level Forum on Aid Effectiveness held in Accra, capital of Ghana, the concept of "effective aid" was further developed. In the *Accra Agenda for Action*, the rights of the majority in developing countries were highlighted to guarantee that "effective aid" is targeted, ensures human rights and gender equality, and helps to promote decent work and sustainable development.

Delegates from more than 160 countries and regions attending the fourth High-level Forum on Aid Effectiveness in Busan, South Korea in 2011 endorsed the *Busan Partnership for Effective Development Cooperation* and put forward new international aid modalities such as aid and development that centered on developing countries. This agreement emphasized the ownership of development priorities by developing countries and a focus on development results rather than process. It stressed the need to establish extensive partnerships, enhance transparency and build up the sense of responsibility. It also proposed to strengthen aid for South–South cooperation and multilateral cooperation and enhance the role of development cooperation in promoting aid.

The most important change made in the agreement is shifting the focus of international aid from "aid effectiveness" to "development effectiveness" so that the goal of aid is concerned with the effectiveness of development in recipient countries. It stressed that the modality and purpose of South–South cooperation is different from that of South–North cooperation and the real purpose of aid is to power the development of recipient countries.

The core of this agreement is aligned with the principle of providing aid upheld by China for a long time, that is, aid is for driving development—the top priority. During the meeting, former British Prime Minister Tony Blair also noted that the aid Africa has received from China in some cases is more effective than it got from Western countries. Though how China exercises its economic clout in Africa has drawn close attention, conventional donors (Western countries) should strengthen their cooperation with China, which is vital to the future of Africa (Cao 2013; Zhong and Li 2013).

The emphasis on effectiveness has undergone a major change, from stressing the central role of donors to that of recipients, and from underscoring aid effectiveness to development effectiveness. What needs to be reiterated is that aid effectiveness can be viewed from the perspectives of both the donor and the recipient, while development effectiveness is assessed from only one perspective, namely the effectiveness of recipients' development.

1.3 Structure of the Book

This book is divided into four parts. The first part is composed of this chapter and Chapter 2, which focus on the origin, basic concept, fundamental thinking, and data sources. If we compare the research on DAHCU to a study of a game of Go, what is discussed in this chapter is a process of choosing points to place the stones, which in Go refers to choosing the best vacant intersections in part of or the whole board to place the stones. We started the research on DAHCU, the core case in this book, at the invitation of the project team. DAHCU also serves as an entry point for us to examine China's influence in Africa and relevant factors. In Chapter 2, we introduce the layout of our research. From the prisms of sociology and anthropology, we collected data by conducting literature search, in-depth interviews and field research. The framework of two-sided four-tiered embeddedness, a theoretical model to help us understand DAHCU, was put forward after we carried out theoretical studies and practices.

The second part includes Chapters 3–5, which examine the framework of two-sided four-tiered embeddedness in the evolution of the theories and practices with regard to international aid. Chapter 3 discusses the development history of aid theories and touches on the overall trend of aid research and major controversies. Chapters 4 and 5 illustrate the environment where DAHCU is undertaken from the angles of the donor and the recipient, respectively.

The third part, Chapters 6–8, discusses DAHCU, its effectiveness and the current situation. Chapter 6 presents the facts related to DAHCU over the past three decades. Based on these facts, Chapter 7 looks at the effectiveness and changes of DAHCU in terms of its impact on resource supply, DAH structure, China–Uganda connections and benefits for Chinese expats. Chapter 8, similar to estimating the scope of each player in Go to determine the strategies to be taken in the next stage, offers an objective understanding and estimate of what has happened and what is happening to DAHCU. The trend of DAHCU is the backdrop against which we are going to take new measures.

The fourth part is the conclusion, which touches on the aid-based opportunities that are identified in the research to help boost cooperation and development. As China-Uganda Friendship Hotel is put into operation, DAHCU is presented with a historical opportunity to shift from sole aid to aid that facilitates cooperation and development. Moreover, it is an optimal time to promote China's more than 60 years' aid experience and extend aid to drive development and cooperation if we are looking at the bigger picture of China's foreign aid.

References

Cao, Li. 2013. From Millennium Development Goals to Busan Declaration: Evolution of International Aid Theory. *Economic Research Guide* 9: 202–204.

Zhang, Xioamin, and Tongquan Sun. 2014. Research One Regulatory System of Britain's Foreign Aid. *Journal of International Economic Cooperation* 5: 50–55.

Zhong, Ling, and Xiaoyun Li. 2013. Review of Busan Declaration and Its Latest Progress. *Journal of Guangxi University* (Philosophy and Social Sciences Edition) 2: 95–98.

CHAPTER 2

Two-Sided Four-Tiered Embeddedness: An Overview of China's Development Aid for Health to Uganda

2.1 Choosing the Right Academic Disciplines: Sociology and Anthropology

Compared with experts who specialize in the research and practices of international relations, diplomacy, and health care, we are familiar with development research but not familiar with the topics, theories, methods and the cutting edge related to development aid. These disciplines therefore have become our research subjects and research into relevant literature is part of our research, which starts from the case study of development aid for health from China to Uganda (DAHCU) from the perspectives of sociology and anthropology.

Most readers may know these two terms, but not many have any idea about the fundamental viewpoints of sociology or anthropology. With a view to helping readers better understand the viewpoints, we believe it is necessary to clarify our choice and views and present the discussion of aid-related topics held in various disciplines and practices. From the perspective of sociology, it is a process to incorporate the discussion into the researchers' choice of theories, which covers researchers' understanding and views of the research subject in terms of theory and practice.

In sociology and anthropology,

1. Every entity that takes action is counted as an actor. In our research, medical personnel that were dispatched to Uganda including doctors, nurses, pharmacists and technicians, medical

Z. Qiu, *When Friendship Comes First*, China and Globalization 2.0,
https://doi.org/10.1007/978-981-32-9308-3_2

teams, hospitals, competent Chinese authority in charge of aid, as well as those in Uganda that are involved in aid, such as individuals, organizations, departments, and the government are all actors.

2. The action taken by actors is social action. Development aid for health in Uganda is complex social action, which is taken at multiple levels by various actors, including individuals, organizations, and governments from both sides.
3. Social action is taken in the context of particular economies and societies. China provides development aid for health in Uganda in the context of political, economic, social and diplomatic environments in China and Uganda. The cultures in both countries vary because of historical and modern influences.
4. Social action will have an impact over other actors. China's development aid for health in Uganda has affected Uganda's politics, economy, society, and diplomacy. As the impact is complicated, we need to identify a perspective to observe a certain type of impact. Generally speaking, sociology and anthropology are inclined to look at the impact from the perspective of ultimate beneficiaries, that is, the society. We call it social impact.
5. Social action not only affects other actors but also affect the actors themselves. China's development aid for health in Uganda will also affect China's diplomacy, foreign aid, healthcare system, donor organizations and individual donors. The feedback of Uganda and relevant actors on aid, in particular, will have an influence over Chinese actors' perception of and judgment about aid and even affect China's diplomacy and domestic politics.

This constitutes actors' social action and social structuration (Giddens 1998). To put it in a simple way, from the perspective of sociology and anthropology, what DAHCU means goes beyond dispatching medical teams for offering treatment, visiting patients, and taking part in healthcare activities, building hospitals and malaria prevention and treatment centers, providing free medical equipment, instruments, and medicine, training healthcare personnel and other forms of giving (Cohen 2013). More importantly, China's development aid for health in Uganda involves actors at different levels in both countries regardless of the aid's form, scale, scope, or duration. It will affect actors in Uganda as well as their Chinese counterparts, even actors elsewhere.

After going through the literature related to DAHCU, we realize only by observing from a theoretical and practical perspective, can we comprehend DAHCU in a systematic manner. In order to allow readers to have a better understanding and agree on the choice of the perspective, it is necessary to illustrate the research process of the literature, which is also a feature of sociological and anthropological research, that is, to present the process of arriving at the research conclusion as part of the research to readers.

From the perspective of actors concerned,[1] we carried out two rounds of literature collection, collation, and study. The first round took place after we accepted this task but before the field survey in Uganda, with a view to getting a basic understanding of DAHCU and relevant research to facilitate us in further conducting literature research and field research. Based on what we had learned, we recognized that DAHCU was similar to the help and giving offered by people out of various reasons. We have learned that actors always provide aid for other actors amid specific situations and the aid is affected by the following factors.

1. Type of aid. Which type of aid can donors provide? And which of them fall into the category of development aid for health?
2. Coverage of aid. What's the coverage of aid that donors are seeking to reach? What types of aid are donors directing to various recipients, respectively?
3. Aim of aid. Which recipients' needs will be met by donors' different types of aid? Will donors take recipients' needs into consideration?
4. Approach to aid. How will donors provide aid?
5. Duration of aid. How long will the aid last and will it be carried out in multiple stages?
6. Systematic features of aid. How are the types, coverage, duration, and aims of aid correlated and is aid provided in a systematic manner?

[1] The "actors concerned" carry different meaning in various disciplines. The most common one is stakeholders used in evaluation research, referring to all the parties that have stakes in the aid.

2.2 Embeddedness of Development Aid for Health

To answer the questions aforementioned, we introduce the concept of embeddedness, which was developed by political scientist Karl Polanyi in 1944 (Polanyi 2007) and dropped out of the attention later. In 1985, sociologist Mark Granovetter explained the relations between humans' economic behaviors with the surroundings with the concept of embeddedness. He argues that humans' economic behaviors are embedded in the social network (Granovetter 1985), thereby establishing embeddedness as an analysis method and making it gradually adopted by social scientists.

Development aid for health provided by China to recipients is not only related to China's overall aid policy, but also affected by the political, economic, social, cultural, and healthcare systems of recipient countries, as well as the official and unofficial aid including development aid for health the countries receive from international organizations and other countries. China's development aid for health to a specific recipient is related to the following factors.

1. Type and make-up of aid. The types of aid received by recipients tend to be complicated, including development aid for health and other types of aid, such as military aid. Besides, among different types of aid, the proportion of development aid is not only related to other types of aid but also influenced by other aid in terms of significance.
2. Coverage of aid. Recipients' aid needs would not cover all the areas of politics, economy, society or health care. However, there should be a scope of needs. Development aid for health is under the scope of recipients' aid needs.
3. Systematic features of aid. Besides the coverage of aid, another concern is the systematic features of recipients' aid needs, that is, whether various types of aid will be integrated as an organic system to power the development of recipients. Development aid for health is an important part, be it systematic or not.
4. Prioritization of aid. Affected by domestic political, economic, social, health, diplomatic, and other factors, the prioritization of needs for different types of aid varies. For sub-Saharan countries, development aid for health is what they in dire need of.

5. Aid modalities. It is a gradual process for recipients to decide what kind of aid is acceptable to them. It is not only related to the international development aid as an ecological behavior but also concerns the political, economic, social, and cultural environments as well as the engagement between recipients and donors.

This is why we have established a framework to help us understand DAH and look at the DAH offered by China in the context of China's aid to Africa and other foreign countries. We believe DAH by China is an integral part of China's aid to Africa and other countries and serves the interests of China's diplomacy because it is under the influence of China's current situation and political environment in particular, thus forming a preliminary analysis framework. According to this framework, DAH by China is embedded in China's aid to Africa and other foreign countries as well as China's domestic politics. That is what the embeddedness of DAH is about.

2.3 Two-Sided Four-Tiered Embeddedness of the Development Aid for Health from China to Uganda

If we look at DAHCU based on embeddedness and from the perspective of recipients and donors, DAHCU falls into the framework of two-sided four-tiered embeddedness.

From China's perspective, DAHCU is an element of China's aid to Uganda (the first tier), a part of China's development aid for health to other countries (the second tier), a component of China's overall foreign aid (the third tier), and a part of China's diplomacy (the fourth tier). It is under the swing of China's current situation, especially China's politics, economy, and society, and follows the fundamental principle of serving the interests of China. It is clear that the first tier falls under the third tier instead of the second tier. DAHCU falls under the first and second tiers and indirectly the third tier. And the third tier falls under the fourth tier. DAHCU does embody China's mission and goals.

From Uganda's perspective, DAHCU is a part of the aid received by Uganda from China (the first tier), a proportion of the DHA received by Uganda from all the donors (the second tier), an element of aid in all forms from all donors (the third tier) and a component of Uganda's

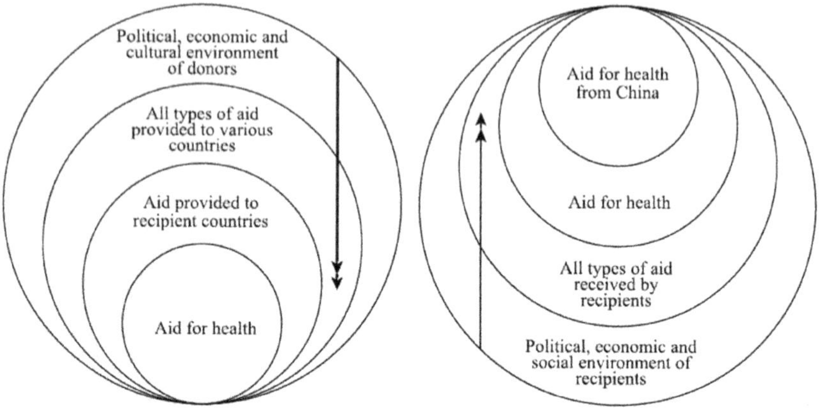

Fig. 2.1 Framework of two-sided four-tiered embeddedness for understanding DAHCU

diplomacy (the fourth tier), impacted by Uganda's politics, economy, and society. The structure here is the same as that in the donor's case. The first tier falls under the third tier instead of the second tier. DAHCU falls under the first and second tiers and indirectly the third tier. And the third tier is part of the fourth tier. Uganda also has its expectations and targets for DAHCU.

From the perspectives of both the donor and the recipient, we put forward the analytical framework of two-sided four-tiered embeddedness to interpret DAHCU, as is shown in Fig. 2.1.

The framework is intended to demonstrate that DAHCU is not an isolated initiative but a factor that influences the donor and the recipient at many levels and is influenced by factors at different levels on both sides. Its effectiveness is a result of its influence over those levels.

Moreover, aid is a progressive activity. "Two-sided four-tiered embeddedness" takes places in tandem for the donor and the recipient when issues such as whether aid should be extended, how to provide aid and how big the scale of aid is determined. The decision-making by China and Uganda is affected by these four components from both sides. Once the aid agreement is concluded and to be implemented, the recipient's four-tiered embeddedness is going to assume a major role. Figure 2.2 illustrates the context in which aid is provided and the effectiveness of aid is evaluated. In a given context, DAHCU affects the recipient on

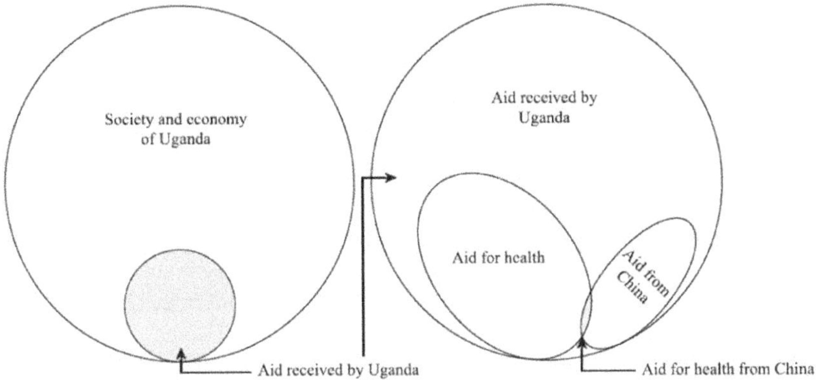

Fig. 2.2 Context of four-tiered embeddedness for DAHCU (*Note* Based on the data available, the proportional relationship of different parts is shown in this figure)

different levels, creating effectiveness for both the recipient and the donor.

It is relevant to highlight that it is an evolving process to develop this framework before the commencement of the research, during the research and after the conclusion of the field survey. It is the result of a theory-building process underlain by empirical facts, constituting the basic perspective adopted to understand DAHCU and its implementation.

2.4 Evaluating the Effectiveness of the Development Aid for Health from China to Uganda

According to the framework of two-sided four-tiered embeddedness, we believe DAHCU has created a main effect on every embedded tier for both the donor and the recipient. The direction and extent of the effects measure the effectiveness. This approach means that there should be a metric for each tier of embeddedness in both China's and Uganda's context to evaluate the effectiveness of DAHCU.

From the donor's point of view, in 1983, China dispatched medical teams to Uganda at the request of the government of Uganda. As shown in the left part of Fig. 2.1, the fourth tier is one part of China's diplomacy. DAHCU reflects China's diplomatic goodwill and similar to placing a stone at a position of no strategic importance in the game of Go. The third tier of DAHCU is a part of China's foreign aid as a type of aid. The second tier is part of China's DAH in terms of coverage by region and type. The first tier is part of China's overall aid to Uganda, which together with other types of aid constitutes the aid where China's relations with Uganda focus.

From the recipient's perspective, when Uganda asked China to send medical teams in 1983, it was suffering from a scarcity of healthcare resources, especially premium human and medical resources. The first tier is the DAH Uganda received from China. The second tier is part of the DAH Uganda received, a subcategory of DAH. The third tier is part of the DAH of all types of aid. The fourth tier is part of Uganda's diplomacy and the aid needed by Uganda.

We will thus find that the effectiveness of DAHCU relies not only on what China has done and how it is done, but also on what the impact DAHCU has over each tier. DAHCU bears different meanings to different embedded tiers of both China and Uganda, which means the effectiveness is reflected in different dimensions. With a view to facilitating the discussion, we focus on the main effect DAHCU has over each tier, thus considering those metrics aforementioned as dimensions of DAHCU effectiveness within the framework of two-sided four-tiered embeddedness, as shown in Table 2.1.

Given that DAHCU is aid on demand and no strings were attached by the donor, we have every reason to assume that the assessment of DAHCU is based on to what extent it has met the needs of Uganda. The extent affects the effectiveness of China's aid to Uganda, China's DAH and China's foreign aid. From Uganda's perspective, the first tier of DAHCU effectiveness is the effectiveness of China's DAH on the healthcare system in Uganda. The second tier is DAH received by Uganda. The third tier is how effective it is among all types of aid,

Table 2.1 Dimensions of DAHCU effectiveness

	First tier	*Second tier*	*Third tier*	*Fourth tier*
China	China's foreign aid	Regions covered by DAH	Types of aid provided	Diplomatic support
Uganda	DAH provided by China	DAH types	Types of aid received	Diplomatic support

i.e., the effectiveness of DAHCU in one tier is attributable to its effectiveness in DAH and the effectiveness of DAH in relation to that of other types of aid. The fourth tier is the effectiveness of China–Uganda diplomatic relations.

Among the four tiers of embeddedness, the third tier involves an array of complex factors. As China merely takes up a minimal proportion of this tier, it is not included in the scope of evaluation. If the effectiveness of DAHCU's two-sided four-tiered embeddedness is expected, the effectiveness of other factors can be interpreted as a form of externality. On the basis of that understanding, we have developed the metrics of evaluating DAHCU effectiveness as follows:

1. Impact on resource supply, i.e., how does DAHCU affect Uganda's healthcare system?
2. Impact on DAH structure, i.e., how does DAHCU fit in with the rest of DAH received by Uganda?
3. Impact on connections between the recipient and the donor countries, i.e., how DAHCU shapes China-Uganda diplomatic relations?
4. Externalities, i.e., what other effects can DAHCU claim to have had?

It should be noted is that these four indicators are derived from the study of DAHCU-related practices so they are different from the five "Partnership Commitments" proposed in the *Paris Declaration*.

What is central to the Partnership Commitments is to leave the decision-making to the recipient countries, or partner countries. First, ownership. Partner countries exercise effective leadership over their development policies, and strategies and coordinate development actions. Second, alignment. Donors base their overall support on partner countries' national development strategies, institutions, and procedures. Six indicators are set under this commitment: (A) Donors align with partners' strategies; (B) Donors use strengthened country systems; (C) Partner countries strengthen development capacity with support from donors; (D) Strengthen public financial management capacity; (E) Strengthen national procurement systems; (F) Untie aid: getting better value for money. Third, harmonization. Donors' actions are more harmonized, transparent and collectively effective. Five indicators are incorporated into this commitment: (A) Donors implement common arrangements and simplify procedures; (B) Complementarity: more effective division of labor; (C) Incentives for collaborative behavior;

(D) Delivering effective aid in fragile states; (E) Promoting a harmonized approach to environmental assessments. Fourth, managing for results: Managing resources and improving decision-making for results. Fifth, mutual accountability: Donors and partners are accountable for development results[2] (He 2011; Wang and Lei 2013; Zhang 2014).

Though we find it not feasible to directly apply these five commitments and eleven indicators to assess the effectiveness of DAHCU, they can be used as a reference for further inspiration. First, DAHCU is run at the invitation of the Ugandan government which put forward the agenda. This complies with the commitment of "ownership." Second, the Chinese government has carried out extensive consultation and coordination with the Ugandan government about the four aspects of DAHCU. It is part and parcel of the development of Uganda's healthcare system. It has been incorporated into Uganda's healthcare system from the onset, which follows the commitment of "alignment." It applies to the donor but not to the recipient country. Third, bilateral procedures in DAHCU are simplified. In the course of dealing with multilateral relations, China has made indirect coordinated efforts through Uganda's healthcare system instead of direct coordination with other donors of DAH in Uganda. This complies with the indicator of "collaborative behavior." However, it may not be transparent enough. Therefore, to a certain extent, it abides by the commitment of "harmonization." Fourth, DAHCU focuses on practice but there is no regular assessment of management for results, which is not in line with the commitment of "managing for results." However, evaluating the effectiveness of DAHCU can be considered an attempt in this regard. Fifth, since 2001, China has started to implement the accountability mechanism. Arguably, DAHCU is in line with the commitment of "mutual accountability."

The gap between the four indicators of DAHCU-related practices and the indicators set in the *Paris Declaration* is attributable to two factors. On the one hand, although the *Paris Declaration* stresses the ownership of recipient countries, it is far from the principles for foreign aid that China proposed in 1964 and has been upholding since

[2]The *Paris Declaration* sets targets specific to each commitment to be achieved before 2010. For more information, refer to *Paris Declaration on Aid Effectiveness (2005)*, *Accra Agenda for Action (2008)*, http://www.oecd.org/dac/effectiveness/34428351.pdf.

then.[3] The principles initiated by China have been a step ahead of the progress made from the *Paris Declaration* to the *Busan Declaration*. On the other hand, the *Paris Declaration* addresses the emphasis on additional conditions placed by developed countries, OECD-DAC member states in particular, and international organizations, in the hope of encouraging donors to reduce and even give up such emphasis and make a shift from the perspective of the donor to that of the recipient to stress aid effectiveness. DAHCU is always about powering the development of the recipient country with no strings attached.

In this context, our proposal of the four indicators for evaluating DAHCU effectiveness can therefore be considered as an effort that goes beyond the partnership commitments set in the *Paris Declaration*. As DAHCU was not designed based on careful planning and no targets were preset, its effectiveness in practice is the effectiveness in real terms.

It should be noted that despite all the efforts, for the fourth type of DAHCU—providing temporary health funding, we failed to obtain specific information and data so this type was excluded from effectiveness evaluation. For the other three types, we will use dimensions of effectiveness listed in Table 2.1 to evaluate.

2.5 Literature Review

2.5.1 Sources of Literature

Based on Fig. 2.1, we sorted out and categorized the literature collected and identified an array of materials for research as follows:

[3] Upon his visit to Ghana on January 16, 1964, Zhou Enlai, then Premier of the People's Republic of China, announced the Eight Principles for Economic Aid and Technical Assistance: (1) equality and mutual benefit; (2) respecting the sovereignty of the recipient countries, and never attach any conditions or ask for any privileges; (3) providing economic aid in the form of interest-free or low-interest loans; (4) helping recipient countries embark step by step on the road of self-reliance and independent economic development; (5) building projects that require less investment while yielding quicker results; (6) providing the best-quality equipment and material of China's own manufacture; (7) seeing to it that the personnel of the recipient country fully master the technique China provides; (8) ensuring the same standard of living for both experts dispatched by China to help in construction in the recipient countries and the experts of the recipient country (For the complete version of the principles, refer to the second footnote in the Introduction section).

1. Academic research. Search for such literature as the books in the library of Peking University, CNKI, especially journals, dissertations, and papers; Jstor, a digital library of academic journals in social sciences, ScienceDirect, NIH, and other related academic literature.
2. Research reports. Search for such literature on the websites of USAID, OECD, WHO, the World Bank and other organizations, publications, databases and the websites, and databases of research institutes.
3. Data. Get access to the databases of the World Bank, OECD, USAID and so on.
4. Policies. Look for relevant information on the websites of China's State Council, Ministry of Commerce, and National Health and Family Planning Commission, USAID, OECD, and so on.

In addition to the materials collected by the team members, we also drew on the recommendations of Dr. Henry Lucas from the Institute of Development Studies, the U.K. After reviewing the literature, we decided on the categories and quantities of literature to be used for research as listed in Table 2.2.

Chinese academic journals, dissertations, and foreign academic journals, as well as books and Chinese newspapers, are major sources of literature, among which foreign literature takes up a significant proportion. The quantity of foreign academic journals is almost twice that of Chinese literature. The numbers of foreign books and reports are larger. Many Chinese dissertations were used because of our limited access to foreign dissertations. It should be noted that as our capabilities for comprehending foreign languages are limited, we only included English literature. Moreover, there is a slight disparity between the actual categories and quantities of literature used for research and those listed in the table.

2.5.2 *Categorization of Literature*

We looked for literature on the following topics:

- Literature on theories, views, and arguments with respect to international aid
- Literature on China's foreign aid
- Literature on aid to Africa from the US
- Literature on aid to Africa from Japan, South Korea and India

Table 2.2 Sources and quantities of literature used for the research on DAHCU

Category	*CNKI*	*Website of the Chinese government*	*Foreign databases**	*Websites of foreign governments*	*Websites of research institutes*	*Borrowed/purchased*
Chinese academic journals	370					
Chinese dissertations	111					
Chinese books						12
Chinese newspapers	75					
Chinese reports					1	
Chinese government reports		4				
Academic journals in foreign languages			699			
Books in foreign languages						47
Government reports in foreign languages				9		
Research reports in foreign languages					21	

Note PubMed, ScienceDirect, ProQuest, Jstor and other foreign databases are used for research

- Literature on aid to Africa from the UK, France, Germany, and other European countries
- Literature on development aid for agriculture, education, and health to Africa
- Literature on aid from China to Uganda.

We sorted through the literature we collected and created an EndNote database.

The literature stored in EndNote database was classified according to the topics aforementioned.

The first category is related to theories and arguments about international aid which is a big topic. The 413 documents on this topic are divided into three types. As some documents touch on more than one topic, the total number of documents in all types is larger than 413. For the first type, there are 270 documents on aid theories, aid activities, aid execution, development facilitation, aid support, recipients, recipients' capabilities to absorb the aid, aid results and so on. The second type includes 95 documents on the economy, trade, economic growth, and poverty. There are 85 documents in third type on politics, government, policies, governance, human rights, democracy, and corruption.

The second category centers on China's foreign aid, especially aid to Africa, with 269 documents covering a wide range of subjects classified into two types. As some documents touch on more than one topic, the total number of documents in all types is larger than 269. The first type includes 96 documents on China's foreign aid, aid strategies, aid policies and aid activities. In the second type, there are 168 documents on bilateral relations and cooperation between China and Africa, China's aid to Africa and relevant experiences and outcomes. The reviews for a book are also included in this category. In 2009, American scholar Bräutigam published a book on China's aid to Africa, triggering the discussion in academia. There are six documents for this book in total.

The third category includes 204 documents related to development aid for health. When we collected the documents, we paid special attention to development aid for health in Africa. We have found that there is a vast body of literature on containing HIV/AIDS in the literature under this category. As the focus of our research does not concern HIV/AIDS, we only selected a few documents. This category centers on China's development aid for health to Africa, including 24 documents on HIV/AIDS, 18 on global health, 78 on development aid for health, 65 on China's medical teams, and 20 on traditional Chinese medicine.

The fourth category includes 408 documents on development aid for Africa from different perspectives, with 19 on theories related to international relations, 75 on Africa, 12 on Western views on development aid, 41 on aid to Africa from Africa, 60 on development aid to Africa from Europe, 99 on development aid to Africa from the US,

52 on comparative studies of aid to Africa from various countries, 42 on development aid for agriculture in Africa, 39 on development aid for education in Africa. The collection of literature on development aid for agriculture and education is intended to be compared with development aid for health.

The fifth category focuses on aid to Uganda. There are 202 documents in total, including 24 on background information of Uganda, 21 on development aid for education and agriculture, 35 on economy, trade, and development aid for development, 40 on healthcare system and development aid for health, 49 on diplomatic relations between China and Uganda, aid to Uganda, and so on, and 16 papers published by medical teams with the data accumulated during the aid operations.

Though literature collection is an energy-consuming and time-consuming process, the literature, academic literature in particular, we collected does not cover every aspect of "two-sided four-tiered embeddedness," because academics tend to focus on issues that interest them while practitioners concentrate on practical matters. If we cannot take a step back from the particular issues we focus on, it will be difficult for us to find inadequacies in the theories and practices regarding development aid. To put it simply, we failed to cover every side of the framework of "two-sided four-tiered embeddedness" is not because we did not work hard to collect materials, but due to the missing content of relevant literature.

That's why we put forward the framework of "two-sided four-tiered embeddedness" in the hope of presenting our views on areas where there is an absence of literature.

2.6 Data Collection, Organization, and Analysis

2.6.1 Methods of Data Collection

Since DAHCU was initiated more than thirty years ago, medical teams have been dispatched to Uganda continuously year after year on a long-term basis while other aspects of aid are rather sporadic. Among all the types of China's foreign aid, China-Uganda Friendship Hospital and the Uganda Malaria Research Center are examples of complete projects, while anti-malaria medicine, instruments, and equipment are phased aid programs.

We adopted different methods of collecting data for different types of DAHCU. As a result different sets of data were collected. Field survey data gathered based on interviews and observations include:

1. A field survey of Jinja Hospital and Jinja where China's medical teams were dispatched to work from 1983 to 2012. We had in-depth interviews with former and incumbent heads of the hospital, current and retired staff members that had close contact with China's medical teams, some of the patients who had received treatment from the medical teams. We also held symposiums with the presence of management team and medical personnel from the hospital, surveyed the outpatient room, treatment center, wards, hospital documents room, operation rooms, outpatient service, pharmacy, acupuncture room, ICU and so on and had brief interviews with patients, interns, and medical personnel.
2. A field survey of China-Uganda Friendship Hospital where China's medical teams are stationed now. We conducted in-depth interviews with some of the managerial personnel, medical personnel and patients and surveyed the facilities, equipment outpatient room, wards, treatment center, operation rooms, outpatient service, pharmacy, and so on in the hospital.
3. A field trip to where Yunnan's medical teams are stationed. We had in-depth interviews with the team leader and some members of the 16th medical team and held discussions with the medical team.
4. A special visit to Economic and Commercial Counsellor's Office of China's Embassy to Uganda. We had in-depth talks with the officials there and looked through DAHCU documents while following the rules.
5. A special visit to the Ministry of Health in Uganda. We paid a visit to officials in charge of receiving aid and conducted brief interviews (due to limited time, in-depth interviews were not an option).
6. Informal interviews with professional personnel and other personnel who were engaged in aid in Uganda on different occasions.
7. In the field survey conducted in China, we had in-depth interviews with officials of the Office of International Cooperation of the National Health and Family Planning Commission, former members of Yunnan's medical teams who had returned to China and experts in international relations.

2.6.2 Data Analysis and Application

As DAHCU is not a common program or a policy and those who are engaged in DAHCU do not adopt the approach of Monitoring and Evaluation (M&E) to recording or collecting data in a systematic way, we cannot use data based on the M&E process.

When we sorted through the data, we had a rough evaluation of the effectiveness of data based on the principle of information saturation, which suggested in terms of exploring and open effectiveness evaluation research, the data we collected met the principle of finite information saturation, that is, we have collected all the possible data.

In the analysis of data, we used three approaches adopted in sociological and anthropological evaluation research.

1. Fact analysis. Based on the basic facts, we discussed the truthfulness of facts within finite range to explore basic facts regarding DAHCU.
2. Comparative analysis. Based on facts of the same nature, we compared different facts in terms of their positions, weights, relations, and implications within a bigger structure and framework. For example, we compared different aspects of DAHCU to determine its focus on Uganda's healthcare system and assess its effectiveness. We also compared DAH from China and the US to get a glimpse into the differences in their focuses and their distinct features of effectiveness.
3. Impact analysis. We analyzed and judged the impacts of DAHCU with four indicators to measure the effectiveness of DAHCU. The principle of finite judgment was strictly adhered to in the analysis to avoid overinterpretation and presumption.

The data used in this book are from a myriad of sources. For those data whose sources cannot be disclosed, we have abided by the code of ethics for social science research, that is, if not necessary, we would opt not to use the data. If necessary, we would not disclose the sources of data. We apologize for the inconvenience this has caused for readers. We have upheld the ethics of research and consider it as the basic principle of protecting the interests of all parties concerned.

References

Cohen, Michael A. 2013. Giving to Developing Countries: Controversies and Paradoxes of International Aid. *Social Research* 80 (2): 591–606.

Giddens, Anthony. 1998. *The Constitution of Society*, trans. Kang Li and Meng Li. DAX Joint Publishing Company.

Granovetter, Mark. 1985. Economic Action and Social Structure: The Problem of Embeddedness. *American Journal of Sociology* 91 (3): 481–510. https://doi.org/10.2307/2780199.

He, Wenping. 2011. From "Aid Effectiveness" to "Development Effectiveness": Evolution of Aid Concepts and Role of Chinese Experience. *West Asia and Africa* 9: 120–135.

Polanyi, Karl. 2007. *The Great Transformation*, trans. Yang Liu and Gang Feng. Zhejiang People's Publishing House.

Wang, Yanlei, and Wei Lei. 2013. Framework Analysis of the Paris Declaration. *Journal of Beijing Union University* (Humanities and Social Sciences Edition) 2: 125–128.

Zhang, Yuting. 2014. Aid Effectiveness Research Within the Framework of the Paris Declaration: A Case Study of Aid to Ethiopia's Education. *Comparative Education Review* 12: 86–91.

CHAPTER 3

Understanding the Basics: Debates in the Theories and Practices of Aid

3.1 "Aid": A Conceptual Analysis

According to a brief review of the history, we know that aid between countries in the modern era is traced back to the Marshall Plan in the 1950s. After the Second World War, the economies of European countries and Japan suffered massively and were in dire need of revival. The US offered aid to these countries, helping them achieve rapid development (Browne 2012). During the Cold War, to build international political alliances and safeguard vested interests, the two camps led by the US and the Soviet Union were proactive in offering development aid to other countries. Meanwhile, aid was indispensable for underdeveloped countries as the savings after the war failed to sustain the economic development or meet the needs of investment (Kasekende and Atingi-Ego 1999).

As the aid target shifted from countries hit hard in the Second World War to developing countries, in the 1960s foreign aid turned into development aid. During this process, suzerains such as the U.S. and those in Europe played a dominant role (Cohen 2013; Lancaster 2007).

Over the past six decades, the scale and coverage of the aid have been expanding. However, more and more problems have surfaced. The debate over aid has been around for a long time. When we sorted through the literature, we found the international community has never reached a consensus about important topics related to aid. We believe it

Z. Qiu, *When Friendship Comes First*, China and Globalization 2.0,
https://doi.org/10.1007/978-981-32-9308-3_3

is necessary to start from basic topics to discuss the structure of aid, such as the purposes, methods, approaches, and outcomes of aid.

This section focuses on the purposes, concepts, methods and political strings attached while the next one touches on the outcomes and impacts.

Since the mission of aid (Musolf 1963) was developed, there has been a debate over the purposes of development aid. To date, we have witnessed development from the *Paris Declaration* to the *Busan Declaration*, but a consensus on the purposes is yet to be reached.

The public debate over the concept may have originated from the 1970s. Abbot, whose paper was on two interpretations of aid, believed most research on aid could be classified into these two broad yet mutually exclusive categories (Abbot 1973). First, some political scientists and economists consider aid as tools of diplomatic policies, which are designed, executed and evaluated according to political standards. Therefore, aid is a political concept and its basic purpose is to reach the political and strategic targets of donors. Second, contrary to the first one, some economists argue that donors should not seek to impose their intentions on recipients via offering aid. Aid is an economic means, used as supplementary resources for recipients and designed to produce extra resources for the development and social transformation of recipients. Therefore, the evaluation of aid should be combined with the efficiency and allocation of aid to meet the criterion of promoting the development of recipients to the maximum extent.

In either interpretation, aid is a tool used to facilitate political development or drive economic growth. The difference is whether there are political conditions attached.

The past few years have seen the debate over aid concepts become more complicated because of the attention to China's aid and China's commitment to its foreign aid concept. This concept is clearly explained in *China's Foreign Aid* published in 2011 and 2014 (Zhang and Huang 2012).[1]

In the white paper published in 2011, the Chinese government has proposed "five commitments": commitment to helping recipient countries build their development capacity, commitment to imposing no

[1] *China's Foreign Aid* is also known as the White Paper on China's Foreign Aid. Up till now, the Chinese government has published two papers, one in April 2011 and the other in July 2014. It is easy to find the text of the white papers using the search engine online.

political conditions, commitment to equality, mutual benefit and common development, commitment to remaining realistic while striving for the best, and commitment to keeping pace with the times and paying attention to reform and innovation. The first three commitments are related to the purposes of aid. In the report of 2014, the Chinese government directed the first three commitments to improving people's lives and advancing economic and social development.

If the previous debate is over political aid and economic aid, China's aid is targeting people's lives, be it designed to drive economic and social development or improve people's living standards. Hu Mei and Liu Hongwu took aid to Africa as examples and compared "democracy-centered aid to Africa" with "living standard-centered aid to Africa." They believe, after the 1990s, the aid strategies of Western countries and China for Africa went through major changes. Promoting democracy is Western countries' priority of their strategies toward Africa and economic aid is used as a tool to improve democracy without taking the urgent needs of Africans into consideration. The focus of China's strategies has been deepening bilateral economic and trade relations and achieving mutually beneficial cooperation, which are rational and pragmatic, delivering benefits to both sides (Hu and Liu 2009).

It should be noted that the theory of political aid, economic aid or livelihood aid is not dominant in the global landscape and transformation of aid. Moreover, every theory is correlated with relevant practices.

The debate has become more diversified recently. After sorting through over 50 aid theories, Sumner and Mallett argue that development aid is a market, in which five factors impact the supply and demand: demand for aid, supply of aid, products or means of aid, decisive factors of aid efficiency, and cost and benefits of aid (Sumner and Mallett 2013). On the contrary, Furia holds that aid is an international gift and offers a special model of gift-offering, including alliance building, understanding of rules, development of topics and governance in an artistic manner (Furia 2015).

A vast body of research connects aid with specific targets, such as democracy (Scott and Steele 2011), human rights (Burton and Lewis 1993), governance (Bräutigam 1992; Busse and Gröning 2009), economic growth (Szmant 1978; Young and Sheehan 2014) and more specific targets, such as education (McGrath 2010), health improvement (McGrath 2010), poverty alleviation (Chong et al. 2009) and so on.

We think that it is necessary to consider the aid targets but it is more important to study aid theories in order to understand the aid concepts of various countries. Of course, theories are not merely bodies of pure logic but summaries of practices and experiences. Every aid concept is related to aid practices and also in line with the values of donors. If aid is not about domination or a great addition but about providing help when one most needs it, no matter which concept it is based on, every type of aid should center on the needs of recipients, make the development of recipients as the goal and be embedded in the social, economic and political landscape of recipients. No matter it focuses on political priorities or economic priorities, the ultimate purpose of aid should be to deliver benefits to the people in recipient countries.

What is ironic is that the dispute centers on the best option to bring benefits to the people. Perhaps, the dispute emerges from the trial-and-error process of offering aid and the experiences of donors instead of those of recipients. Incorporating the experiences and wills of recipients into aid programs is probably the best approach to allowing the people there to gain benefits from aid.

In 2011, OECD-DAC proposed a change from "aid effectiveness" to "development effectiveness," suggesting a shift to prioritizing the needs and development of recipients. In a certain sense, this is a response to the debate over the concept of aid for decades (He 2011).

Whether there are political conditions attached or not and which areas should the aid cover are two overarching questions of aid practices. If there are political conditions attached, what will they be like and how will they be attached; if not, how will be aid provided and what areas will be given priority. These are the questions to be answered in aid practices. Literature of the past decades all touch on these topics and is interwoven with the literature of aid results. We have selected the most important for discussion.

The practice of attaching political conditions attached to aid operations may date back to the 1990s when the IMF and the World Bank asked recipient countries to carry out restructuring and reform of their budgets and governance, which is also known as the first generation of conditions attached (Stiles 1990). The second generation of conditions attached includes political reform, such as democracy, human rights, administrative accountability and so on (Stokke 1995). The second generation focuses more on government efficiency (Molenaers et al. 2015). Koch found that the conditions attached have become more diversified, and conceptualized them as beforehand-positive conditions, such as pre-ratification conditions and selective conditions, afterward-positive conditions, such as incentivizing conditions, beforehand-negative conditions, such as intensifying conditions, beforehand-negative conditions, such as intensifying conditions, and afterward-negative conditions, such as sanctioning conditions and oversight conditions. During the discussion, researchers stressed the need to distinguish between political conditions from policy conditions (Koch 2015).

World Development is a mainstream journal on aid. In terms of articles with the keyword "conditional" or "conditionality," the first three articles were published in 1979. In the 1980s, there were 50 such articles including 15 articles in 1987, the largest number during this period. There were 94 articles in the 1990s, and five years saw the publication of over 10 articles. In 1990 and 1997, for example, 14 articles were published, registering the largest number. A total of 77 articles were published in the first decade of the twenty-first century, and three years saw the publication of over 10 articles, such as 16 in 2002, the largest number during that period. Since 2010, 63 such articles have been published, with four years witnessing more than 10 articles published. In 2015, there were 25 such articles, the peak of this period, and 12 articles in 2016. This set of data represents a change of the international community's attention toward "conditions attached." Arguably, we have seen an upswing in the attention in recent years.

We also found that literature connecting aid with democracy did date back to the 1990s (De Waal 1997; Hyden and Reutlinger 1992), but linking aid with management appeared in the 1950s toward the end of postwar aid (King 1953). As early as in the 1980s, there were systematic discussions on political conditions attached to aid (Cohen et al. 1985) and development (Yeats 1982). The earliest documents connecting aid with human rights (Burton and Lewis 1993) and governance (Bräutigam 1992; Busse and Gröning 2009) were published in the 1990s. All the literature allows us to know about the types and modalities of political conditions attached to aid.

The US and the EU are the entities that are the first to have provided aid with the largest scale. According to their aid practices, the aid covers agricultural development, livelihood improvement, family planning, education enhancement, nutrition improvement, HIV/AIDS prevention and treatment, and so on. OCED classifies aid into the following areas: (1) social infrastructure and services, such as education, health, population policies, water and sanitation, etc.; (2) economic infrastructure and services, such as transport and storage, communications, energy generation, distribution and efficiency, banking and financial services, and business and other services; (3) production sectors, including agriculture, industry, trade policy and regulations and trade-related adjustment, tourism, etc.; (4) cross-cutting sectors, such as general environmental protection; (5) commodity aid and general program assistance such as general budget support, developmental food aid, and other commodity assistance; (6) humanitarian aid, such as emergency response, reconstruction relief and rehabilitation, disaster prevention and preparedness; and (7) other sectors. The aid can also be classified into social infrastructure, production, and humanitarian aid.

From the timing of these categories in literature, we found that production sectors used to be the priority of aid and social infrastructure and services came next. Take the US aid to Africa as an example. The USAID programs of aid to Africa and the timing of relevant literature suggest that in the beginning, aid was directed to agricultural development, such as agricultural technology and materials; then came humanitarian aid such as subsistence aid; it was then expanded to social infrastructure such as basic education, educational facilities and human resources training. In the health sector, the focus was on chronic diseases and epidemics. After 2007, literature covering HIV/AIDS prevention and treatment, malaria prevention and treatment, safe drinking water, family health, health promotion, social health campaign takes up a dominant proportion.

However, it is a regret that among the existing literature, there is no systematic research on the changes of the timing and prioritization of aid over the past six decades, the resources consumed by different areas within a certain period of time and the factors that influence the three dimensions mentioned above. Zhang Bin and Zhang Yun have studied the areas and countries of the US foreign aid in recent years (Zhang and Zhang 2016), but they failed to look into and analyze the aid trends of a longer term.

We think that understanding such topics within the framework of "two-sided four-tiered embeddedness" is vital to comprehending the development patterns of aid, the influences of recipients and donors over aid, and the changes of the relations between recipients and donors. It concerns our knowledge of the diachronic features of aid and the grounds for devising aid policies in the future.

3.2 The Effects of Aid and How They Are Determined

No matter what concepts aid is based on or which areas aid is provided to or what methods are adopted or whether there are political conditions attached to aid, the focus on aid effects is a common concern for both recipients and donors. It also involves different understanding about aid effects and works in line with the framework of "two-sided four-tiered embeddedness," that is, a multi-tiered embedded "effect structure."

First, overall effect. It includes evaluating aid effects from both a national and international perspective within a given period of time, such as the influences over politics, economy, society, and diplomacy. It also covers assessing the evolution of aid's overall effects from a diachronic perspective.

Second, effects of different types of aid. Within a specified period, different types of aid take up different shares of the overall. There are also performance differences among different types of aid, that is, the evaluation of cost per unit of production. Time-based evaluation and comparison of the same program during different periods of time is also included.

Third, effects of certain type(s) of aid to a particular recipient. Certain type(s) of aid targets a particular recipient, usually a sovereign country or a region. For a particular recipient, the major focuses are: the comparison of effects of different types of aid coming from the same donor, time-based changes of aid effects of one donor and time-based changes of the effects of different types of aid. In some cases, the same type of aid will be offered to multiple recipients, such as the development aid for health to Africa where China has dispatched medical teams. More correlations are involved with aid effects under such circumstances. Meanwhile, there are evaluations and time-based comparisons of the effects of aid from different donors.

Fourth, the effects of a certain aid program. A certain aid program is targeted at a particular recipient and related to the types of aid provided by donors, types of aid received by recipients, various types of aid received by recipients from different donors, complicating the dimensions of evaluations and comparisons.

This poses many challenges to a systematic evaluation of aid effects, such as the choice of standards, and how to measure effects and make comparisons. Perhaps because of such challenges, the evaluation of aid effects represented by the literature is complex from any perspective.

Despite that, some keywords used in the evaluation of aid effects can be summarized.

In the case of aid with political conditions attached, besides the overall evaluation of the effects of political conditions (Fisher 2015; Ohler et al. 2012), keywords include democracy (Kersting and Kilby 2014; Knack 2004; Kono and Montinola 2009; Kosack 2003; Resnick and Van de Walle 2013; Scott and Steele 2011), human rights (Lebovic and Voeten 2009; Demirel-Pegg and Moskowitz 2009; Carey 2007; Gomez 2007), governance (Bräutigam and Knack 2004; Busse and Gröning 2009; Winters and Martinez 2015), corruption (Acht et al. 2014; Bauhr et al. 2013; Dietrich 2011; Okada and Samreth 2012), politics (Boone 1996; Dutta et al. 2013; Reinsberg 2014; Woods 2005), government (Ayittey 2003; Khan and Hoshino 1992; Ouattara 2006), policies (Anonymous 2011; Blackorby et al. 1999; King 2011; Lambert 1996; Muravchik 1996), and reform (Collier and Dollar 2001; Crawford 2001; Hsieh 2000).

As for aid focusing on economic development, keywords are reform (Ayittey 2003; Baccini and Urpelainen 2012; Heckelman and Knack 2008; Stein 1994), economy (Bräutigam 1992; Burhop 2005; Feeny and Fry 2014; Francken et al. 2012; Schwalbenberg 1998), growth (Arndt et al. 2015; Mekasha and Tarp 2013; Minoiu and Reddy 2010; Young and Sheehan 2014; Kourtellos et al. 2007), industry (Liu et al. 2014; Museru et al. 2014; Papanek 1973; Phelps et al. 2009), trade (Bearce et al. 2013; Jakupec and Kelly 2016; Lim et al. 2015; Rotberg 2009), development (Zhang 2012; Atwood et al. 2008; Leonard 2005; Miller 2014; Smith 2010), privatization (Due 1993; Ghosh and Rondinelli 2003), and income distribution (Ali and Isse 2007; Chong et al. 2009; Lof et al. 2014; Saghafi and Nugent 1983).

In terms of aid focusing on livelihood improvement, poverty (Agénor et al. 2008; Bhagwati 2010; Cogneau and Naudet 2007; Collier and Dollar 2001), education (King 2010; McGrath 2010; Mundy et al. 2010) and health (Adelman and Norris 2001; Bendavid 2014; Mishra and Newhouse 2009; Roodman 2012) are the keywords.

The evaluation of donors' aid overall effects usually appears in national reports of donors, such as *China's Foreign Aid* (2011 and 2014) published by the Chinese government, annual performance reports and financial reports published USAID and thematic reports released by

OECD-DAC. However, in these reports, the evaluation of recipients and donors are very complicated and a consensus is not easy to reach.

The evaluation of the effects of different types of aid is included in the reports of administrative agencies and management bodies of donors and focuses on the specific aid programs or the goals aid campaigns seek to achieve. There are seldom systematic evaluation reports. For instance, the Chinese documentary *Chinese Angels-50 Year Chronicle of Chinese Medial Teams* is an evaluation of Chinese medical teams rather than an overall assessment of China's development aid for health. USAID seldom has an evaluation of aid for agriculture or health.

Recipient-specific reports prepared by donor countries are also absent. This is not unique to China. The absence of such reports is also common among other major donors. Some donors provide data of aid programs, such as the data of aid programs to Uganda and finance. Data by aid recipients, years and types is accessible on the websites of USAID and OECD, but there is rarely such data or report on the evaluation of aid effects.

The evaluation of aid effects from the perspective of recipients is even more scarce. Take Uganda for example, we haven't found annual aid effect evaluation report or report on certain types of aid published by the Ugandan government or relevant authorities or evaluation report on the effects of all types of aid from a certain donor published or evaluation or comparison reports on the effects of the same type of aid from different donors by any agency in Uganda.

In contrast, there is a vast body of evaluation reports of specific aid programs including the reports on aid effects. These reports are mainly issued by donors and focus on aid effects from the perspective of donors such as USAID. According to the US laws, all the programs funded by public finances are subject to audit and evaluation. USAID has a series of guidelines, tools, and training for program evaluation. Only a small proportion of program evaluation reports are provided by recipients, but because of the support from donors, such reports still center on the perspective of donors.

No matter what the focus is or at which level the evaluation is conducted, once the evaluation is directed at aid effects, it is difficult to make evaluations. Sumner and Mallett studied post-2000 literature on poverty reduction aid and summarized over 50 results of effect evaluation (Sumner and Mallett 2013) but no two results are consistent.

Among the literature on effect evaluation, from the perspective of donors, such views as low aid efficiency (Gulrajani 2011) or zero efficiency (Smith 2010) and unsustainable debts of recipients, and aid turning recipients into countries of net capital outflow (Zalanga 2014) prevail. There are even notions like dead aid (Moyo 2009) and aid is white men's burden (Easterly 2006).

A massive amount of research from the perspective of recipients concludes that aid is effective, especially according to evaluation reports from international organizations such as the World Bank and IMF. After conducting analysis with data of OECD, Cohen pointed out aid is effective for the development of developing countries (Cohen 2013). The analysis of OECD-DAC data by Arndt and others suggests over the past 40 years, aid effects have become more remarkable. Data shows that aid has not only facilitated the growth but also promoted the economic structure transformation and society improvement (Arndt et al. 2015). Even if aid is divided into development aid and nondevelopment aid, research by Minoiu and others demonstrates the contribution of development aid to economic growth between 1960 and 1990 was positive and incremental (Minoiu and Reddy 2010).

Therefore, according to the framework of "two-sided four-tiered embeddedness," a systematic evaluation of aid effects is a wish, because there are multiple complex factors involved. Jones' error correction model shows us that there is no perfectly designed aid (Jones 2015). Hence, no systematic evaluation. The vast body of evaluation focuses on the effect of a certain program, especially the evaluation conducted by OECD-DAC, USAID and international organizations such as the World Bank and IMF. The evaluation of the effects of a certain aid program is a common method of managing aid. It should be noted that the evaluation of one aid program's effects does not incorporate complete or major correlated factors or disengage from the influences of other factors. Therefore, regardless of the results, it is advisable that the readers adopt a prudent attitude.

No matter what effects aid produces, it is the reality. The factors that influence aid effects are the concerns for both the donor and the recipient. Within the framework of "two-sided four-tiered embeddedness," all these factors are related to every tier of embeddedness. Regrettably, the existing literature puts more emphasis on the environmental factors of donors, executioners, and recipients, so there is no systematic discussion.

In terms of quantity, the literature related to donors accounts for the majority. In terms of content, the literature is related to the intention donors have for aid (Lskavyan 2014). Fuchs and others studied the budgets of 22 member countries of DAC from 1976 to 2011 and found that excluding the fixed effects of donors, the influences of colonial history and execution bodies were not significant, the impacts of GDP per capita were weakened and donors' budget deficit would reduce its aid scale (Fuchs et al. 2014). Brech and others examined the data of 23 member states of OECD-DAC from 1960 to 2009 and found left-wing governments would more than often adopt the bilateral model to aid underdeveloped and medium and low-income counties, that is, hypothesis of party politics (Brech and Potrafke 2014). This approach is also deployed to observe China's foreign aid, which is believed that China, as a donor, has staged a reform quietly. The aid system established by the western countries has lost its appeal and influence, because since the 1980s, aid from the western countries hasn't focused on the needs of recipients but their own intentions and attached strings. In stark contrast, emerging donors don't emphasize their intentions or impose attached strings, merely asking recipients to support donors' diplomatic policies. Moreover, the focus of aid is on trade and investment, offering technology, recommendations and professional help to recipients so that recipients find the aid more helpful and meet their needs. Naturally, the revolution took place quietly (Woods 2008).

Besides, other important aspects of aid are donors' domestic environment (Fu and Lv 2011; Jiang 2015; Lancaster 2007; Otter 2003; Taw 2011; Tingley 2010), public support (Otter 2003) and attention to aid effects.

Once again, we have witnessed the impacts of political aid, economic aid, livelihood aid and other concepts over aid and aid effects. At the same time, we have found under different circumstances the intentions of donors will lead to various effects. According to Woods' analysis and Moyo's argument, we found when recipients are left with no choices, donors, with the money, will impose their intentions and act in an aggressive manner. In order to get aid, recipients have to accept donors' intentions. If donors have choices, donors' intentions won't be absolutely aggressive and recipients are allowed to choose the donors that are suitable and beneficial to them. Against the backdrop of such a logic, China's aid has broken down the western countries' monopoly over aid and delivered a blow to the existing aid system. Therefore, considering aid as a market (Sumner and Mallett 2013) is an effective description of the current and future aid.

Another factor influencing aid and aid effects is recipients. The attention to recipients covers the environment such as climate and population (Walker 1986) and the gains and spending of recipients. According to Martins' research, two-thirds of aid resources have flown to low-income countries. And most of the resources received by recipients are spent on public investment without surplus (Martins 2011). The attention is also expanded into absorption capability and the capability of using resources. A large number of studies have found that the returns rate of capital is declining gradually. Fenny, among others, thinks the influencing factors include capital, policies and institutions, macroeconomy, funders' practices, social and cultural factors. They concluded from the research that absorption capability severely impacted the capability to receive aid and aid efficiency. Recipients' human resources, infrastructure, policies and institutions, and funders' practices are important components of recipient' absorption capacity (Feeny and de Silva 2012).

Based on the examination of China's agriculture aid to Africa since the 1960s, Tang Xiaoyang argues that the unique environment in rural Africa has imposed a challenge to China and points out that as aid cannot be accommodated to the local society, it cannot lead to transformative changes, which is a major factor influencing aid activities and aid effects. He suggests a renewed review of the function of aid as well as the evaluation standards of aid effects (Tang 2013).

Easterly, a former economist of the World Bank, participated actively in aid operations and worked on a massive amount of literature on aid. In the discussion about influencing factors of aid and aid effects, he noted that practice is the most important factor (Easterly 2006; Easterly and Williamson 2011). In 2007, he published *The White Man's Burden* which was groundbreaking in the realms of aid in the west, suggesting there are too many wrong practices in aid in the West while too few right and good examples. The most primary cause is the disengagement of designers and searchers. Easterly for sure is against grand designs and believes the ones that of great help are the searchers. In aid, planners announce grand focuses however fail to motivate others to practice. Searchers find feasible ways to practice and get rewards. Planners raise their expectations but fail to be responsible for realizing such expectations. Searchers shoulder the responsibility and engage themselves in practices. Planners decide where aid goes to, while searchers know what is needed. Planners design the global blueprint, while searchers are deploying local conditions. Planners are not in touch with the reality without knowledge of activities on the ground, while searchers know everything about the reality on the ground. Planners never bother to care whether plans are achieved, while searchers know whether their targets are satisfied. Therefore, what really helps is delivering aid directly to the poor, that's where practice comes to play (Easterly 2009). Easterly's notion of searchers includes donors' searchers and recipients' searchers and shifts its focus on searcher to agency. The former emphasizes more on individuality and the possibility of exploration, the latter focuses more on the possibility of initiative and organization.

Amartya Sen, the Nobel laureate in economics, wrote a book review about it, and holds that aid practices are not as easy as depicted by Easterly. However, what he agrees with Easterly is that the failure of many grand plans is down to overlooking the complexity of institutions and incentives and ignoring the creativity of individuals. What needed is social measures instead of bureaucracy. Sen also holds that Easterly completely ignores economic problems of different types (Sen 2006).

Connecting planners with searchers is exactly what China has been doing. On the one hand, China provides aid to recipients. On the other hand, China has dispatched its experts, professionals to recipient countries, working on different areas and teaching its practices to the beneficiaries in recipient countries to achieve effective interaction between plans and practices.

Angeles, as well as others, emphasized the influences of the elite from recipient countries. According to them, if the elite, between donors and aid beneficiaries, are influenced by the economy and power rather than beneficiaries, there is a high chance that aid is misused. The data on former colonial countries shows that the number of former colonists staying in the former colonies and aid efficiency are negatively correlated, and the results are stable (Angeles and Neanidis 2009).

Ni Guohua and others studied the influences of the group of experts over aid performance and argued that the professional technical capability, gender, age, and confidence of experts dispatched abroad have a significant impact over the cooperation capability of the experts and experts with proficiency in communication, coordination and languages are more popular among recipients (Ni et al. 2014). In research on China's aid to Africa for agriculture, Xu among others discussed the aid-related behaviors of state-owned agricultural companies' managers, especially the relations between the headquarters and farms. They pointed out that as a business borderland, even though managers don't settle down there, aid effects are not affected because they work closely with locals in their work (Xu et al. 2014).

In the discussion about factors related to aid effects, we have found that without relatively systematic study, thematic exploration focuses on donors' political trends, domestic politics, donors' aid modalities, recipients' politics, economy, social environment, human capital, infrastructure and institutional environment. Literature on both the donor and the recipient centers on the practices of offering and receiving aid and points out that execution impacts aid efficiency (Dietrich 2011; Broughton et al. 2016). Besides, groups have also drawn attention, including donors' executioners, recipients' agencies and so on (Herman and Martín-Cruz 2013; Easterly and Williamson 2011).

What remains unclear is how to measure aid effects. As what has been discussed before and shown by the framework of "two-sided four-tiered embeddedness," aid effects have a multi-tiered embedded structure. Regrettably, at any level, even the bottom level of the programs, the existing literature from both donors and recipients fail to reach a consensus on the standards of measuring aid effects. If we take a rough review of the discussion on factors that influence aid, every piece of literature sounds reasonable. However, it is difficult to identify the connection between different literature.

What inspired us is that when we evaluate the effectiveness of development aid for health from China to Uganda, we do not have any effectiveness evaluation criteria to follow; instead, we need to establish applicable effectiveness evaluation criteria according to China's practices in development aid for health.

3.3 Foreign Aid: A Changing Landscape

On the basis of examining the history of aid, Sumner and Mallett point our clearly that the landscape of official development aid (ODA) has undergone historic transformation (Sumner and Mallett, 2013). They cited the data of the World Bank and noted that in 1990, 90% of impoverished people (with USD 1.25 every day) lived in low-income countries. In 2008, three-quarters of impoverished people lived in medium-income countries. Same changes have also occurred over the past decades in the distribution of undernourished people, shifting from low-income countries to middle-income countries. Poverty and development have become domestic problems for middle-income countries rather than international problems. In the meanwhile, impacts of emerging donors such as private organizations and funds in China are expanding in the ODA. The arrival of emerging donors is reshaping the landscape of international aid.

Among such changes, like Moyo, both Severino and Ray hold that traditional ODA has died (Severino and Ray 2009, 2010) and the goals, participants and methods of aid should be redefined and changed, which they call the threefold revolution of ODA. This is because, if those struggling with poverty live in middle-income countries cannot benefit from economic development, economic growth may not necessarily resolve problems confronted by traditional aid such as resurfacing poverty and malnutrition. The major solutions will be domestic governance, taxation and redistribution policies adopted by middle-income countries rather than ODA. Bilateral aid is obviously not the effective way to solve the problems plaguing middle-income countries. Multilateral cooperation has become an important trend.

In the context of such changes, donors need to adapt to new situations and reconsider the goals, allocation and means of aid. While discussing the key features, targets, and means of traditional development aid, Sumner and Mallett developed "Aid 2.0," that is to adapt to new development aid (Sumner and Mallett 2013).

Jones, who has tracked data of the past five decades and discussed major problems of aid and believed that the fact that every country deployed error correction model in its ODA means it is a long-term trend in bilateral aid. Within a short span of time, different donors represent differences. In light of the long-term trend, it means: First, aid behaviors vary among different countries during different periods of time. Second, besides the heterogeneity of recipients, donors especially big donors compete against each other, for instance, compete in expanding or contracting the scale of aid. Third, domestic macroeconomy has a short-term impact over aid activities, however the crisis of the banking system seems to have no negative impacts over aid. Fourth, aid has been more and more related with security, the democracy, and economic growth of recipients (Jones 2015).

If error correction model demonstrates a kind of social fact, Dollar and Levin identified another social fact. After surveying the development aid between 1984 and 2003, they found the selectivity of aid had been strengthening, which means it is a new phenomenon to connect the institutions of the donor and the recipient. According to research, both bilateral and multilateral aid is related to the democracy, property right and rule of law of recipients and multilateral aid is more selective than bilateral aid. From 1984 to 1989, bilateral and multilateral aid is significantly negatively correlated to the rule of law of recipients, as well as recipients' economic governance, that is worse economic governance leads to more aid, which has little to do with the democracy of recipients. However, from 2000 to 2003, multilateral aid was positively correlated to economic governance, i.e., better economic governance leads to more aid. Bilateral aid was also positively correlated to economic governance. However, the statistics does not show significant results (Dollar and Levin 2006). This finding is highly consistent with the finding of Bräutigam (2006).

The third possible fact is connecting aid with security. The latest work of Brown and Grävingholt focuses on this topic. As the international security landscape evolves, they have found the threat to security is not from rival countries, but from fragile politics, governments and the spread of terrorism around the world. They think recipients are reflecting under the circumstances of aid efficacy and realizing without security, there is no development and vice versa, which has become a more remarkable trend. Therefore, they put forward an argument targeting ODA policies of the western countries, i.e., "aid securitization" and cited the data of OECD between 1990 and 2013 to demonstrate this trend (Brown and Grävingholt 2016).

Thérien has sought to find the factors that influence aid-related phenomena such as error correction, selectivity, and connection with security. After looking through the evolution of aid since it was initiated, he established an ideal model and put forward the understanding of decades of aid cannot be detached from ideologies. Left and right ideologies have been the inclinations of aid and directly impacting the trends of aid. After the second World War, aid was initiated by the left wing, and aid from 1950 to 1970 was influenced by the right-wing ideology. Before 1955, 90% of aid was provided by the USA, the UK, and France. From 1970 to 1980, aid was questioned and the left-wing ideology called for the establishment of a new international economic order. The era from 1980 to 1990 was once again dominated by the right-wing ideology. Neo-liberalists argued the role played by countries should be weakened. From 1990 until now, the pendulum seems to be swinging back to human development (Thérien 2002). Such judgments are arbitrary and ideal, however simplifying and clarifying the changes of ideologies in aid.

These analysis and judgments greatly inspire us to understand China's foreign aid.

First, as the international aid landscape evolves, it is high time to reflect on traditional methods of aid. Over the past decades, aid-related changes have been occurring in the economic area, the distribution of poor people and politics, economy and security of recipients and neighboring areas. Of course, international aid is not limited to economic aid. ODA of the 1960s covered almost every aspect such as politics, economy, culture, health care, military, and so on. The takeaway of economic aid may not necessarily be applicable to other areas, however, it serves as a warning, meaning that it will be difficult to reach the goals of aid with the same methods, content and scale, because in the framework of two-sided four-tiered embeddedness, the yardstick of reaching donors' aid goas is to satisfy the needs of recipients and prioritize aid on a short-term and long-term basis.

Second, if we agree that the development of aid is a process of trials, then we measure the gains and loss of previous aid programs, lessons are more important than experience, because experience cannot guide current or future aid. Donors are developing and recipients are developing, too. To design aid in the future, we need to understand not only the evolution of the macro landscape interpreted by Sumner and Mallett, but also understand the phenomenon observed by Jones through the data of the past five decades, i.e., the aid provided by each other is not the same and the aid provided by one country is different at different times. In the future, aid should be provided through trials. Therefore, in the framework of two-sided four-tiered embeddedness, what is needed is more interaction and communication between the donor and the recipient and prediction about the possible efficacy of aid with different purposes, content, and means. Whether multilateral cooperation is needed or how such cooperation is conducted is still a process of trials in the future.

Because of these two judgments of the aid landscape, other discussions have become limited and overly specific, such as the discussion about neocolonialism (Pfaff 1995), the discussion about aid missions since the 1960s (Clad and Stone 1992; Musolf 1963), the discussion about the support of aid from various actors such as NGOs (Dicklitch and Rice 2004; Nunnenkamp and Ohler 2012; Paxton and Knack 2012), the discussion about factors that influence aid scale (Kilby 2011), the discussion about conflicts between the donor and the recipient (Balla and Reinhardt 2008; de Ree and Nillesen 2009; Nielsen et al. 2011), the discussion about power asymmetry in rural aid (Nielsen and Yamamoto 2013), the discussion about appearance and reality (Gerhart 1999), the discussion about the relations between aid and public goods (Hatzipanayotou and Michael 1995; Lei et al. 2007) and so on.

To our regret, there is almost no Chinese literature touching on important topics such as ODA's development landscape and trends.

References

Abbot, George C. 1973. Two Concepts of Foreign Aid. *World Development* 1 (9): 1–10. https://doi.org/10.1016/0305-750x(73)90153-8.

Acht, Martin, Toman Omar Mahmoud, and Rainer Thiele. 2014. Corrupt Governments Receive Less State-to-State Aid: Governance and the Delivery of Foreign Aid Through Non-state Actors. *Journal of Development Economics.* https://doi.org/10.1016/j.jdeveco.2014.11.005.

Adelman, Carol C., and Jeremiah Norris. 2001. Usefulness of Foreign Aid for Health Care in Less-Developed Countries. *The Lancet* 358 (9299): 2174. https://doi.org/10.1016/S0140-6736(01)07212-9.

Agénor, Pierre-Richard, Nihal Bayraktar, and Karim El Aynaoui. 2008. Roads out of Poverty? Assessing the Links Between Aid, Public Investment, Growth, and Poverty Reduction. *Journal of Development Economics* 86 (2): 277–295. https://doi.org/10.1016/j.jdeveco.2007.07.001.

Ali, Abdiweli M., and Hodan Said Isse. 2007. Foreign Aid and Free Trade and Their Effect on Income: A Panel Analysis. *The Journal of Developing Areas* 41 (1): 127–142. https://doi.org/10.2307/40376162.

Angeles, Luis, and Kyriakos C. Neanidis. 2009. Aid Effectiveness: The Role of the Local Elite. *Journal of Development Economics* 90 (1): 120–134. https://doi.org/10.1016/j.jdeveco.2008.05.002.

Anonymous. 2011. Rethinking Aid Policy: Working with Recipient Communities. *Harvard International Review* 32 (4): 78–79.

Arndt, Channing, Sam Jones, and Finn Tarp. 2015. Assessing Foreign Aid's Long Run Contribution to Growth and Development. *World Development* 69: 6–18. https://doi.org/10.1016/j.worlddev.2013.12.016.

Atwood, J. Brian, M. Peter McPherson, and Andrew Natsios. 2008. Arrested Development: Making Foreign Aid a More Effective Tool. *Foreign Affairs* 87 (6): 123–132. https://doi.org/10.2307/20699376.

Ayittey, George B.N. 2003. Aid and Reform in Africa: Lessons from *Ten Case Studies. Journal of Economic Literature* 41 (1): 248–250.

Baccini, Leonardo, and Johannes Urpelainen. 2012. Strategic Side Payments: Preferential Trading Agreements, Economic Reform, and Foreign Aid. *The*

Journal of Politics 74 (4): 932–949. https://doi.org/10.1017/S0022381612000485.

Balla, Eliana, and Gina Yannitell Reinhardt. 2008. Giving and Receiving Foreign Aid: Does Conflict Count? *World Development* 36 (12): 2566–2585. https://doi.org/10.1016/j.worlddev.2008.03.008.

Bauhr, Monika, Nicholas Charron, and Naghmeh Nasiritousi. 2013. Does Corruption Cause Aid Fatigue? Public Opinion and the Aid-Corruption Paradox1. *International Studies Quarterly* 57 (3): 568–579. https://doi.org/10.1111/isqu.12025.

Bearce, David H., Steven E. Finkel, Anibal S. Perez-Linan, Juan Rodrfguez-Zepeda, and Lena Surzhko-Harned. 2013. Has the New Aid for Trade Agenda Been Export Effective? Evidence on the Impact of Us AfT Allocations 1999–2008. *International Studies Quarterly* 57 (1): 163–170. https://doi.org/10.2307/41804855.

Bendavid, Eran. 2014. Is Health Aid Reaching the Poor? Analysis of Household Data from Aid Recipient Countries. *PLoS ONE* 9 (1): 1–9. https://doi.org/10.1371/journal.pone.0084025.

Bhagwati, Jagdish. 2010. Banned Aid: Why International Assistance Does Not Alleviate Poverty. *Foreign Affairs* 89 (1): 120–125. https://doi.org/10.2307/20699788.

Blackorby, Charles, Walter Bossert, and David Donaldson. 1999. Foreign Aid and Population Policy: Some Ethical Considerations. *Journal of Development Economics* 59 (2): 203–232. https://doi.org/10.1016/S0304-3878(99)00010-3.

Boone, Peter. 1996. Politics and the Effectiveness of Foreign Aid. *European Economic Review* 40 (2): 289–329. https://doi.org/10.1016/0014-2921(95)00127-1.

Bräutigam, Deborah. 1992. Governance, Economy, and Foreign Aid. *Studies in Comparative International Development* 27 (3): 3.

Bräutigam, Deborah. 2006. State-Building and the Origin of 'Good' Institutions. *Conference Papers-American Political Science Association*, 1.

Bräutigam, Deborah, and Stephen Knack. 2004. Foreign Aid, Institutions, and Governance in Sub-Saharan Africa. *Economic Development and Cultural Change* 52 (2): 255–285.

Brech, Viktor, and Niklas Potrafke. 2014. Donor Ideology and Types of Foreign Aid. *Journal of Comparative Economics* 42 (1): 61–75. https://doi.org/10.1016/j.jce.2013.07.002.

Broughton, Edward I., Martin Muhire, Esther Karamagi, Herbert Kisamba, and Sarah Smith Lunsford. 2016. *The Effectiveness and Efficiency of Implementing the Chronic Care Model for HIV Care in Uganda*. Washington, DC: USAID.

Brown, Stephen, and Jorn Grävingholt. 2016. *The Securitization of Foreign Aid*. New York: Palgrave Macmillan.

Browne, Stephen. 2012. *Aid and Influence: Do Donors Help or Hinder?* Hoboken: Taylor & Francis.

Burhop, Carsten. 2005. Foreign Assistance and Economic Development: A Re-evaluation. *Economics Letters* 86 (1): 57–61. https://doi.org/10.1016/j.econlet.2004.06.007.

Burton, A. Abrams, and Kenneth A. Lewis. 1993. Human Rights and the Distribution of U. S. Foreign Aid. *Public Choice* 77 (4): 815–821. https://doi.org/10.2307/30027190.

Busse, Matthias, and Steffen Gröning. 2009. Does Foreign Aid Improve Governance? *Economics Letters* 104 (2): 76–78. https://doi.org/10.1016/j.econlet.2009.04.002.

Carey, Sabine C. 2007. European Aid: Human Rights Versus Bureaucratic Inertia? *Journal of Peace Research* 44 (4): 447–464. https://doi.org/10.2307/27640540.

Chong, Alberto, Mark Gradstein, and Cecilia Calderon. 2009. Can Foreign Aid Reduce Income Inequality and Poverty? *Public Choice* 140 (1/2): 59–84. https://doi.org/10.2307/40270909.

Clad, James C., and Roger D. Stone. 1992. New Mission for Foreign Aid. *Foreign Affairs* 72 (1): 196–205. https://doi.org/10.2307/20045506.

Cogneau, Denis, and Jean-David Naudet. 2007. Who Deserves Aid? Equality of Opportunity, International Aid, and Poverty Reduction. *World Development* 35 (1): 104–120. https://doi.org/10.1016/j.worlddev.2006.09.006.

Cohen, Michael A. 2013. Giving to Developing Countries: Controversies and Paradoxes of International Aid. *Social Research* 80 (2): 591–606.

Cohen, John M., Merilee S. Grindle, and S. Tjip Walker. 1985. Foreign Aid and Conditions Precedent: Political and Bureaucratic Dimensions. *World Development* 13 (12): 1211–1230. https://doi.org/10.1016/0305-750x(85)90122-6.

Collier, Paul, and David Dollar. 2001. Can the World Cut Poverty in Half? How Policy Reform and Effective Aid Can Meet International Development Goals. *World Development* 29 (11): 1787–1802. https://doi.org/10.1016/s0305-750x(01)00076-6.

Crawford, Gordon. 2001. *Foreign Aid and Political Reform: A Comparative Analysis of Democracy Assistance and Political Conditionality*. Basingstoke: Palgrave.

Demirel-Pegg, Tijen, and James Moskowitz. 2009. Us Aid Allocation: The Nexus of Human Rights, Democracy, and Development. *Journal of Peace Research* 46 (2): 181–198. https://doi.org/10.2307/25654379.

de Ree, Joppe, and Eleonora Nillesen. 2009. Aiding Violence or Peace? The Impact of Foreign Aid on the Risk of Civil Conflict in Sub-Saharan Africa. *Journal of Development Economics* 88 (2): 301–313. https://doi.org/10.1016/j.jdeveco.2008.03.005.

De Waal, Alex. 1997. Democratizing the Aid Encounter in Africa. *International Affairs* 73 (4): 623–639.

Dicklitch, Susan, and Heather Rice. 2004. The Mennonite Central Committee (MCC) and Faith-Based NGO Aid to Africa. *Development in Practice* 14 (5): 660–672. https://doi.org/10.2307/4029894.

Dietrich, Simone. 2011. The Politics of Public Health Aid: Why Corrupt Governments Have Incentives to Implement Aid Effectively. *World Development* 39 (1): 55–63. http://dx.doi.org/10.1016/j.worlddev.2010.06.011.

Dollar, David, and Victoria Levin. 2006. The Increasing Selectivity of Foreign Aid, 1984–2003. *World Development* 34 (12): 2034–2046. https://doi.org/10.1016/j.worlddev.2006.06.002.

Due, Jean M. 1993. Liberalization and Privatization in Tanzania and Zambia. *World Development* 21 (12): 1981.

Dutta, Nabamita, Peter T. Leeson, and Claudia R. Williamson. 2013. The Amplification Effect: Foreign Aid's Impact on Political Institutions. *Kyklos* 66 (2): 208–228. https://doi.org/10.1111/kykl12018.

Easterly, William. 2006. *The White Man's Burden: Why the West's Efforts to Aid the Rest Have Done So Much Ill and So Little Good*. Oxford: Oxford University Press.

Easterly, William. 2009. Can the West Save Africa? *Journal of Economic Literature* 47 (2): 373–447. https://doi.org/10.2307/27739927.

Easterly, William, and Claudia R. Williamson. 2011. Rhetoric Versus Reality: The Best and Worst of Aid Agency Practices. *World Development* 39 (11): 1930–1949. https://doi.org/10.1016/j.worlddev.2011.07.027.

Feeny, Simon, and Ashton de Silva. 2012. Measuring Absorptive Capacity Constraints to Foreign Aid. *Economic Modelling* 29 (3): 725–733. https://doi.org/10.1016/j.econmod.2012.01.013.

Feeny, Simon, and Tim R.L. Fry. 2014. How Sustainable is the Macro-economic Impact of Foreign Aid? *Journal of Policy Modeling* 36 (6): 1066–1081. https://doi.org/10.1016/j.jpolmod.2014.11.001.

Fisher, Jonathan. 2015. 'Does It Work?': Work for Whom? Britain and Political Conditionality Since the Cold War. *World Development* 75: 13–25. https://doi.org/10.1016/j.worlddev.2014.12.005.

Francken, Nathalie, Bart Minten, and Johan F.M. Swinnen. 2012. The Political Economy of Relief Aid Allocation: Evidence from Madagascar. *World Development* 40 (3): 486.

Fu, Ruiwei, and Xiaoqing Lv. 2011. China's Policy on Global Health and Foreign Aid in Africa. Reports of the Center for and International Studies.

Fuchs, Andreas, Axel Dreher, and Peter Nunnenkamp. 2014. Determinants of Donor Generosity: A Survey of the Aid Budget Literature. *World Development* 56: 172–199. https://doi.org/10.1016/j.worlddev.2013.09.004.

Furia, Annalisa. 2015. *The Foreign Aid Regime: Gift-Giving, States and Global Dis/Order*. New York: Palgrave Macmillan.

Gerhart, Gail M. 1999. Aid to Africa: So Much to Do, So Little Done. *Foreign Affairs* 78 (6): 163.

Ghosh Banerjee, Sudeshna, and Dennis A. Rondinelli. 2003. Does Foreign Aid Promote Privatization? Empirical Evidence from Developing Countries. *World Development* 31 (9): 1527–1548. https://doi.org/10.1016/s0305-750x(03)00107-4.

Gomez, Simon Peter. 2007. Human Rights and the Allocation of Foreign Aid: A Cross-National Analysis of the Last Years of the Cold War, 1980–1989. *The Social Science Journal* 44 (2): 275–285. https://doi.org/10.1016/j.soscij.2007.03.018.

Gulrajani, Nilima. 2011. Transcending the Great Foreign Aid Debate: Managerialism, Radicalism and the Search for Aid Effectiveness. *Third World Quarterly* 32 (2): 199–216. https://doi.org/10.1080/01436597.2011.560465.

Hatzipanayotou, Panos, and Michael S. Michael. 1995. Foreign Aid and Public Goods. *Journal of Development Economics* 47 (2): 455–467. https://doi.org/10.1016/0304-3878(95)00020-Q.

He, Wenping. 2011. From "Aid Effectiveness" to "Development Effectiveness": Evolution of Aid Concepts and Role of Chinese Experience. *West Asia and Africa* 9: 120–135.

Heckelman, Jac C., and Stephen Knack. 2008. Foreign Aid and Market Liberalizing Reform. *Economica* 75 (299): 524–548. https://doi.org/10.2307/40071816.

Hermano, Vmtor, and Natalia Martm-Cruz. 2013. How to Deliver Foreign Aid? The Case of Projects Governed by the Spanish International Agency. *World Development* 43: 298–314. https://doi.org/10.1016/j.worlddev.2012.10.017.

Hsieh, Chang-Tai. 2000. Bargaining over Reform. *European Economic Review* 44 (9): 1659–1676. https://doi.org/10.1016/s0014-2921(99)00012-4.

Hu, Mei, and Hingwu Liu. 2009. Ideology First or Livelihood First: A Comparative Study on Western and China's Policies on Aid to Africa after the Cold War. *World Economy and Politics* 10: 17–24.

Hyden, Goran, and Shlomo Reutlinger. 1992. Foreign Aid in a Period of Democratization: The Case of Politically Autonomous Food Funds. *World Development* 20 (9): 1253–1260. https://doi.org/10.1016/0305-750x(92)90076-8.

Jakupec, Viktor, and Max Kelly (eds.). 2016. *Assessing the Impact of Foreign Aid: Value for Money and Aid for Trade*. Amsterdam: Academic Press.

Jiang, Huajie. 2015. Reexamination of the History of China's Medical Teams to Africa (1963–1983): A Discussion on Effectiveness and Sustainability of International Aid. *Foreign Affairs Review—Journal of China Foreign Affairs University* 4: 61–81.

Jones, Sam. 2015. Aid Supplies over Time: Addressing Heterogeneity, Trends, and Dynamics. *World Development* 69: 31–43. https://doi.org/10.1016/j.worlddev.2013.12.014.

Kasekende, L.A., and Atingi-Ego, M. 1999. Uganda's Experience with Aid. *Journal of African Economies* 8 (4): 617.

Kersting, Erasmus, and Christopher Kilby. 2014. Aid and Democracy Redux. *European Economic Review* 67: 125–143. https://doi.org/10.1016/j.euroecorev.2014.01.016.

Khan, Haider Ali, and Eiichi Hoshino. 1992. Impact of Foreign Aid on the Fiscal Behavior of LDC Governments. *World Development* 20 (10): 1481–1488. https://doi.org/10.1016/0305-750x(92)90068-7.

Kilby, Christopher. 2011. What Determines the Size of Aid Projects? *World Development* 39 (11): 1981–1994. https://doi.org/10.1016/j.worlddev.2011.07.023.

King, J.R. 1953. Science Versus Administration in Certain U. S. Foreign Aid Efforts. *Science* 117 (3047): 568–569. https://doi.org/10.1126/science.117.3047.568.

King, Kenneth. 2010. China's Cooperation in Education and Training with Kenya: A Different Model? *International Journal of Educational Development* 30 (5): 488–496. https://doi.org/10.1016/j.ijedudev.2010.03.014.

King, Kenneth. 2011. The New Aid Architecture in Ghana: Influencing Policy and Practice? *The European Journal of Development Research* 23 (4): 648–667. https://doi.org/10.1057/ejdr.2011.26.

Knack, Stephen. 2004. Does Foreign Aid Promote Democracy? *International Studies Quarterly* 48 (1): 251–266. https://doi.org/10.2307/3693571.

Koch, Svea. 2015. A Typology of Political Conditionality Beyond Aid: Conceptual Horizons Based on Lessons from the European Union. *World Development* 75: 97–108. https://doi.org/10.1016/j.worlddev.2015.01.006.

Kono, Daniel Yuichi, and Gabriella R. Montinola. 2009. Does Foreign Aid Support Autocrats, Democrats, or Both? *The Journal of Politics* 71 (2): 704–718. https://doi.org/10.2307/30218980.

Kosack, Stephen. 2003. Effective Aid: How Democracy Allows Development Aid to Improve the Quality of Life. *World Development* 31 (1): 1–22. https://doi.org/10.1016/s0305-750x(02)00177-8.

Kourtellos, Andros, Chih Ming, and Xiaobo Zhang. 2007. Is the Relationship Between Aid and Economic Growth Nonlinear? *Journal of Macroeconomics* 29 (3): 515–540. https://doi.org/10.1016/j.jmacro.2007.02.07.

Lambert, Marie-Laurence. 1996. Foreign Aid and Tuberculosis Control Policy in the Federated States of Micronesia. *The Lancet* 347 (8997): 334–335. https://doi.org/10.1016/S0140-6736(96)90516-4.

Lancaster, Carol. 2007. *Foreign Aid: Diplomacy, Development, Domestic Politics.* Chicago, IL and London: University of Chicago Press.

Lebovic, James H., and Erik Voeten. 2009. The Cost of Shame: International Organizations and Foreign Aid in the Punishing of Human Rights Violators. *Journal of Peace Research* 46 (1): 79–97. https://doi.org/10.2307/27640800.

Lei, Vivian, Steven Tucker, and Filip Vesely. 2007. Foreign Aid and Weakest-Link International Public Goods: An Experimental Study. *European Economic Review* 51 (3): 599–623. https://doi.org/10.1016/j.euroecorev.2006.03.008.

Leonard, David K. 2005. Foreign Aid and Development: Lessons Learnt and Directions for the Future. *The Journal of Modern African Studies* 43 (1): 153–154.

Lim, Sijeong, Layna Mosley, and Aseem Prakash. 2015. Revenue Substitution? How Foreign Aid Inflows Moderate the Effect of Bilateral Trade Pressures on Labor Rights. *World Development* 67: 295–309. https://doi.org/10.1016/j.worlddev.2014.10.025.

Liu, Xiangbo, Xiaomeng Zhang, and Chi-Chur Chao. 2014. Foreign Aid, Leisure Effort Choice, and Economic Growth. *Economic Modelling* 43: 435–438. https://doi.org/10.1016/j.econmod.2014.09.006.

Lof, Matthijs, Tseday Jemaneh Mekasha, and Finn Tarp. 2014. Aid and Income: Another Time-Series Perspective. *World Development*. https://doi.org/10.1016/j.worlddev.2013.12.015.

Lskavyan, Vahe. 2014. Donor-Recipient Ideological Differences and Economic Aid. *Economics Letters* 123 (3): 345–347. https://doi.org/10.1016/j.econlet.2014.03.016.

Martins, Pedro M.G. 2011. Aid Absorption and Spending in Africa: A Panel Cointegration Approach. *The Journal of Development Studies* 47 (12): 1925–1953. https://doi.org/10.1080/00220388.2011.579115.

McGrath, Simon. 2010. Beyond Aid Effectiveness: The Development of the South African Further Education and Training College Sector, 1994–2009. *International Journal of Educational Development* 30 (5): 525–534. https://doi.org/10.1016/j.ijedudev.2010.03.011.

Mekasha, Tseday Jemaneh, and Finn Tarp. 2013. Aid and Growth: What Meta-Analysis Reveals. *The Journal of Development Studies* 49 (4): 564–583. https://doi.org/10.1080/00220388.2012.709621.

Miller, Daniel C. 2014. Explaining Global Patterns of International Aid for Linked Biodiversity Conservation and Development. *World Development* 59: 341–359. https://doi.org/10.1016/j.worlddev.2014.01.004.

Minoiu, Camelia, and Sanjay G. Reddy. 2010. Development Aid and Economic Growth: A Positive Long-Run Relation. *The Quarterly Review of Economics and Finance* 50 (1): 27–39. https://doi.org/10.1016/j.qref.2009.10.004.

Mishra, Prachi, and David Newhouse. 2009. Does Health Aid Matter? *Journal of Health Economics* 28 (4): 855–872. https://doi.org/10.1016/j.jhealeco.2009.05.004.

Molenaers, Nadia, Sebastian Dellepiane, and Jorg Faust. 2015. Political Conditionality and Foreign Aid. *World Development* 75: 2–12. https://doi.org/10.1016/j.worlddev.2015.04.001.
Moyo, Dambisa. 2009. *Dead Aid: Why Aid Is Not Working and How There Is Another Way for Africa*. London: Allen Lane.
Mundy, Karen, Megan Haggerty, Malini Sivasubramaniam, Suzanne Cherry, and Richard Maclure. 2010. Civil Society, Basic Education, and Sector-Wide Aid: Insights from Sub-Saharan Africa. *Development in Practice* 20 (4/5): 484–497. https://doi.org/10.2307/20750147.
Muravchik, Joshua. 1996. Affording Foreign Policy: The Problem Is Not Wallet, But Will. *Foreign Affairs* 75 (2): 8–13. https://doi.org/10.2307/20047484.
Museru, Malimu, Francois Toerien, and Sean Gossel. 2014. The Impact of Aid and Public Investment Volatility on Economic Growth in Sub-Saharan Africa. *World Development* 57: 138–147. https://doi.org/10.1016/j.worlddev.2013.12.001.
Musolf, Lloyd D. 1963. Overview Overseas: Dilemma for Aid Missions. *Public Administration Review* 23 (4): 219–226. https://doi.org/10.2307/973896.
Ni, Guohua, Jing Zhang, Dong Ding, and Fengtian Zheng. 2014. Influence of Personal Traits of Experts Aiding Africa on Their Performance: An Empirical Analysis Based on Cross-Sectional Data of 100 Experts. *World Agriculture* 9: 163–169.
Nielsen, Richard A., Michael G. Findley, Zachary S. Davis, Tara Candland, and Daniel L. Nielson. 2011. Foreign Aid Shocks as a Cause of Violent Armed Conflict. *American Journal of Political Science* 55 (2): 219–232. https://doi.org/10.1111/j.1540-5907.2010.00492.x.
Niyizonkiza, Deogratias, and Alyssa Yamamoto. 2013. Grassroots Philanthropy: Fighting the Power Asymmetries of Aid in Rural Burundi. *Social Research* 80 (2): 321–336.
Nunnenkamp, Peter, and Hannes Ohler. 2012. Funding, Competition and the Efficiency of NGOs: An Empirical Analysis of Non-charitable Expenditure of Us NGOs Engaged in Foreign Aid. *Kyklos* 65 (1): 81–110. https://doi.org/10.1111/j.1467-6435.201.00528.x.
Ohler, Hannes, Peter Nunnenkamp, and Axel Dreher. 2012. Does Conditionality Work? A Test for an Innovative Us Aid Scheme. *European Economic Review* 56 (1): 138–153. https://doi.org/10.1016/j.euroecorev.2011.05.003.
Okada, Keisuke, and Sovannroeun Samreth. 2012. The Effect of Foreign Aid on Corruption: A Quantile Regression Approach. *Economics Letters* 115 (2): 240–243. https://doi.org/10.1016/j.econlet.2011.12.051.
Otter, Mark. 2003. Domestic Public Support for Foreign Aid: Does It Matter? *Third World Quarterly* 24 (1):115–125. https://doi.org/10.2307/3993633.

Ouattara, B. 2006. Foreign Aid and Government Fiscal Behaviour in Developing Countries: Panel Data Evidence. *Economic Modelling* 23 (3): 506–514. https://doi.org/10.1016/j.econmod.2006.02.001.

Papanek, Gustav F. 1973. Aid, Foreign Private Investment, Savings, and Growth in Less Developed Countries. *Journal of Political Economy* 81 (1): 120–130. https://doi.org/10.2307/1837329.

Paxton, Pamela, and Stephen Knack. 2012. Individual and Country-Level Factors Affecting Support for Foreign Aid. *International Political Science Review/Revue internationale de science politique* 33 (2): 171–192. https://doi.org/10.1177/0192512111406095.

Pfaff, William. 1995. A New Colonialism? Europe Must Go Back into Africa. *Foreign Affairs* 74 (1): 2.

Phelps, Nicholas A., John C.H. Stillwell, and Roseline Wanjiru. 2009. Broken Chain? AGOA and Foreign Direct Investment in the Kenyan Clothing Industry. *World Development* 37 (2): 314.

Reinsberg, Bernhard. 2014. Foreign Aid Responses to Political Liberalization. *World Development*. https://doi.org/10.1016/j.worlddev.2014.11.006.

Resnick, Danielle, and Nicolas Van de Walle. 2013. Democratic Trajectories in Africa: Unravelling the Impact of Foreign Aid. A Study Prepared by the United Nations University World Institute for Development Economics Research (UNU-WIDER).

Roodman, David. 2012. Doubts About the Evidence That Foreign Aid for Health Is Displaced into Non-health Uses. *The Lancet* 380 (9846): 972–973. https://doi.org/10.1016/s0140-6736(12)61529-3.

Rotberg, Robert I. 2009. *China into Africa: Trade, Aid, and Influence*. Washington, DC: Brookings Institution Press.

Saghafi, Massoud Mokhtari, and Jeffrey B. Nugent. 1983. Foreign Aid in the Form of Commodity Transfers That Increase the Income Gap Between Rich and Poor Countries: The Chichilnisky Theorems Revisited. *Journal of Development Economics* 13 (1–2): 213–216. https://doi.org/10.1016/0304-3878(83)90061-5.

Schwalbenberg, Henry M. 1998. Does Foreign Aid Cause the Adoption of Harmful Economic Policies? *Journal of Policy Modeling* 20 (5): 669–675. https://doi.org/10.1016/s0161-8938(97)00111-7.

Scott, James M., and Carie A. Steele. 2011. Sponsoring Democracy: The United States and Democracy Aid to the Developing World, 1988–2001. *International Studies Quarterly* 55 (1): 47–69. https://doi.org/10.2307/23019513.

Sen, Amartya. 2006. The Man Without a Plan: Can Foreign Aid Work? *Foreign Affairs* 85 (2):171–177. https://doi.org/10.2307/20031920.

Severino, Jean-Michel, and Olivier Ray. 2009. The End of ODA: Death and Rebirth of a Global Public Policy, vol. 167. Working Paper, Center for Global Development.

Severino, Jean-Michel, and Olivier Ray. 2010. The End of ODA (Ii): The Birth of Hypercollective Action, vol. 218. Working Paper, Center for Global Development.

Smith, Clark. 2010. *Ineffectiveness of Official Development Assistance in Ethiopia and Sudan*. Rochester: Social Science Research Network. SSRN-ID2317463.

Stein, Howard. 1994. Theories of Institutions and Economic Reform in Africa. *World Development* 22 (12): 1833–1849. https://doi.org/10.1016/0305-750X(94)90177-5.

Stiles, Kendall W. 1990. IMF Conditionality: Coercion or Compromise? *World Development* 18 (7): 959–974. https://doi.org/10.1016/0305-750X(90)90079-D.

Stokke, Olav. 1995. *Aid and Political Conditionality*. London: F. Cass, in association with The European Association of Development Research and Training Institutes (EADI).

Sumner, Andrew, and Richard Mallett. 2013. *The Future of Foreign Aid: Development Cooperation and the New Geography of Global Poverty*. New York: Palgrave Macmillan.

Szmant, H.H. 1978. Foreign Aid Support of Science and Economic Growth. *Science* 199 (4334): 1173–1182.

Tang, Xioayang. 2013. Evolution and Effect of China's Agricultural Aid to Africa. *World Economy and Politics* 5: 55–69.

Taw, Jennifer Morrison. 2011. Distributive Domestic Response. *Review of International Studies* 37 (3): 1357–1382. https://doi.org/10.2307/23025424.

Thérien, Jean-Philippe. 2002. Debating Foreign Aid: Right Versus Left. *Third World Quarterly* 23 (3): 449–466. https://doi.org/10.2307/3993536.

Tingley, Dustin. 2010. Donors and Domestic Politics: Political Influences on Foreign Aid Effort. *The Quarterly Review of Economics and Finance* 50 (1): 40–49. https://doi.org/10.1016/j.qref.2009.10.003.

Walker, Brian W. 1986. The African Environment and the Aid Process. *International Journal* 41 (4): 734–747.

Winters, Matthew S., and Gina Martinez. 2015. The Role of Governance in Determining Foreign Aid Flow Composition. *World Development* 66: 516–531. https://doi.org/10.1016/j.worlddev.2014.09.020.

Woods, Ngaire. 2005. The Shifting Politics of Foreign Aid. *International Affairs (Royal Institute of International Affairs 1944–)* 81 (2): 393–409. https://doi.org/10.2307/3568895.

Woods, Ngaire. 2008. Whose Aid? Whose Influence? China, Emerging Donors and the Silent Revolution in Development Assistance. *International Affairs (Royal Institute of International Affairs 1944–)* 84 (6): 1205–1221. https://doi.org/10.2307/25144989.

Xu, Xiuli, Gubo Qi, and Xiaoyun Li. 2014. Business Borderlands: China's Overseas State Agribusiness. *IDS Bulletin* 45: 114–124. https://doi.org/10.1111/1759-5436.12097.

Yeats, Alexander J. 1982. Development Assistance: Trade Versus Aid and the Relative Performance of Industrial Countries. *World Development* 10 (10): 863–869. https://doi.org/10.1016/0305-750X(82)90061-4.

Young, Andrew T., and Kathleen M. Sheehan. 2014. Foreign Aid, Institutional Quality, and Growth. *European Journal of Political Economy* 36: 195–208. https://doi.org/10.1016/j.ejpoleco.2014.08.003.

Zalanga, Samuel. 2014. Rural Development in Africa: An International Political Economy Perspective on the Significance of Healthcare in Human Development. *Journal of Third World Studies* 31 (1): 17–50.

Zhang, Haibing. 2012. Development-Oriented Aid: A Study of China's Model of Aid to Africa. *World Economic Research* 12: 78–83.

Zhang, Bin, and Yun Zhang. 2016. The US Foreign Aid and Its Inspiration for China. *World Agriculture* 7: 102–105.

Zhang, Yanbing, and Ying Huang. 2012. Differences in Foreign Aid Concepts Between China and the West. *Modern International Relations* 2: 41–47.

CHAPTER 4

Aid Recipients' Experience and Analysis

4.1 DAH in Africa

Within the framework of "two-sided four-tiered embeddedness," the first tier through which the development aid for health from China to Uganda (DAHCU) program is embedded in the aid received by Africa. Although such aid has an unprecedented influence on the continent, it won't be discussed at length in the book for the following two reasons. First, the aid received by Africa constitutes the first tier in which the DAHCU program is embedded. Compared with the two inward tiers, it wields less significant impact on the understanding of the program. Second, the actors of aid for Africa (donors and recipients) come in a great number, demonstrate quite different attributes, and feature extremely complicated structures/relations, thus requiring separate research. Considering these, we directly discuss the development aid for health (DAH) received by Africa.

In the past two decades, the DAH from the international community to Africa has improved remarkably in both quantity and quality. DAH used to be insensitive to politics and weak in political influence (Obermann 2007). However, as the calls for improving the health conditions worldwide grow louder, DAH begins to draw more attention with each passing day. As a result, related aid funds grow rapidly and account for an increasingly prominent proportion in the total aid. Moreover, its ties with politics become strikingly close, as well. Since efficient DAH can help recipients improve multiple health indicators greatly (Afridi and

Z. Qiu, *When Friendship Comes First*, China and Globalization 2.0,
https://doi.org/10.1007/978-981-32-9308-3_4

Ventelou 2013), they hence get the chance to gain related experience and knowledge. In this sense, DAH is recognized as a form of aid which can lead to a win-win outcome for donors and recipients.

While going through the existing literature, we spot in the database of the Development Assistance Committee (DAC), affiliated to the Organization for Economic Cooperation and Development (OECD), the data on DAH from DAC member states to Africa. Not complete as expected, these data tell a lot about how much DAH the continent has received, its developments in this regard over the past several decades, major sources of aid, and health fields to which such aid has gone. Unfortunately, we don't find any literature which can shed some light on the big picture of DAH received by Africa, or any literature about the effect of aid from the overall perspective. So there is no ready answer to the questions about how to understand and interpret the related data. In this context, we attempt to draw a sketch of DAH received by Africa with the literature that expounds similar topics, and on the basis to examine DAH from China to Africa.

4.1.1 DAH in Africa

According to the existing literature, the research on DAH methods and contents usually starts from the perspective of aid recipients. Figure 4.1 exhibits a part of an aid method to some extent (Dieleman et al. 2016). It is convinced by some people that two obviously different types of relations exist in DAH. They are the North–South relations and the South–South relations. Under the North–South relations, there coexist North-American pattern, Japanese pattern and European pattern, while Indian pattern and Chinese pattern can be found as part of the South–South relations (Xia and Chen 2016).

The North-American pattern is represented by the United States. Its basic features are affluent funding, wide participation, strong political strings attached, particular attention to institutional development in recipients, and call for multiple channels. Take HIV/AIDS prevention and treatment for example. The US President's Emergency Plan for AIDS Relief (PEPFAR) committed USD 5.4 billion to HIV/AIDS programs at its very beginning. Its expenditures went up by 20% every year from 2004 to 2009. Its annual budget was around USD 6.7 billion from 2009 to 2015 (Bendavid 2016). Like its other forms of assistance which bring a vast amount of funding to Africa, the US DAH focuses on

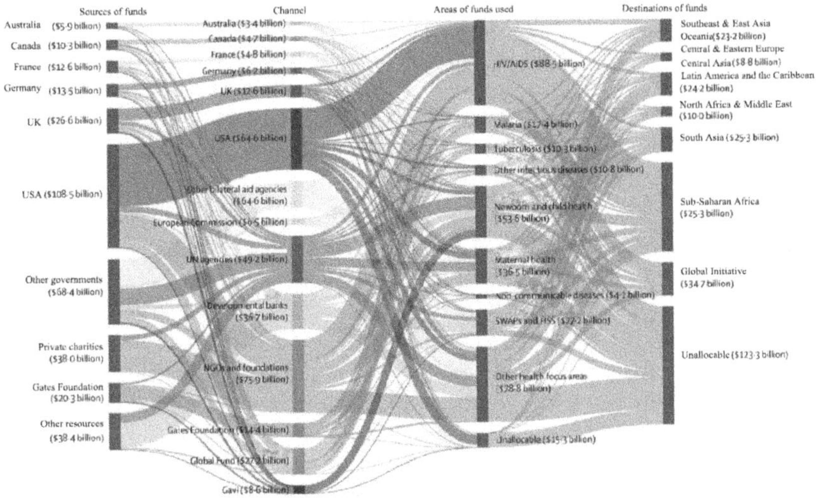

Fig. 4.1 Flows of DAH funds (2000–2013) (*Source* Dieleman et al. [2016: 2540])

how recipient countries develop their own healthcare system and expand the coverage of their health insurance programs. The first aspect receives the most attention. For instance, when it comes to the Ugandan medical care infrastructure, the US advocates a political overhaul in the recipient country. Specifically, improvements on human rights situation and democratic reforms are two preconditions for the provision of aid (Xia and Chen 2016).

In other words, while offering DAH, the US prefers to directly intervene with the system of recipient countries. Unlike that, the Japanese pattern tends to interweave its political and economic interests with its aid programs. This determines that safeguarding its economic benefits plays a decisive role in Japan's efforts to offer DAH (Schraeder et al. 1998). Besides, the ways Japan chooses to extend DAH are consistent with its approaches to other forms of assistance. For fear that aid may lead to complaints among African countries, and thus hinders the realization of its well-knitted economic and political appeal, the country adopts a primary approach to DAH which helps to maintain balance. Moreover, same as the US, Japan's DAH programs also advocate capacity building and institutional development. For instance, it provided Kenya with

JPY 2.8 billion to manufacture blood screening kits in 1982. Eight years later, it funded the Kenyan Medical Research Center in its infectious disease research, managing to lower down the HIV/AIDS screening cost by a margin that ranged between 1/3 and 1/2 (Xia and Chen 2016).

The European pattern differs from the US and Japanese pattern. It is primarily characterized by the widespread fields covered, rich strata, diversified channels, and sound supervision. The African healthcare system basically continues the model that formed in the colonial era. A large number of health personnel received education and trainings in Europe. In addition, the European Union (EU) has established a health personnel exchange platform. The DAH programs run by Europe almost cover all major aspects concerning the health of a person throughout his entire life from the cradle to the grave, which include development of healthcare system, immunization, infectious disease prevention and treatment, maternal and child health, mental health, and medical service. The EU has even struck the clinical trials partnership with 47 sub-Saharan African countries, 17 of which are OECD–DAC member states (Xia and Chen 2016). To put it simply, Africa still remains the backyard of Europe in terms of DAH, especially in basic medical service and institutional development.

A look into the South–South relations reveals that India maintains the oldest ties with Africa. With respect to DAH, continuing its overall principle for aid, India makes full use of its advantages in history, geography and ethnic group. In specific fields of aid, it resorts to its technological strength. Mainly relying on technology export like medical and personnel training, the country integrates its DAH programs with other forms of assistance. The Pan African e-Network project seeks to connect the 53 African countries through a telecommunications network. In addition to basic educational resources, it also offers medical services and medical personnel trainings. As part of the project, the remote courses are delivered by seven Indian universities, and the remote medical services are rendered by 12 Indian hospitals. The project links these Indian facilities with 53 teaching centers, state hospitals, five regional universities, and five regional hospitals based in African countries. As of early 2011, the network had possessed 169 remote terminals, and held 1127 healthcare trainings. On top of the project, India has also sent medicine and medical personnel to Africa, and also hosted the healthcare trainees from African countries, covering such sectors as infant health care, maternal health, and women health (Xia and Chen 2016).

4.1.2 DAH Trends and Methods

A glimpse into the trend of various types of aid received by Africa demonstrates that since the 1990s, the aid has taken on a continuously expanded scale. In 1990, the aid amounted to USD 5.66 billion; that number doubled to reach USD 10.52 billion in 2000; and it even sky-rocketed to USD 26.87 billion in 2010, a figure roughly five times that in 1990. With regard to the sources of aid funds, both the funds from bilateral and regional banks, World Bank, United Nations (UN) organizations, regional foundations, and private foundations, and those from other nongovernmental organizations were on the rise. Of these, the bilateral aid funds increased fastest (Dieleman et al. 2016; Murray et al. 2011).

Nevertheless, since 2010, DAH has seen its funding growth slower than expected. The annual growth rate from 2000 to 2009 stood at 11.3%, while that for the period of 2010–2015 was merely 1.2%. Furthermore, the purposes of aid funds have changed as a whole. In 2015, 29.7% of these funds were invested in HIV/AIDS prevention and treatment; 17.9% went to the field of infant health; and 9.8% were spent on improving mental health. In the decade from 2000 to 2009, the aid funds in favor of UN Millennium Development Goals (MDGs) grew in an amount of USD 290 million every year, demonstrating a remarkable difference with those contributing to the realization of other goals. Over the same period, HIV/AIDS, malaria and tuberculosis became the center of attention. From the year of 2010, mental health and infant health won more aid funds at a faster rate (Dieleman et al. 2016). As illustrated in Fig. 4.2, the US continued to be the largest aid donor in the period from 2000 to 2013, granting DAH funds in a total amount of USD 108.5 billion; of the received aid funds, USD 25.3 billion found their way to the sub-Saharan Africa, and the amount of funds whose application defied explicit explanation reached as high as USD 123.3 billion. Each aid donor had their respective focus. According to Fig. 4.2, NGOs and foundations paid much of their attention to HIV/AIDS, the Global Alliance for Vaccines and Immunization (GAVI) had special regard to new-born health, and the World Bank concentrated its efforts on sector-wide approaches and healthcare system strengthening (SWAps/HSS).

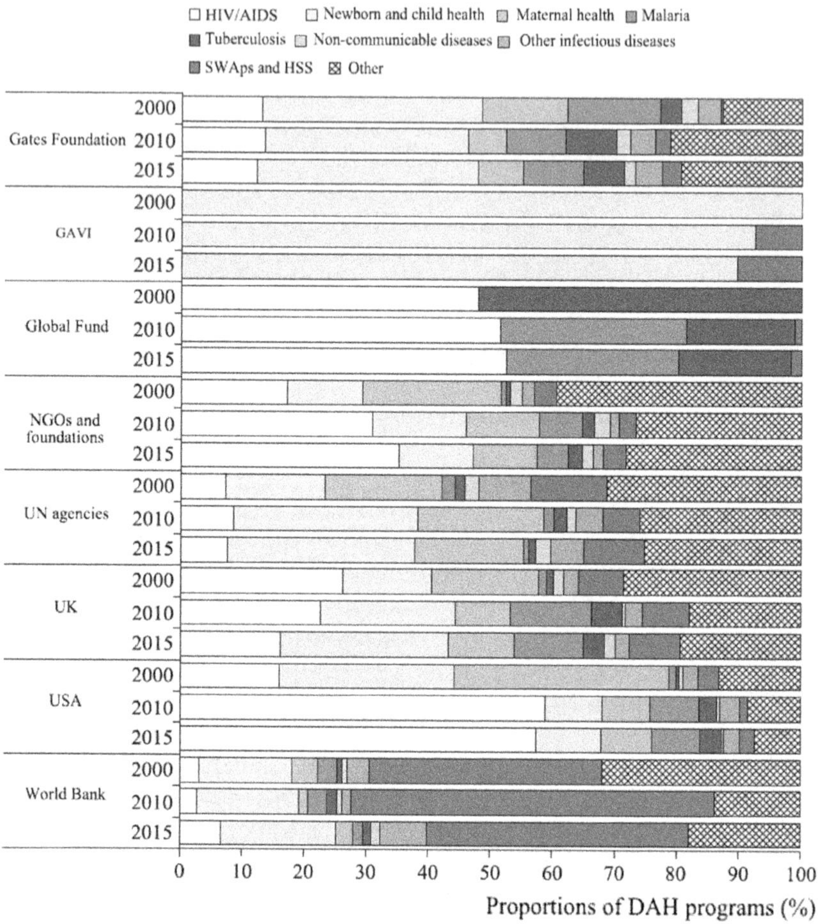

Fig. 4.2 DAH priorities of different donor countries or organizations (*Source* Dieleman et al. [2016: 2541])

4.1.3 Effects of DAH

When it comes to evaluating the effects of DAH, the literature from the perspective of aid recipients discusses the overall achievement but fails to make country-by-country introduction. For instance, while analyzing how aid influenced education and health in a total of 65 low-income countries defined by the World Bank at five-year intervals divided from 1960 to 2001, the research finds aid worked on the two sectors, and that its effects on life expectancy were quite remarkable (Ziesemer 2016). The data of the 34 sub-Saharan African countries from 1990 to 2012 suggest that DAH sharply reduced the health outcomes of recipient countries, by cutting down the HIV/AIDS transmission rate and the infant mortality rate by 8.3 and 64%, respectively. These positive effects were achieved through improving women's education and increasing health expenditures. They had nothing to do with whether a state could remain politically stable. In other words, countries could demonstrate the same improvement trend, no matter whether they suffer from a civil war or not (Yogo and Mallaye 2015). The research on the mortality rate of children aged below five in the 49 aid recipient countries from 1993 to 2012 also holds that every extra one dollar of health aid means a 5.7‰ drop in mortality rate (Bendavid 2014). As revealed by the findings of analysis into the effects of health aid granted to the sub-Saharan African countries, more aid in drinking water and disinfection facilities can improve people's access to drinking water, although there is no linear relationship between the improvement and the use of facilities (Ndikumana and Pickboum 2015; Botting et al. 2010).

To tackle with the threats to human health, some researchers take the fight against Ebola virus for example, and hold that faced up with threat of the virus, the world made its joint actions later than it should have done. If DAH is divided into global aid and country-specific aid, it will be evident that the first type only accounts for 21% and the second type makes up a lion's share of 79%. Of the global aid, only 14% goes to public products (Schaferhoff et al. 2015). As held by the extended research, the effects of the existing DAH, if any, are mainly reflected in the health situation of specific countries. From the dimension of human health, no country has attached adequate importance to the public products that matter all over the world.

As to the application of these research findings, there is one point to be added. The analysis of data from six different sources indicates these data vary greatly. This is especially true for country-specific data. Therefore, it is suggested that to answer a specific question requires choosing data prudentially, because improper data may mislead readers (Van de Maele et al. 2013).

4.2 DAH in Uganda

4.2.1 *Reasons for Which the Basic Health Subsectors Failed to Get Aid*

Over the past several decades, Uganda received a rapidly increasing amount of DAH, which even outnumbered its expenditures on health. The eleven years from 1999 to 2009 witnessed the country's DAH funds surged from USD 180 million to USD 450 million. Even so, Ugandan basic health subsectors still failed to get the aid as they needed.

One reason for this situation is that only a miserably small proportion of these aid funds was at the discretion of the Ugandan government. A close look into the data from different sources helps us extract multiple sets of indicators (Table 4.1). As shown by Table 4.1, DAH accounted for a stably high proportion in the various forms of assistance that came to Uganda. In the two decades covered by the form, the gross aid amount received by Uganda nearly doubled from USD 830 million to USD 1.63 billion. Of it, DAH rose by 3.5 times, outperforming other forms of assistance in both speed and amount. The proportion of DAH reached its peak in 2014, which was 39%.

The high percentage and massive amount of DAH theoretically means that the Ugandan healthcare system has the chance to plan its healthcare service as a whole and make full use of these funds. However, the reality that came into our sight just told a very different story. As shown by the data from 1995 to 2014, the DAH funds were allocated to the different health subsectors of the country in sharply varying proportions, thus revealing no regular pattern to follow. The unpredictable changes to such proportions might be understandable. For instance, in a certain period, massive investments need to be made to solve major issues confronting health policy and administration, and such investments will cease after the entry into a phase of regular maintenance and sustainable development. Even so, the percentage of funds for basic health insurance should reveal some patterns. Leaving population growth aside, if the guarantee measures are being refined, the spending on the basic health subsectors will increase accordingly. If the rapid population growth and the to-be-improved basic health indicators are taken into account, such spending should be scaled up proportionately. However, the data available only expose some random changes.

Does this mean the Ugandan government ran the country poorly? Things aren't that simple. In the decade from 1999 to 2009, the health

Table 4.1 DAH received by Uganda and major designated fields of use (1995–2014) (in million US dollars)

Year	*Aid received*	*DAH received*	*Health policy regarding DAH*	*Basic health-care service with DAH*	*Infrastructure construction with DAH*	*Health education with DAH*	*Educational training with DAH*	*Health workforce engaged in DAH*	*Infectious disease control with DAH*	*Malaria control with DAH*	*AIDS control with DAH*
1995	833.16	128.14	16.10	10.76	78.76				0.59		11.25
1996	673.69	111.51	65.28	6.50	4.07	2.96		2.12	4.85		9.30
1997	813.05	66.41	26.86	4.97	1.60	0.33	0.29	0.14	5.16		2.79
1998	655.38	113.70	3.44	7.07	1.93	0.08	0.07	0.45	17.51		20.35
1999	605.03	91.28	2.81	0.75	42.88	0.84	0.84	1.19	2.75		23.12
2000	853.28	208.22	113.40	33.25	15.35	0.03	0.09	2.74	6.30		17.65
2001	822.19	239.59	99.36	10.35	1.00	0.08	6.05	29.68	17.97		55.10
2002	725.39	174.37	76.95	10.55	0.65	0.47	0.02	2.11	2.96		63.37
2003	997.65	302.47	59.48	128.77	1.94	0.42	0.01	2.12	4.58		94.11
2004	1216.02	322.00	7.23	8.51	0.13	1.45	0.39	2.35	6.41	28.33	207.51
2005	1192.16	385.32	51.90	18.16	7.54	0.19	10.98	0.11	14.31	78.70	151.65
2006	1586.43	276.56	9.62	3.91	7.80	0.14	0.43	1.70	5.08	0.04	213.61
2007	1737.30	377.66	45.79	19.79	1.01	0.11	0.98		2.85	26.06	251.11
2008	1641.47	623.78	41.07	64.88	1.90	0.71	1.50	0.42	6.32	79.56	397.72
2009	1784.70	457.89	12.30	14.33	1.72	0.24	1.19	0.63	4.80	97.80	287.89
2010	1688.02	521.01	23.75	19.56	105.48	2.11	0.81	6.42	7.20	40.86	259.99
2011	1572.81	530.22	17.78	22.42	0.41	2.88	2.53	1.14	3.42	82.13	318.18
2012	1641.76	635.52	19.72	53.81	86.97	2.97	0.09	0.16	0.98	103.97	262.07
2013	1700.74	552.44	8.44	34.98	19.16	1.86	1.02	0.30	1.99	54.32	323.96
2014	1632.93	420.40	9.59	49.39	0.34	1.76	0.46	0.16	4.39	46.96	241.48

Source Online databases of the OECD and the World Bank

expenditures of Uganda soared from USD 210 million to USD 580 million. Amid the spike, the Ugandan government maintained its health budget share at 8–11%. So it was non-government funding that grew at the fastest pace. The government health budget came from the following three sources: poverty action funds, general resources, and project-based resources. Of these, the DAH funds always accounted for more than 50%, and the project-based funds attained a share that ranged between 34 and 59%. To put it simply, a roughly 10% share of the total health expenditures was included into the government budget. Among the government health budget, DAH occupied more than a half, the majority of which came from related projects. In this way, the total funds that were truly used to provide basic health insurance only took up a miserably low proportion in the gross health expenditures. If you have no hand, you can't make a fist. The reason for this staggering situation is not the inaction of the Ugandan government, but the extremely limited resources available. The rocky proportions of expenditures for basic healthcare service as shown in Table 4.1 reveal that the Ugandan healthcare system provided the fragile and unstable basic health insurance for its people.

Another contributing factor is about the preference of aid donors. The international community tends to focus their attention on the effectiveness of aid. In this context, what gets more attention is the intention of those who offer aid, especially their interest in disease research. This has channeled aid funds into the fight against certain types of disease like HIV/AIDS. In 2003, Uganda received some USD 220 million in DAH. Of it, USD 60 million, or a 27% share, went to the HIV/AIDS control. In 2009 when the received DAH amounted to USD 450 million, USD 310 million was spent on HIV/AIDS prevention and treatment, taking up a 69% share of the total. A part of the money that flowed to the HIV/AIDS fight was PEPFAR's funding. Given the flow of massive DAH into some certain disease control campaigns, the aid used for general healthcare services shrank from 74 to 31% (Stierman et al. 2013; Juliet et al. 2009).

Among the project-based funding, the money spent on HIV/AIDS control accounted for 35% in 2003, the proportion reached its peak in 2007, which was 70%, and it declined somewhat to 67% in 2009. Thereby, the researchers hold that the failure for Uganda's key health subsectors to draw sufficient attention is largely attributed to the interventions from donors (Stierman et al. 2013; Juliet et al. 2009).

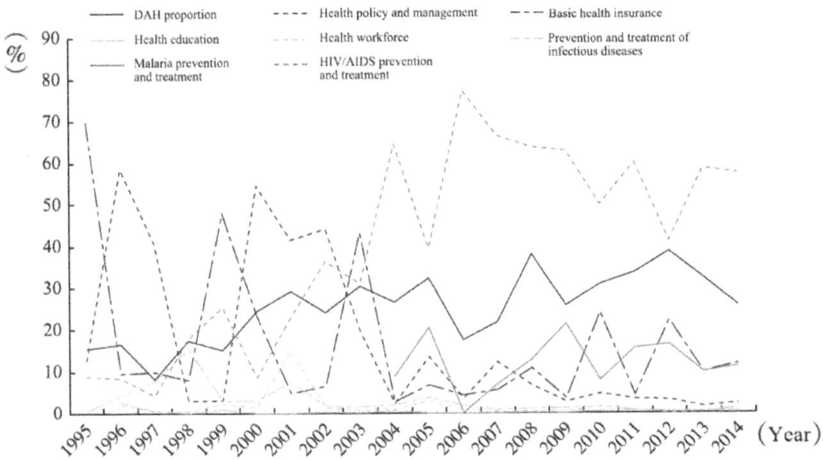

Fig. 4.3 Purposes of health aid Uganda received and their proportions, 1995–2014 (*Source* Online databases of the OECD and the World Bank)

The conclusion of the existing research that the will of donors directly affects how healthcare services and resources are allocated in Uganda has been verified by the data available in Table 4.1 and Fig. 4.3. Take malaria control and HIV/AIDS control as two examples. Back to 2004, the proportion of money spent on malaria control in DAH was nothing but zero, but it soared to 21.4% in 2009, which was its highest level. The percentage remained above 6.9% in other years. The funds that went to the HIV/AIDS fight took up a lion's share of 77.2% in 2006. The proportion averaged 40.2% over 20 years for HIV/AIDS control, and 11.9% over 10 years for malaria control. The two consumed over a half of DAH combined. Over the surveyed 20 years, the money invested in the most underfunded basic health sub-sectors only accounted for 16.4% of the total DAH, a level proportionate to the health policy and administration overheads; the input to health workforce which played the most pivotal role in basic health care only took up a 1.7% share; and likewise, that went for infectious disease control only stood at 2.9%.

If put Uganda's situation under the landscape of international aid, you will realize that the extent to which donors' interventions impact there may have gone far beyond our observation. According to the OECD's data, since 1960, the aid received by Uganda has long remained

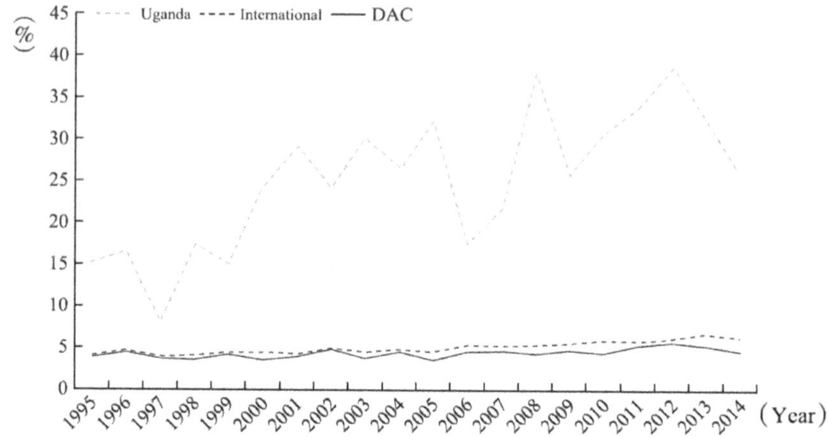

Fig. 4.4 Proportion of DAH received by Uganda in its total assistance, proportion of DAH in global aid, and proportion of DAH in the aid from DAC, 1995–2014 (*Source* Online databases of the OECD and the World Bank)

relatively stable among the sub-Saharan African countries. The proportion of the Ugandan aid in the total received by the countries in the region ranged between 0.43 and 6.56%, and averaged 2.96%. For much of the period, it stayed at 3% roughly. Its proportion in the gross international aid also demonstrated a fairly steady status, by ranging between 0.09 and 1.61%, averaging 0.78%, and moving around 1% for much of the time.

This means DAH has an independent influence in Uganda. With respect to international aid, the data on DAH appeared for the first time in 1971. Back that year, the proportion of DAH in global aid was merely 0.8%. In the subsequent few years, the percentage went up slowly. By 1995, it was about 5%. Over the period from 1971 to 1995, the ceiling was reached in 1983, and it grew to 6.7%. As a matter of fact, this is still the highest level today. Furthermore, DAH took up a lower share in the assistance offered by the DAC state members. Figure 4.4 exhibits the trend of comparable changes in Uganda. It can be observed that DAH makes up a lion's share in the aid received by the country. Plus, DAH plays an absolutely important role in Uganda's expenditures on health, by accounting for some 90% of its total health spending. In this sense, the interventions from donors are magnified further.

Against such background, some researchers have made dedicated studies into the influence of aid agreements, and concluded that the practice of deciding how to aid and whether to continue aiding based on the performance of recipients had indeed intervened with the operation and efficiency of their health sector. By employing the agent theory and realistic evaluation, some other researchers have made the following findings. The official evaluation mechanism for the performance of the health sector and the related projects falls short of objective criteria. Different donors neither hold structural and systematic discussions nor reach any consensus. While deciding standards to evaluate whether recipients' performance lives up to expectation, they usually neglect the actual needs, and fail to measure how things progress. Even though the performance is quite poor, there is no punishment and their aid will continue. For this, the donors often defend themselves by citing other reasons. For instance, their doing is based on trust and aims to sustain relationships over the long term. Therefore, the performance results, satisfactory or not, have no substantial bearing on aid (Mwenda and Tangri 2005). However, there exist opposite views (Matsiko 2010). Other people insist that how efficiently the health sector operates concerns the entire system and the neglect of the system itself turns out to be a factor jeopardizing the efficiency (Juliet et al. 2009).

Another piece of research on the factors affecting the efficiency of aid suggests that given the governance inefficiency of low-income countries, recipient countries are unable to execute the quantity-backed decisions. Besides, it also holds that Uganda should give its health priorities to disease prevention and control and family planning, because these fields exert long-standing influences on its healthcare system; and the ceaseless debates over the healthcare service topics have evolved into the flight of different donors for power in essence. Therefore, it is imperative to refocus on local people and solve actual problems plaguing them (Colenbrander et al. 2015).

Even so, the research on the effectiveness of DAH in Uganda indicates that DAH has taken effect in the following two aspects. First, it reduced the harm brought by diseases remarkably as a whole. Second, it helped the Ugandan people lift the economic burden of disease. Additionally, the research also reveals that the more aligned with community needs the aid is, the more obvious its effect is. Therefore, besides countries, more aid should be able to reach the hands of beneficiaries directly (Odokonyero et al. 2015). The statistics of the UN also attest the noted improvement in Uganda's health indicators. In the sub-sector of primary health care, the local people who had access to safe water reached 40% in 1990 and 79% in 2015; the tuberculosis control rate stood at 75% in 1990 and 93% in 2015; the diphtheria-tetanus-pertussis (DTP3) immunization coverage reported 45% in 1990 and 78% in 2015; and the measles immunization coverage was 52% in 1990 and 82% in 2015 (United Nations 2016).

As believed by some people on the Ugandan side, the current state in the country is a far cry from the expectations of the government and the UN MDGs. Uganda has allocated 10% of its government budget to its health sector, which means some USD 15 dollar per-capita expenditure on health. But there is a staggering gap between USD 34, which is recommended by the World Health Organization (WHO).[1] More than that, Uganda also has to deal with many other unfavorable factors such as rapid population expansion and rising medical costs. According to some researches, even though the country faces the pressure from raising health funds, the pressing thing is about how to use the existing resources and help its people get the most out of the healthcare system. To solve this problem, the Ugandan government must put the three missions below high on its agenda: optimizing and managing the supply of health workforce and medical resources, making full use of DAH-related resources, and lowering down the ever-growing medical costs facing its people (Okwero et al. 2010).

To coordinate the aid resources, the Ugandan government has kept negotiating with its major donors. The outcome of these efforts is the Uganda Joint Assistance Strategy which came out formally in 2005 (Uganda et al. 2005). It represents a milestone in the country's progress over aid strategy and management. Its point is to pool the aid from different sources together for coordinated use and maximum effect. In 2006, the strategy was assessed and spoken highly of by the African Development Bank. It was expected to coordinate aid effectively (Puetz 2006).

However, as we observed, it hasn't taken any effect in DAH so far.

[1] These data are slightly different from those cited in the prior part from other sources. But there are no impairment on the basic judgment of the big picture, which goes as the Uganda health situation has improved remarkably over the past few decades.

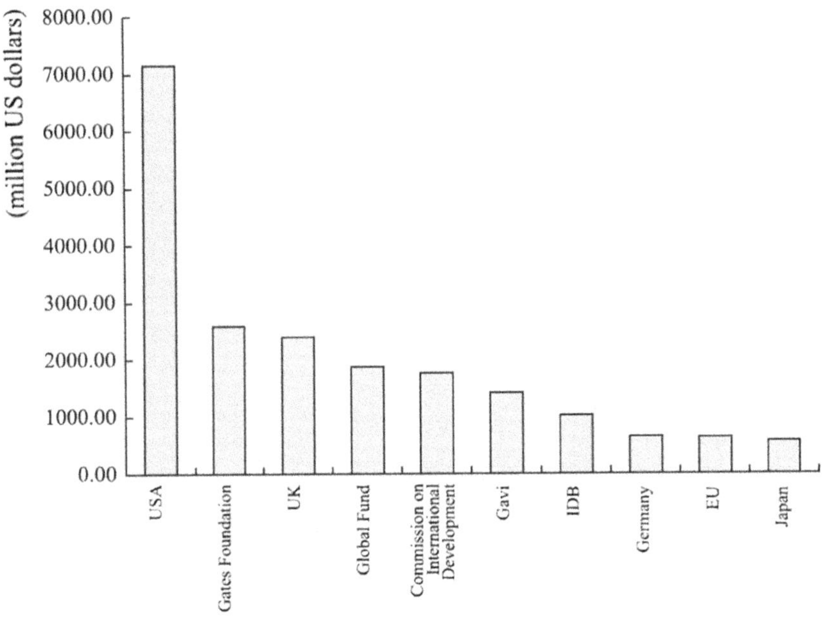

Fig. 4.5 Top ten DAH donors among the DAC members, 2013 (*Source* OECD database)

The most prominent feature of DAH is still the free will of donors. Perhaps it is in this context that the DAH aligned with Uganda's actual needs from China is emerging so strikingly.

4.2.2 *DAH from the US to Uganda*

Choosing the US as the reference is based on the following two considerations. First, by comparing and analyzing the data on DAH offered by OECD, we find out the US serves as a major DAH donor; and among the DAC member states, other countries are nowhere near the US in terms of DAH amount (Fig. 4.5). Second, when it comes to the DAH received by Uganda, the US also comes as the biggest donor. As illustrated in Fig. 4.6, America's DAH amount overpasses that of other aid providers overwhelmingly. Therefore, by choosing the US as the frame of reference, we tend to compare China's DAH in Uganda with the largest donor all over the world.

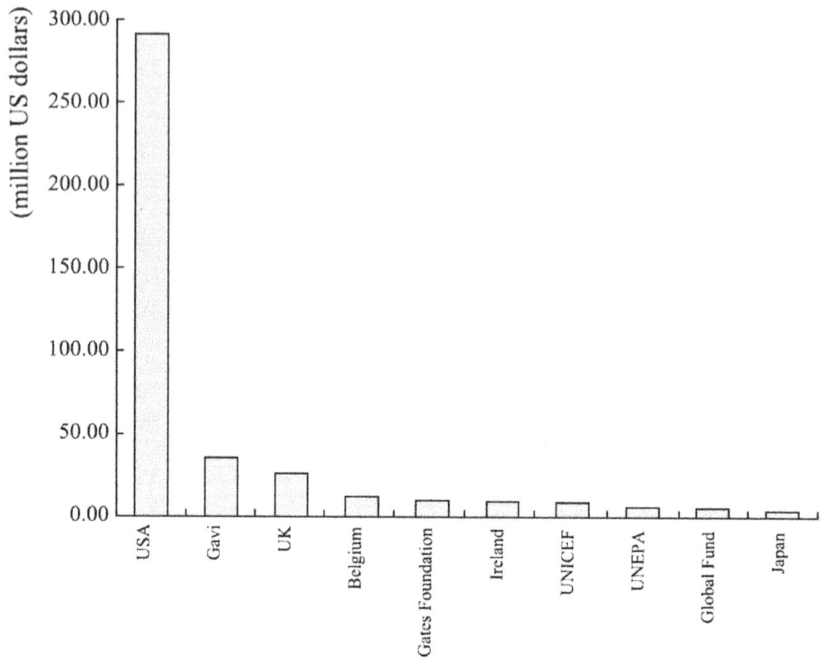

Fig. 4.6 Top ten DAH donors in Uganda, 2013 (*Source* OECD database)

What are the characteristics of the DAH from the US to Uganda? Due to the limited Source, we are unable to go through all data on DAH the US offers to Uganda. Focusing on the obtained data, we sort through the 48 aid missions America conducted in Uganda from 2005 to 2015. These missions are available on the website of the US Agency for International Development (USAID). By analyzing these data, we arrive at our basic judgment on DAH from America to Uganda.

Firstly, keenly aware of the health state of the Ugandan people. From 2011 to 2013, the US committed about USD 1.7 million to conducting the Uganda Demographic and Health Survey, with a view to getting a whole picture of local people's health state. This follow-up survey commenced in 1988. It was hosted by Uganda's Ministry of Health with the support of Uganda's Ministry of Finance, Planning and Economic Development, the Geography Department of Makerere University, the Institute of Statistics and Applied Economics of Makerere University, and other institutions. On the US side, the Institute for Resource Development and Columbia University took part in the program. After that, another three surveys of the same sort followed in 1995, 2000/2001 and 2006. That taking place in 2011 was the fifth one. The 20-year-old demographic and health survey is expected to help the US have the trend and status quo of the Ugandan population and their health state at its fingertips.

Secondly, getting a full picture of family planning, maternal and infant health, and population nutrition. In the period from 2007 to 2015, America channeled USD 350 million in aid to seven programs, which covered maternal and infant health, family planning, food and nutrition, disadvantaged children and their families, and fistula treatment. Of these, the family planning program operated as part of the Family Health International (FHI). Apart from the aforesaid five programs, there were three others dedicated to influence on and support for kids. Out of them, two's funding remained unknown; the remaining one was targeted at orphans and vulnerable children, and operated in cooperation with the UN International Children's Emergency Fund (UNICEF).

Thirdly, directly involved in managing the healthcare service supply chain of Uganda. Over the period from 2009 to 2013, the US struck partnerships with Uganda's supply chain by providing funds in an unknown amount. One of these partnerships was between the US Department of Defense and the Uganda's People's Defence Force.

Fourthly, committing the most funds to combating and studying HIV/AIDS. A decade witnessed the launch of 48 programs. Out of them, 20 fell under the category of HIV/AIDS prevention and treatment. There emerged new programs almost every year. By putting the four ones with unknown expenditures aside, these efforts brought aid in USD 470 million to the country. They covered every aspect of HIV/AIDS fight such as infection prevention, consulting and testing, partner communication, alleviative treatment, health advocacy, supervision assessment, community involvement, service enhancement, state support, collaboration among public sectors, targeted medical service and lab service, and project management.

Fifthly, attaching particular importance to malaria prevention and treatment. A total of seven themed programs kicked off in 10 years. Three of them provided data on expenditures, which amounted to USD 79 million. These endeavors covered many aspects as diverse as malaria monitoring, cooperation among disease control bodies, community-wide fight, and indoor mosquito eradication. On top of these, there were other malaria combating efforts. One example of these was the assessment of long-lasting mosquito nets (USAID 2015).

Sixthly, limited attention paid to tuberculosis. Over the 10 years, only one project was about tuberculosis prevention and treatment. But it involved huge funding, which totaled USD 225 million. The main point of the program was to facilitate the implementation of the National Tuberculosis and Leprosy Control Program (NTLP) in Uganda. In the five years from 2009 to 2014, the program was divided into four complementary projects—Prevent, Identify, Respond and Predict—to finance the response to pandemic threats. The purpose by doing so was to build up capacity for rising to sudden epidemic outbreaks. Besides, there were also programs on management of zoonotic disease, enhancement of medical service, guarantee of rights to getting essential medicines, and health advocacy in private sectors. Of these, the project for guaranteeing access to essential medicines alone sent USD 39 million to Uganda.

According to the classification of DAH by the OECD, of the 48 projects, 12 fitted under the category of health policy and administration (eight of them had no data on expenditures available and the remaining four spent USD 103 million in total); one was grouped under the category of basic health care, and received the funding of some USD 29 million; one came under the category of basic setting, and incurred expenditures in about USD 100,000; two were about health education, and cost funds in USD 116 million; one fell under the category of educational training worth USD 350,000 roughly; one was in the category of infectious disease, and won USD 225 million in funding; and the number and overheads of projects under the categories of malaria control and HIV/AID control are mentioned as above.

Seen from the funding structure alone, 30 of the 48 projects had data on expenditures available. They incurred the total expenses of USD 1182 million, with the average registering USD 39 million. If the average is used to reckon the missing values, the total funding of the 48 projects would approach USD 1.6 billion. In other words, USD 160 million was spent every year. And that is supposed to a very conservative estimate.

As a matter of fact, to comprehend the influence of the US on how DAH was allocated in Uganda, we need to take into account the overall landscape of how Uganda received DAH and how the US offered assistance to Uganda. As the data of OECD have told us, of the aid totaling

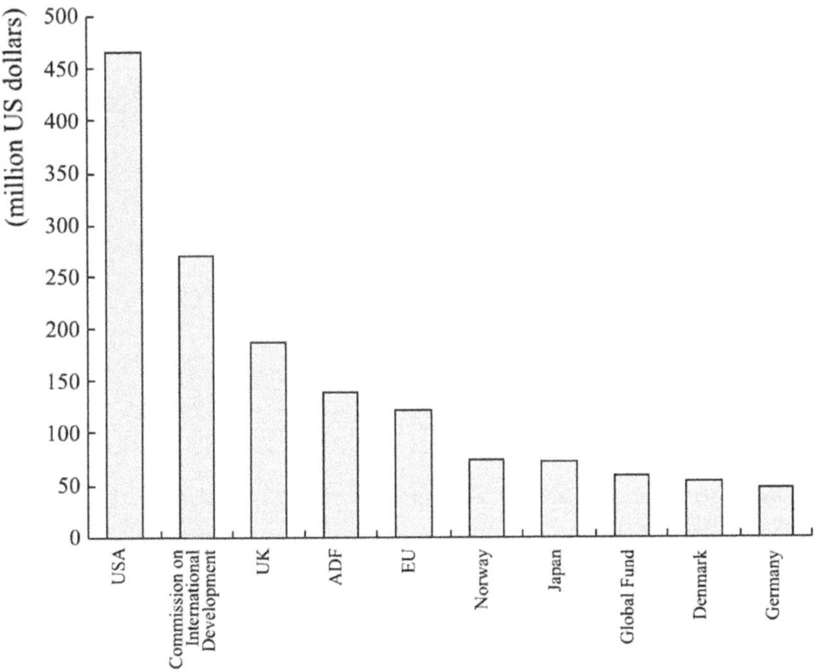

Fig. 4.7 Top ten aid donors in Uganda, 2014 (*Source* OECD database)

USD 1632 million received by Uganda in the fiscal year of 2013–2014 (Table 4.1), the top ten donors contributed USD 1490 million in funding, which accounted for 91.2% of the total. Of the top ten aid donors, the US offered the assistance worth USD 465 million, or 28.5% of the total. Other countries have lagged far behind it (Fig. 4.7).

The more detailed data of the recent five years further reveal that the US has provided Uganda with DAH in a total amount of USD 259 million every year, a level higher than the average of the previous period. The American DAH to Uganda can be divided into eight categories: democracy and governance, economic development, education, environment, health development, humanism, peace and security, and project management, which are slightly different from those of OECD. Among those categories, health development takes up the biggest share, followed by economic development. Figure 4.8 exhibits the changes in the

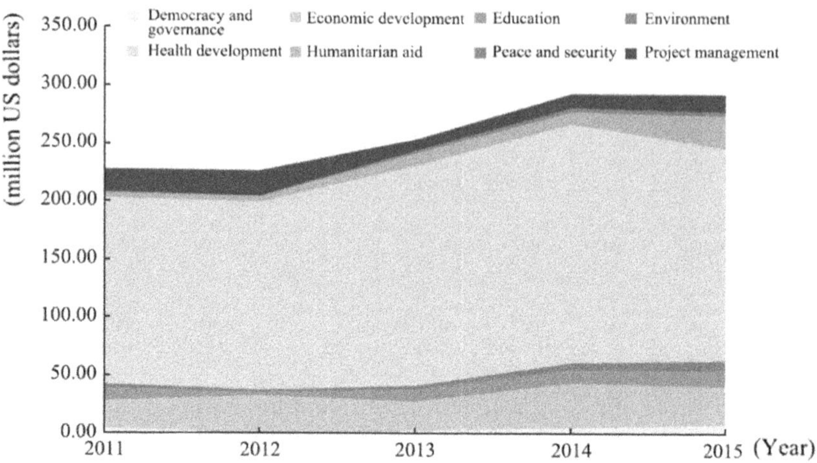

Fig. 4.8 Structure and size of the aid from the US to Uganda, 2011–2015 (*Source* USAID database)

size and structure of the aid from the US to Uganda in 2011–2015. Of it, DAH took up a share that edged up.

DAH can be further divided into such smaller groups as family planning (fertility planning), maternal and infant health, nutrition, tuberculosis prevention and treatment, HIV/AIDS prevention and prevention, malaria prevention and prevention, water and sterilization, and others. A glimpse into Fig. 4.9 can awaken us clearly to the facts that the fights against HIV/AIDS and malaria consumed the majority of the DAH funding; then came family planning and maternal & infant health; and nutrition started to occupy a considerable share in the recent three years.

All the above are our primary observations for the aid from the US to Uganda. As exposed by the literature review, the aid received by Uganda always accounted for about 10% of its GDP over the period from 1998 to 2006 (Guloba et al. 2010); its proportion in GNI reached the highest level in 1992, at 26.1%; and that number was 14% in 2000, 16.4% in 2006 and 6.19% in 2014.[2] This means international aid plays a crucial role in Uganda's economic development. More importantly, DAH

[2]World Bank: http://data.worldbank.org.cn/indicator/DT.ODA.ODAT.GN.ZS?locations=UG&view=chart.

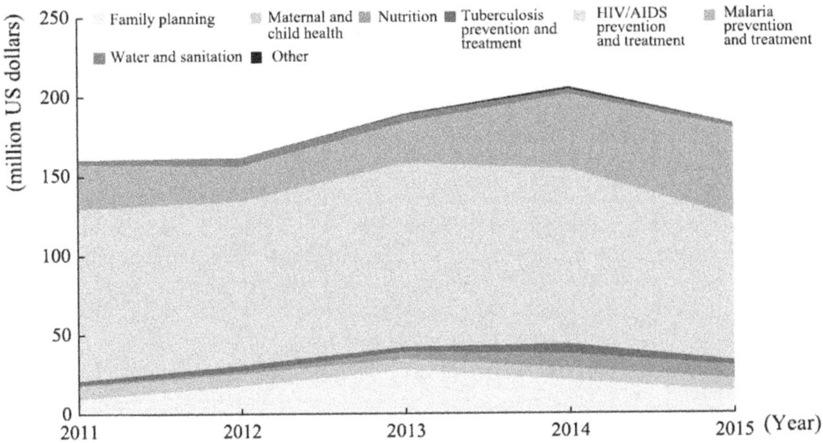

Fig. 4.9 Structure and size of the DAH from the US to Uganda, 2011–2015 (*Source* USAID database)

matters for its healthcare system. From the perspective of expenditures on health, it is even dominant in the country's healthcare system. There is one point worth particular attention. That is the US turns out the biggest donor, whether in terms of overall aid or DAH. Aligned with the judgment of the existing literature, the DAH from the US to Uganda embodies the strong will of the US—particularly high attention to HIV/AIDS and malaria. Over a half of the DAH has been spent on reducing the prevalence of these diseases.

References

Afridi, Muhammad Asim, and Bruno Ventelou. 2013. Impact of Health Aid in Developing Countries: The Public vs. the Private Channels. *Economic Modelling* 31: 759–765. https://doi.org/10.1016/j.econmod.2013.01.009.

Bendavid, Eran. 2014. Is Health Aid Reaching the Poor? Analysis of Household Data from Aid Recipient Countries. *PLoS One* 9 (1): 1–9. https://doi.org/10.1371/journal.pone.0084025.

Bendavid, Eran. 2016. Past and Future Performance: PEPFAR in the Landscape of Foreign Aid for Health. *Current HIV/AIDS Reports*: 1–7. https://doi.org/10.1007/s11904-016-0326-8.

Botting, M.J., E.O. Porbeni, M.R. Joffres, B.C. Johnston, R.E. Black, and E.J. Mills. 2010. Water and Sanitation Infrastructure for Health:

The Impact of Foreign Aid. *Global Health* 6: 12. https://doi.org/10.1186/1744-8603-6-12.

Colenbrander, S., C. Birungi, and A.K. Mbonye. 2015. Consensus and Contention in the Priority Setting Process: Examining the Health Sector in Uganda. *Health Policy and Planning* 30 (5): 555–565. https://doi.org/10.1093/heapol/czu030.

Dieleman, Joseph L., Matthew T. Schneider, Annie Haakenstad, Lavanya Singh, Nafis Sadat, Maxwell Birger, Alex Reynolds, Tara Templin, Hannah Hamavid, Abigail Chapin, and Christopher J.L. Murray. 2016. Development Assistance for Health: Past Trends, Associations, and the Future of International Financial Flows for Health. *The Lancet* 387 (10037): 2536–2544. http://dx.doi.org/10.1016/S0140-6736(16)30168-4.

Guloba, Madina, Nicholas Kilimani, and Winnie Nabiddo. 2010. *Impact of China-Africa Aid Relations: A Case Study of Uganda*. Economic Policy Research Centre (EPRC).

Juliet, Nabyonga Orem, Ssengooba Freddie, and Sam Okuonzi. 2009. Can Donor Aid for Health Be Effective in a Poor Country? Assessment of Prerequisites for Aid Effectiveness in Uganda. *The Pan African Medical Journal* 3 (9): 9.

Matsiko, Charles W. 2010. *Positive Practice Environments in Uganda: Enhancing Health Worker and Healthcare System Performance*. Geneva, Switzerland: The Global Health Workforce Alliance.

Murray, C.J.L., B. Anderson, R. Burstein, K. Leach-Kemon, M. Schneider, A. Tardif, and R. Zhang. 2011. Development Assistance for Health: Trends and Prospects. *The Lancet* 378 (9785): 8–10. https://doi.org/10.1016/s0140-6736(10)62356-2.

Mwenda, Andrew M., and Roger Tangri. 2005. Patronage Politics, Donor Reforms, and Regime Consolidation in Uganda. *African Affairs* 104 (416): 449–467. https://doi.org/10.2307/3518724.

Ndikumana, Léonce and Lynda Pickbourn. 2015. The Impact of Foreign Aid Allocation on Access to Social Services in Sub-Saharan Africa: The Case of Water and Sanitation, vol. 400. Working Paper, Political Economy Research Institute, Umass Amherst.

Obermann, Konrad. 2007. Global Health and Foreign Policy. *The Lancet* 369 (9574): 1688. http://dx.doi.org/10.1016/s0140-6736(07)60769-7.

Odokonyero, Tonny, Alex Ijjo, Robert Marty, Tony Muhumuza, and Godfrey Owot Moses. 2015. Sub-national Perspectives on Aid Effectiveness: Impact of Aid on Health Outcomes in Uganda. Working Paper No. 18, AidData.

Okwero, Peter, Ajay Tandon, Susan Sparkes, Julie McLaughlin, and Johannes G. Hoogeveen. 2010. *Fiscal Space for Health in Uganda*, vol. 186. Washington, DC: The World Bank.

Puetz, Detlev. 2006. *Uganda Joint Assistance Strategy: A Review of the Harmonization Process in Five Countries*. Abidjan: African Development Bank Group.

Schaferhoff, Marco, Sara Fewer, Jessica Kraus, Emil Richter, Lawrence H. Summers, Jesper Sundewall, Gavin Yamey, and Dean T. Jamison. 2015. How Much Donor Financing for Health Is Channelled to Global Versus Country-Specific Aid Functions? *The Lancet* 386 (10011): 2436–2441. https://doi.org/10.1016/S0140-6736(15)61161-8.

Schraeder, Peter J., Steven W. Hook, and Bruce Taylor. 1998. Clarifying the Foreign Aid Puzzle: A Comparison of American, Japanese, French, and Swedish Aid Flows. *World Politics* 50 (2): 294–323. https://doi.org/10.2307/25054039.

Stierman, E., F. Ssengooba, and S. Bennett. 2013. Aid Alignment: A Longer Term Lens on Trends in Development Assistance for Health in Uganda. *Global Health* 9 (1): 7. https://doi.org/10.1186/1744-8603-9-7.

Uganda, African Development Bank, Australia, Germany, The Netherlands, Norway, Sweden, United Kingdom, and The World Bank. 2005. *The Uganda Joint Assistance Strategy*. Kampala.

United Nations. 2016. *African Statistical Yearbook 2016*. Scanprint, Denmark.

USAID. 2015. *Mass Distribution of Long Lasting Insecticidal Nets for Universal Coverage in Uganda Evaluation Report*. Washington, DC: USAID.

Van de Maele, Nathalie, David B. Evans, and Tessa Tan-Torres. 2013. Development Assistance for Health in Africa: Are We Telling the Right Story? *Bulletin of the World Health Organization* 91: 483–490. https://doi.org/10.2471/blt.12.115410.

Xia, Qingjie, and Yujiang Chen. 2016. Models of Health Aid to Africa in the World and China's Investment in Health Aid to Africa. *International Aid* 2: 18–32.

Yogo, Urbain Thierry, and Douzounet Mallaye. 2015. Health Aid and Health Improvement in Sub-Saharan Africa: Accounting for the Heterogeneity Between Stable States and Post-conflict States. *Journal of International Development* 27 (7): 1178–1196. https://doi.org/10.1002/jid.3034.

Ziesemer, Thomas. 2016. The Impact of Development Aid on Education and Health: Survey and New Evidence for Low-Income Countries from Dynamic Models. *Journal of International Development* 28 (8): 1358–1380. https://doi.org/10.1002/jid.3223.

CHAPTER 5

Donors' Experience and Analysis

5.1 China's Aid to Africa

Within the framework of "two-sided four-tiered embeddedness," the understanding of China's aid to Africa may shed some light on the understanding of its aid, in particular development aid for health (DAH) for Uganda. If knowing nothing about the DAH programs China has run in Africa, one cannot get a full picture of the DAH Uganda has received from China. Considering the literature written in Chinese and English languages comes in various types, we screen the data available based on their relevancy to the abovementioned framework, in the hopes of holding logical and well-structured discussions as far as possible. Likewise, given the discreteness of the research, it is impossible for us to create a continuously integral system.

Africa is also called Afrikyah on a full name basis. At 30.2 million square kilometers, it covers 20.4% of the earth's total land areas, and is the second largest continent of the world. According to the statistics of the United Nations (UN 2016), the population of Africa was 940 million in 2006 and 1.18 billion in 2015, including 450 million economically active population. So Africa is the second most populous continent across the globe. Africa is geographically divided into five main regions: North Africa, East Africa, West Africa, Central Africa and South Africa. It is home to 54 countries and regions.

North Africa, customarily called "Africa in the north of Sahara," refers to the African regions flanking the Tropic of Cancer and consists of seven

Z. Qiu, *When Friendship Comes First*, China and Globalization 2.0,
https://doi.org/10.1007/978-981-32-9308-3_5

countries such as Egypt, Sudan and South Sudan as well as the Madeira Islands and the Azores Islands of Portugal in the Atlantic. Among its 192 million population, 70% are Arabians.

East Africa means the regions from the Horn of Africa down to Southeast Africa along the Indian Ocean. It encompasses 20 countries and regions, and internally divided into four geographical parts, which are the Horn of Africa (four countries), six island countries in the Indian Ocean, East Africa Community (six countries) and Southeast Africa (four countries). Since civil disorder has been long rampant in some places of the region, there are no accurate demographic data on it.

West Africa stretches all the way from Lake Chad in the east to the Atlantic in the west and from Gulf of Guinea in the South to the Sahara Desert in the north. It has a total of 17 countries and regions, home to some 340 million population.

Central Africa stands as a collection of nine countries and regions located in the center of the continent, with a population of 200 million roughly. Due to wars, the region has been divided recklessly. Therefore, the existing demographic statistics cannot be attributed to clear sources.

South Africa refers to the southern part of Africa. According to the regional definition of the US, it includes five countries. Founded in 1980, the Southern African Development Community (SADC) comprises 15 member states. No demographic data on it are available.

In the aid to Africa, there is another frequently used concept. It is the sub-Saharan Africa, which is made up of 49 countries and regions to the south of the desert.

Aid for and cooperation with Africa has always been a significant part of China's foreign aid, if not the most important part. This holds true whether before or after the introduction of the policy on reform and opening up in 1978.

As indicated by China's Foreign Aid (white paper) which the Chinese government in released in April 2011 for the first time,

> China's foreign aid began in 1950, when it provided material assistance to the Democratic People's Republic of Korea (DPRK) and Vietnam, two neighboring countries having friendly relations with China. In 1956, following the Asian-African Conference in Bandung, Indonesia in 1955, China began to aid African countries. In 1964, the Chinese government declared the Eight Principles for Economic Aid and Technical Assistance to Other Countries, the core of which featured equality, mutual benefit

> and no strings attached. Hence the basic principle for China's foreign aid was formulated. In October 1971, China established relations of economic and technical cooperation with more developing countries, and funded the Tanzania-Zambia Railway (TAZARA) and other major infrastructure projects. All of these efforts laid a solid foundation for China to maintain the long-term friendly cooperation with developing countries.

The 2011 whiter paper also points out that financial resources provided by China for foreign aid mainly fall into three types: grants (aid gratis), interest-free loans, and concessional loans; China offers foreign aid in eight forms: complete projects, goods and materials, technical cooperation, human resource development, metical teams sent abroad, emergency humanitarian aid, volunteer programs in foreign countries, and debt relief; and complete projects account for 40% of China's foreign aid expenditures, which has always ranked the first place among all forms of aid. By the end of 2009, China had financed a total of 2025 complete projects. The top two sectors to which these projects went were public facility and industry. The top three subsectors which received the most projects were the light industry under the industry sector (320), the science, education, culture and health under the public facility sector (236), and the transportation under the economic infrastructure sector (201), respectively.

As the second white paper released in July 2014 further points out, over the three years from 2010 to 2012, China undertook the construction of 580 complete projects overseas. Out of these, 360 projects fell in the public facility sector, and 156 went to the economic infrastructure sector, two of which were the top two fields receiving the most projects of the sort. As to subsectors, hospitals, schools and civil buildings under the public facility sector all saw the number of complete projects received exceeding 80, and transportation under the economic infrastructure sector had such projects in the number of over 70. Therefore, it can be concluded that China's foreign aid has benefited local people's livelihood prominently.

When it comes to geographical distribution, the 2011 white paper suggests, by the end of 2009, Africa had been the continent that got the most financial aid from China, which accounted for 45.7% of its total. The 2014 white paper further indicates that over the three years from 2010 to 2012, the aid funds channeled to infrastructure had taken up a 44.8% share of China's total foreign aid; and the proportion of those flowing to Africa in the total further climbed up to 51.8%. It therefore can be seen that aid to Africa is foremost in China's foreign aid. Given the abovementioned features of China's foreign aid, we can also hold that aid to people's livelihood also occupies a marked position in China's aid to Africa.

What is worth mentioning is none of the existing academic works written in Chinese language is dedicated to depicting China's foreign aid, and the only academic paper that discusses about this (Zhang 2006) was written ten years ago. By contrast, English-written works and articles expounding on this theme have sprung up continuously. Some typical examples in this regard are the book of Deborah Bräutigam published in 2009 and the three-volume book that was published by John Copper (2016). Two of them offer a systematic account of China's foreign aid and diplomacy.

The existing literature roughly discusses China's foreign aid from multiple perspectives such as strategy, policy, activity, effect, diplomatic ties established thereof, forms of cooperation, and experience. The literature on aid to Africa comes in the largest quantity. Some of them serves as holistic researches on aid to Africa (Harneit-Sievers et al. 2010; Dreher et al. 2015; Hu 2011; Schiere et al. 2011; Strauss 2009), some study country-specific aid, fields of aid, and purposes of aid (Stein 2002), and some even compare aid to African countries with that to other countries, thus summing up related experience (Rupp 2013; Bräutigam and Tang 2009; Niu 2014).

5.1.1 *Principles Underlying China's Aid to Africa*

Among the literature on China's aid to Africa, the largest proportion of it deals with the principles that underpin the aid, which comes in both Chinese and English languages. The most elaborately discussed topics roughly fall into two categories: (1) analysis of no political strings attached and (2) emphasis of aid to people's livelihood. The two types of literature have been both discussed above. This part only introduces some key and new ideas contained there.

While offering aid to Africa, China follows a clear guiding principle which is no political strings attached at all. After looking back into the 60-plus years' aid China has provided for Africa, Ma Rao attempts to testify that China has never attached any political strings to its aid to Africa; and instead it respects the sovereignty of African countries and supports them in exploring for a path of development fit for themselves. China's theory and practice, on the one hand, relieves the pressure on political elite. On the other hand, it holds stronger attraction and appeal for the general public, thus reducing the prejudice, estrangement, and misunderstanding that arise from the lack of communication (Ma 2016).

Different from Ma Yao, Chen Luqi tries to prove by comparing China's aid to Africa offered before and after the Forum on China-Africa Cooperation (FOCAC) that the principles China follows to offer its aid to African countries are respecting their sovereignty, giving priority to their development, and helping aid recipients build up capacity for developing themselves independently (Chen 2009). What has echoes of this standing is a report made by Dreher et al. According to the report, aid on demand more often means the assistance to the places where political leaders of African countries were born. To prove their viewpoint, the researchers collected the birthplaces and tribal groups of 117 African leaders, and coded the 3553 geographical locations the 1955 development assistance projects funded by China all over the continent from 2000 to 2012. The comparison of these data reveals that the places where the incumbent leaders of African countries were born received more assistance than others, yet this was not true for the tribal groups to which these leaders affiliated (Dreher et al. 2015). Its findings seem to be a negative comment on China's aid principles. Actually, we can see through the seemingly negative presentation a more accurate statement on the aid principle that China's assistance to Africa is more to promote its regional development rather than to expand some tribal groups. Allowing some regions to grow first and then lead others just happens to be the path of development China has embarked on. In this sense, the relevancy between leaders' birthplaces and destinations of China's aid might be nothing but a coincidence.

The question about whether people's livelihood or democracy should play a leading role in aid is mentioned again in an article written by Chen Shuisheng and Xi Guigui together (2013). A close look into China's practice in hosting human resource trainings, sharing experience in development, and offering other forms of aid across Africa awakens He Wenping to the fact that China has always adhered to the aid principle of "teaching people how to fish rather than give them a fish directly" (He 2011). As observed by Hu Mei from the course of China's aid to Africa, the aid principles adopted by China have demonstrated the features of South–South cooperation since the very beginning. In other words, China has put itself in the position of other developing countries to cement the Sino-African relations. Equality, mutual assistance, respect and sincerity as advocated by China in the 1960s are at the core of its principles underpinning its aid to Africa. By saying so, it means the South–South aid and the South–North aid have different logical starts. China has always striven to renew its friendship with African countries, borne what they really need in its mind, and helped its African friends to develop their economies and other aspects on their own.

When it comes to aid for Africa, China's act has a big lead over its theory. China fails to talk and exchange with the Western as much as it should be, although it has emphasized its aid principles (Hu 2011). For example, with respect to the attitude toward benefit, it advocates that "the gentlemen love fortune, in a proper way" (Sautman and Hairong 2007). In the view of Leinira Lopes Sanches, an African student who studied in China, the 2006 FOCAC actually announced the Chinese model for aid; it looks like a contest between Beijing Consensus and Washington Consensus (Lopes Sanches 2009); but it is actually a rivalry between the Chinese and Western aid principles.

After combing through the course of China's aid for Africa, Shu Yunguo believes that China's aid to African countries fully embodies the basic aid principles the country has followed. That is, aid is not benediction but mutual support. On this basis, China has always tried to impart means of development, offer what is in dire need, and honor promises to the letter in its aid practice (Shu 2010).

China's aid principles displayed in the specific practice are to act concretely and improve people's livelihood, in the view of Wang and Liang (2010). Unlike the Western countries that used to deem their aid to African as a relationship between a donor and recipient, China tends to treat Africa like a marketplace with great prospects and a real partner. It is China's aid that has helped turn Africa from a troubled continent into a promising land. Therefore, Wang Yuhong suggests that China's aid to Africa practices a philosophy of harmonious development (Wang 2012). In the view of Zhang Haibing, it represents a model of assistance plus cooperation, which aims to enable recipient countries to realize independent development. Therefore, China follows a develop-oriented principle, while offering aid to Africa (Zhang 2012).

Gu and Carty's research offers another perspective into this. As they are convinced, China's programs of aid and economic cooperation in Africa have reached the fields and regions which the Western countries would like to set aside for themselves. Furthermore, China deems aid recipient countries as equal partners and never imposes its own standards on them. There have emerged the governance principles which take local people seriously and actually work (Gu and Carty 2014). The researchers with the same opinions also suggest that an outstanding manifestation of China's aid principles is the emphasis on the Sino-Africa partnership (He 2012; Rotberg 2009; Strauss and Saavedra 2009). That is to say, the reason for which China's aid to Africa can be interpreted into a partnership lies in that it allows recipient countries to govern themselves with their own methods.

Deborah Bräutigam and Tang Xiaoyang study how China's aid principles evolve by peeping through the changes in the means of aid for agriculture the country has offered to Africa. As they believe, since the 1980s, China has advocated blurring the boundaries of aid, South–South cooperation, and investment. In the meantime, it also applied this concept into the practice of establishing agricultural experiment stations in Africa. With the model where the public and private sector are mixed, landowners, farmers, and investors emerge as a community of shared interest. In this way, their partnership can bring actual benefits, thus promoting sustainable development (Bräutigam and Tang 2009).

Amid the discussions about the history and reality of China's aid to Africa, Strauss also realizes that no interference, mutual benefit, friendship enhancement, and no strings attached altogether constitute an aid principle China has followed persistently and consistently. At the same time, she also points out that the emphasis of this principle not only serves as an extension of the history, but also goes in parallel with the Chinese culture and the diplomatic philosophy worshiped by the Chinese people (Strauss 2009)

Within the framework of comparing the foreign aid practice of China and the West, Jiang Lei and Wang Haijun discuss about the different attitudes of the two sides toward political strings attached to aid. As they note, China believes attaching strings to aid amounts to the interference with the internal affairs of aid recipient countries. In this sense, attaching political strings become a negative idea. To the opposite, the Western community thinks political strings attached are a prerequisite for their aid objectives to come true. Under this context, attaching political strings is transformed into a positive thing. Neither of the above two attitudes is advisable. Instead, political strings attached should exist as a neutral concept (Jiang and Wang 2011).

The examination of the above discussions allows us to realize the principles China upholds in its aid to Africa awaken can be summed up as follows: no political strings attached, equality and mutual benefit, emphasis of imparting means of development, pursuit for joint growth, and establishment of partnership with Africa. It is fair to say that this aid principle is primarily conditional on relations of cooperation for joint development. On the Chinese front, Africa is a partner and a close friend. The way the Chinese people make friends just constitutes the cultural foundation of its aid to Africa.

With regard to the issue on political strings attached or not, we think the completely opposite attitudes of China and the Western countries tell a lot about their varying perceptions of who should play a dominant role in the course of seeking for growth. China's proposition for no political strings attached is based on its understanding of what China and even the rest of developing world has gone through and achieved in their pursuit for development. According to China, aid recipient countries should decide their path of development, because no one could replace them to realize their development. Assistance functions as a catalyst to endogenous growth. And it never plays a decisive role. As believed by the advocate of political strings attached, aid donors should dominate the course of development, or at least that role should be played by aid recipients under their guidance. In the view of China, the so-called guidance proves to be nothing but the neglect to the mastership of recipient countries and the interference with their internal affairs. Putting aid donors at a superior position is a practice that is unacceptable for China.

In the meantime, we also hold that the principles that underpin China's aid to Africa have evolved over time (Kobayashi 2008). Settings and objectives of aid vary in different period of time. In the process of evolution, the overall tenet remains unchanged. Under this premise, specific principles are embodied through various aid programs, and have developed their own features step by step (Bräutigam 2011). For instance, the eight new measures to boost China's aid to Africa announced by the Chinese government in 2009 represents a further development to its previous edition that the government declared in 2006. Behind the changes in specific measures stands the evolution of aid principles. Nevertheless, China has always pursued the Eight Principles for Economic Aid and Technical Assistance to Other Countries which was put forth in 1964.

Of course, China's aid principles have also sparked wide controversy in the international community. This is especially true, as to whether political strings should be attached. So to say, as long as aid to Africa continues, the controversy over aid principle will not cease. Neither does the debate over whether political strings attached do favor to the development of Africa.

5.1.2 Practice of China's Aid to Africa

China's practice in providing assistance for Africa began in the 1950s. It is a gradually evolving process, accompanied by the enhancement of partnership between China and Africa.

Someone divides the evolution of Sino-Africa partnership into three phases. The first phase lasts from 1950 to 1979. During this phase, the relationship between the two sides was chiefly characterized by the dominant position of political and strategic considerations. Their ties were profoundly affected by ideology at that time. The second phase is the period of 1979–1999. With the advent of this phase, China and African countries both adjusted their strategies, and began to take economic development as their top priority. Against such a backdrop, they tried to deepen their economic cooperation on multiple levels, thus contributing to a better global environment and a fairer world. In this phase, China also commenced exploring for the markets and resources of African countries. While guaranteeing the development of Chinese society and economy, it sought for African countries' support over the Taiwan issue. The years from 2000 to date constitute the third phase, when China has attempted to strike a new type of strategic partnerships with African countries. As driven by the partnerships, the two sides would seek for collaboration in many fields as diverse as politics, economy, education, science, culture, health, society, and security under the principle of pursuing sincerity, friendship, equality, mutual benefit, common prosperity, close cooperation, learning from each other, and joint development (Harneit-Sievers et al. 2010).

As an official text, *China's Foreign Aid* also offers a summary account of how China's aid to Africa has developed historically, and notes that all means of aid as proposed by the country have been tested in the actual practice. Egypt became the first African country to be assisted by China in 1956. By 1970, China had entered relations of economic and technical cooperation with a total of 17 African countries. By the end of 2012, it offered assistance to 53 African countries by funding more than 1000 projects which involved industry, agriculture, technology and facility, culture, education and health, and many other sectors. The course of China's aid to African countries has gone through three historical phases. 1956–1976: a phase of commencement. In this period, China's aid to Africa was characterized by free assistance. The country was aimed to establish and develop friendly relations with African countries, shatter the US or Soviet blockade, and win itself more diplomatic space. 1976–2000: a phase of adjustment. In the beginning of the period, China started to get rid of the constraints of political interest and ideology. As a result, it diverted much of its aid from supporting African countries' struggle for national independence and liberation to fueling economic development on both sides. And the unilateral aid was replaced by various forms of assistance and cooperation. Since 2000: a phase of development. In response to new changes in both sides, China began to adopt a diversity of means and launched various projects to offer Africa aid. Under this circumstance, there emerged a host of approaches to assistance and cooperation, which included grants, free-interest loans, subsidized loans, technical assistance, project construction, direct factory construction, expert guidance, labor service, personnel cultivation, technical training, guidance for technical management, provision of concessional loans, construction of investment and trade promotion centers, debt relief for highly indebted poor countries, trainings of economic and trade officials, emergency rescue after natural disasters (Ma 2016; Shu 2010). Instead of three phases, some researcher divides China's aid to Africa into two phases. The two-division results are similar in nature. And the minor difference results from the slightly different dividing criteria. For instance, He Xianfeng uses the year of 1978 when the policy on reform and opening up was adopted as a dividing line between the two phases (He 2011).

By comparing the course of how the Sino-Africa partnership develops and the course of China's aid to Africa, we can find that the two overlap and relate with each other greatly. Cooperation and assistance coexist and grow together. Mutual support and promotion just stands as a practical feature of China's aid. The feature has been institutionalized by the FOCAC since 2000. Besides, it has also been embodied through a series of achievements made after the birth of the event. For example, the Chinese government announced eight measures to boost its aid to

Africa at Beijing Summit as part of the FOCAC, which took place in November 2006. Three years later, on the 4th Ministerial Conference of the event it rolled out eight new measures with a view to seeking for practical cooperation with African countries. On the 60th anniversary of China's foreign aid, the *International Business Daily* released a feature article to compare the old and new eight measures. According to the article, the eight measures put forth at the Beijing Summit had been executed as scheduled. As a result, China's aid to Africa doubled in 2009 over 2006. The two sides saw their cooperation going deeper in such fields as infrastructure construction, human resource development, agriculture, medical service, and education. The new eight measures that advocates practical collaboration is proceeding orderly. It goes on particularly smoothly in agriculture, health, education, domestic installations, and human resource development (*International Business Daily* 2010).

In addition to the complete projects involved with the infrastructure sector for example as introduced in *China's Foreign Aid*, the most eye-catching part of China's practice in offering aid to Africa is the Green Revolution, a term coined by Bräutigam. As early as the 1990s, Bräutigam had set her eyes on China's aid for agriculture in Africa. Her doctoral thesis is developed around China's Aid for agriculture and Africa's Green Revolution. As she points out, the Western countries think the resolution to Africa's political issues is possible only when the continent handles such local problems as poorly developed policies, low human capabilities, and resistant attitudes toward development properly. Participation, accountability, transparency, and rule of law may be some feasible options. However, China's development assistance for agriculture in West Africa attests that for West African countries, modeling after China to develop irrigable farmlands and grow crops on them is a political decision of great importance, even measured by the Western standards. This is because by doing so, they could guarantee the supply of crops and further the political stability (Bräutigam 1998). The practice of bringing multiple stakeholders under a framework of development not only fuels the development of agriculture but also gives birth to the Green Revolution (Bräutigam and Tang 2009). While promoting agricultural technology, their efforts to transform agriculture into industrialized operations even provide a feasible way to help Africa realize self-sufficiency in grains, which is a green dream of the continent (Bräutigam and Zhang 2013). What China has done to improve people's livelihood through aid in Africa could set a good example for Latin-American countries as well (Bräutigam and Gallagher 2014).

Besides, there are some other high-profile aid practices, which involve the light industry (He 2013), special economic zone (Bräutigam and Tang 2011), direct investment (Ju 2010), and other fields.

To extract other features from China's practice in offering aid to Africa, you can refer to the opinions of He Xianfeng, who proposes nonpolitical operation, cooperation for joint development, and aid to improve people's livelihood (He 2011).

5.1.3 Controversy over China's Aid to Africa

As China's aid to Africa goes wider and more influential, it is drawing wider attention and provoking more fierce controversy with each passing day. As someone points out, "if we set eyes on China's desires for natural resources of Africa and its intervention with local efforts for self-governance and sustained development, China can be said to play a role of devil there; however, when it comes to the contributions to Africa's infrastructure construction, creation dividend, and long-term economic growth, China can be hailed as a noble angle for what it has done there" (Sun 2014). In the meantime, the presence of China in Africa has been under the close watch of the entire world. For the Western realists, the China-Africa cooperation turns out to be a challenge for the Western world (Schiere et al. 2011). The considerable controversy in this regard may involve the following five aspects.

(1) China's Motivations

In the early days of its founding, the new China started to offer assistance to African countries. In return, they provided an important source of political support in China's regaining its legal seat in the UN and promoting the "One China" principle. In this sense, China's aid to Africa may be explained as a policy or program that is devised based on the country's need for lifting its position in the international geopolitics (Liu et al. 2014). Or it can be comprehended as an attempt the new China has made to export the socialist experience and ideology and get itself involved in the world affairs (Wang and Sun 2014).

According to a commonly held view, China uses its aid to Africa as a diplomatic instrument to secure its national interests (Zafar 2007).

Africa is richly endowed with energy and other natural resources, and presents huge market prospects, all of which are necessary for China to sustain its high-speed economic growth (Power et al. 2012). China has racked up considerable benefits from Africa in the abovementioned three aspects over recent years. The European Development Cooperation to 2020 (EDC 2020) project includes five papers related with China (Grimm 2008; Hackenesch 2011; Grimm 2011; Grimm et al. 2009; Humphrey 2011), all of which deal with the relations between Europe and China in terms of aid to Africa. European experts believe that the primary objectives of China's aid to Africa are about economic benefits, diplomatic interests (like Taiwan issue), international position, and other factors leftover from the past. Of these, economic benefits come with the foremost significance.

There are mainly two types of means to gain resources in exchange of aid. First, the explicit means. The loans China provides for African countries are guaranteed with their natural resources (like petroleum) (Bräutigam and Gallagher 2014), through which China therefore has direct access to African resources as it may need (Moyo 2012). Second, the implicit means. China's aid helps the recipient countries to bolster up their soft power (Li 2013; Luo 2007; Wei 2011; Yu 2014; King 2013; Kurlantzick 2007; McGiffert 2009; Rebol 2011). To facilitate its acquisition of natural resources from Africa, China makes efforts to develop the strong willingness of African leaders to cooperate with it and build a good reputation across the continent.

In the view of some critics and scholars, China's aid to Africa is in the nature of new colonialism (Pfaff 1995; Lo 2012; Li 2012). Only seeking for interests in Africa, China has neglected a variety of bad consequences its development efforts brought about to the African societies like environmental pollution, overdevelopment, exploitation of local labor, and trade asymmetry (Schiere et al. 2011). Some researchers even claim that China's assistance to Africa is a new form of imperialism (Bello 2007); China deems Africa as its second continent (French 2014); and its aid is typical of resource diplomacy (Power et al. 2012).

Absolutely, there are some opposite voices that utter China's conducts conform to the logics of market, capital and free trade. For instance, we cannot criticize that the arrival of Chinese enterprises who employ Chinese workers for their projects in Africa impedes the employment of local workers and the development of local companies. As pointed out by Bräutigam et al., China's access to African resources is based on market principles, instead of plundering them (Bräutigam and Gallagher 2014). As viewed by Xi Qie et al., China's aid to Africa has nothing to do with resource snatch or squeeze of other countries out of the continent, because China always practices the principle of equality and mutual trust that underpins the South–South cooperation (Xie et al. 2012). Starting from the phenomenon of widespread stigmatization, Xiao Yang holds that aid to Africa involves fights for reputation and rights/interest; and China needs to maintain its reputation while offering its assistance to the continent (Xiao 2013).

It should be noted that China purses multiple objectives in instituting its policy toward Africa. Due to the absence of near-term strategies, China has been less trusted and more misunderstood by African countries and other actors worldwide (Dent 2011; Song 2014; Wang 2013; Huang and Lang 2010; Li and Wu 2009). If China's gaining economic profits in Africa hurts its friendly relations with African countries, its means this is a process incurring more political risk.

As Li Anshan thinks, China is more a doer than a talker, compared with others in the rest of the world. The publicity of its aid to Africa proves to be a weak spot of China. So it requires an overarching state strategy to do better in this regard. China brings concrete benefits to Africa with its courteous and moderate actions. What it needs to do better is establish a good state image by appropriately publicizing the contents of aid, means of aid, and aid recipients (Li 2008a, b). He also writes a book review for Deborah Brautigam's the *Dragon's Gift: The Real Story of China in Africa*, to refute the new colonialism as claimed by the Western scholars (Li 2010).

(2) Environmental impact

While offering its aid to Africa, China has conducted many projects which are closely related to local environment. Some of them are about infrastructure construction, metal smelting, and mining of natural resources. The consequences caused by the infrastructure projects on African ecology have aroused widespread attention. Take the dam construction project China Three Gorges Corporation (CTG) has undertaken in the Democratic Republic of the Congo for example. The project has led to water/soil erosion and other environmental pollution problems. The performance of CTG in Africa has the public think that it is unable to protect African environment while advancing construction.

Similarly, the mining and metal smelting projects launched by other Chinese companies also exposed the aid recipient countries to pollutions like the release of sulfur from the copper and cobalt smelting process and the use of hydrargyrum in the gold refining process. All these discharges do harms to the local environment. Besides, the improper deforestation speeds up the drainage of resource reserves. Some researchers suggest that while providing its aid to Africa, China works hard to maintain good relations with local governments, and renders them unable to play their monitoring functions, thus damaging local environment directly (Harneit-Sievers et al. 2010; Chan-Fishel and Lawson 2007).

(3) Corruption

China's aid to Africa also faces the problem of inefficiency, like that provided by the international community. The emphasis of no political strings attached to aid wins China from Africa more beneficial offers, opportunities of investment and trade, and debt relief than Western countries (Jakobson 2009). At the same time, China tends to closely team up with political elites of recipient countries, in carrying out its aid programs (Angeles and Neanidis 2009). Those political elites will significantly influence the effect of aid by considering their own power and interests. Some research findings reveal that under this circumstance, the aid method of no political strings attached adopted by China will lead to corruption. Furthermore, China's reluctance to disclose aid-related data is more likely to breed corruption in the aid recipient countries (Alden 2005; Rimmer 2000).

According to some researchers in the opposite, China's practice of involving its own companies and workers in the aid projects reduces the funds that flow to the recipient countries, thus curbing the possibility of corrupting local officials (Bräutigam 2010). One of the challenges confronting China is how to strike a balance between not intervening with internal affairs of the recipient countries and encouraging them to adopt better policies (Schiere et al. 2011).

(4) Effects on economic development of recipient countries

The actual effect of China's aid to Africa is also under considerable debate for now. As claimed by some researches, China's infrastructure aid projects represented by the Tanzania-Zambia Railway help the recipient countries get rid of bottlenecks holding back their trade and economic development (Bräutigam, 2009; Smith 2010). However, the opinion is divided as to how the arrival of Chinese companies affects the development of local economies. Bilateral partnerships make the bulk of China's cooperation projects with African countries. In the view of some people, the approach to cooperation based on national interests results in the unbalanced development and instability within different regions of the continent (Schiere et al. 2011), which goes against the regional integration in Africa.

The state-owned enterprises (SOEs) of China that extend their business presence to Africa usually come in large sizes and employ a considerable amount of labor. And most of these companies are engaged in capital-intensive industries such as petroleum. By contrast, private Chinese companies participate in a wider range of market competition there (Warmerdam and van Dijk 2013; Diana 2013; Ju 2010). China's enterprise investment in Africa on the one hand has bridged the shortage of Africa in industrial production capacity and improved the living standards of local people. On the other hand, it has also squeezed the room for survival of local companies, especially small and medium-sized enterprises (SMEs). Unemployment, poor working conditions, and low wages also bring some African countries like Zambia and Senegal into social conflicts (Harneit-Sievers et al. 2010). Besides, some others also point out that China exports goods of inferior quality to African countries, and therefore jeopardizes the healthy development of local industries (Gadzala 2010).

(5) Challenge to traditional aid donors

The greater controversy exists about the influence of emerging aid donors represented by China on the aid market. As more Chinese companies find their way to Africa, China's imports from the continent grow rapidly. In the meantime, the traditional aid donors see their share in African market on the decline. In this context, they become increasingly concerned about that China is likely to turn the aid framework they have built upside down. (OECD 2012; Cheru and Obi 2010; Golley and Song 2011; Hu et al. 2014; Schiere 2014; Zhang 2007). Some researchers comment that China wages a quiet revolution in the aid filed (Woods 2008). The European researchers widely believe that China's aid to Africa is bound to challenge the aid norms and commercial interests established by the EU or its member states and even the entire Western world (Grimm et al. 2009; Grimm 2011).

Since China barely disclosed its data on bilateral cooperation, plus the inconsistency between the forms of its aid in a considerable part and the statistics of the OECD on official development assistance, China's aid to Africa falls short of transparency, and scholars thus hold divergent judgments about its share in bilateral cooperation. To tackle with this problem, Bräutigam argues that the aid to Africa from emerging donors like China only accounts for a small proportion of the total, and it doesn't crucially differ from that offered by the DAC countries. Therefore, the international aid framework won't be shaken (Bräutigam 2010, 2012). Besides, Liao Lan and Liu Jing also review the prevailing comments of the Western scholars against China's aid to Africa, by criticizing and refuting its lack of transparency, irresponsible provision of enormous loans, and snatch of natural resources. But as agreed by these scholars with one accord, China's aid to Africa plays a supplementary but not succedaneous role in terms of amount. It is noteworthy that China has changed the ways aid donors and recipients interact, as an important force of emerging aid donors (Liao and Liu 2012).

Generally speaking, the facts that underlie various controversy over China's aid to Africa all turn out to be the problems exposed from the development process. As Dent indicates, the too much concern over China's development stands as an extension of realism. On the one hand, the US encourages the studies in search for rivals, while valuing and maintaining its hegemony. On the other hand, to protect its unilateralism, America exceedingly simplifies what other actors have done, and deliberately overstates the threats these actors pose on it (Dent 2011).

In addition to *China's Foreign Aid*, the Chinese government releases another white paper entitled *China-Africa Economic and Trade Cooperation*,[1] to more explicitly expound its stand, principles and practice in this regard. The 2010 white paper tries to highlight the trade

[1] *China-Africa Economic and Trade Cooperation* is also known as a White Paper. So far, the Chinese government has released two editions of this document, in December 2010 and August 2013.

Both are available online.

2013 edition: http://english.gov.cn/archive/white_paper/2014/08/23/content_281474982986536.htm.

2010 edition: https://www.fmprc.gov.cn/ce/cebw/eng/xwdt/t785012.htm.

balance, mutual investment and mutual benefit between China and Africa, and exhibits the priorities of its investment there go to infrastructure construction, development capability building, and improvement of people's livelihood. It is a clear statement on China's stand in its aid to and cooperation with African countries. The 2013 white paper reiterates the importance of the above three aspects, and takes a further step to stress China's involvement in two traditional dimensions of aid to Africa: agricultural cooperation and grain security. Compared with the 2010 edition, the 2013 white paper realizes a significant progress, by emphasizing multilateral cooperation.

Regardless of wherever data are obtained and however they are analyzed, the existing academic literature, we believe, explicitly attests that the mainstream conclusions are completely in line with the Chinese government's standing, opinion, and practice.

5.1.4 *Foreign Aid to Africa: China vs. Other Countries*

Comparative studies into foreign aid to Africa from China and other countries constitute a significant part of the literature on China's aid to Africa. They are also an important content within the framework of the two-sided four-tiered embeddedness. In other words, China's aid to Africa is embedded into both the world's aid that goes to the continent and China's aid to all other countries. For the latter aspect, the book has made a full review and exploration in its previous parts. For the former point, we will comb through related researches and viewpoints thereinafter from the dimension of aid donors. It should be noted here that out of the collected literature, the pieces published in Chinese language come in a larger number than those written in English language.

(1) Foreign aid to Africa: China vs. the US

The US is one of the world's first countries that offer aid to Africa. It also ranks the first among all donors in terms of the resources invested and the coverage of these resources. Among the OECD-DAC member states, America contributed more than 50% aid funds of the organization's total between 1950 and 1968; the proportion long-ranged between 20 and 30% over the period from 1974 to 1991, and dropped and moved between 10 and 20% in the decade of 1991–2000; and it has gone back to above 20% since 2001. Seen from the OECD-DAC data in previous years, although the ratio of the US aid funds to the organization's total went through fluctuations, the US position as the biggest aid donor has never been shaken. The only exception took place in the 1990s when it was outperformed by France for the time being. From 2000, the US's proportion went up rapidly, which enabled the gross aid made by the DAC member states to present a steep growth curve.[2]

Furthermore, the US is also one of the first countries that have converted foreign aid into an institutionalized and legalized mechanism. Starting from the Marshall Plan, the US began incorporating foreign aid into its legal system step by step. The US Congress adopted the Foreign Assistance Act in 1961. Amended for many times, the law has grown from 49 pages in the very beginning to more than 400 pages today. It now sets out a total of 108 program goals and priorities, involving 37 departments and 60 offices of the US government. On top of the basic statute, the country also enacted 20-plus authorized acts to prescribe foreign aid in terms of specific region, practice and issue from 1945 to 2014. Besides laws and acts promulgated by the Congress, executive orders issued by the president of the US constitute another source of policies on foreign aid, and also serve as important tools to execute related legislation. Two examples under this category are the 2009 Presidential Study Directive on US Global Development Policy and the 2010 Presidential Policy Directive on US Global Development. The last but not the least, there is also a type of suggestive guiding opinions, that is, Presidential Initiatives, such as the US Global Health Initiative and the Feed the Future Initiative proposed by the former US president Barack Obama.

The United States Agency for International Development (USAID) operates as the primary agency of the country to implement its foreign aid programs Founded in 1916, USAID still manages the overwhelming foreign aid projects of the US. Besides it, the US State Department, Department of Defense, Department of Agriculture, Treasury Department, Millennium Challenge Corporation (MCC) and other short-term or temporary agencies also get themselves in foreign aid through specific programs.

[2]The OECD-DAC data can be obtained directly from the OECD website. Search by theme, and you can get related figures and graphics and download data by visiting https://data.oecd.org/.

All these organizations team up or work together through a variety of foreign aid projects of the US. Each project has their own specified account, no matter where their funds come. Some types of dedicated accounts include development assistance, disaster rescue, crisis foundation, global health, migrant and refugee assistance, narcotic control and law enforcement, peacekeeping operations, military assistance, and food for peace program. This operating mechanism is especially true for the funds from government spending.

In short, the US foreign aid is based on its legal system where the Foreign Assistance Act functions as the foundation and presidential directives and initiatives serve as strong supplements. All of these ensure a smooth transition from legislation to enforcement. On the legal basis, foreign aid is mainly given out by the USAID, and these projects are participated in or led by related government departments. A large category of foreign aid projects has a dedicated account or foundation to finance them. Each project must go through a complete set of legal and administrative procedures from proposal to conclusion. As prescribed by the General Accounting Office for project funding, every foreign aid project shall be subject to evaluation before they are concluded, so as to have their effects and influences assessed properly.

Aid to Africa comes as part of the US's vast foreign aid system. After the end of the Cold War, America's aid to Africa demonstrated a turning point in policies (Walle 2010; Johnson 2010), and shifted its focus somewhat (Fleck and Kilby 2010; Chhotray and Hulme 2009). In the opinions of Liu Guijin, Africa, especially sub-Sahara Africa, has long been positioned low in the US external strategy; but this situation has been ended and evolved into the opposite direction since its counterterrorist campaign was unveiled. In the wake of the 9/11 attacks, the US further specified the four pillars of its strategy toward Africa, which are to (1) strengthen democratic institutions; (2) spur economic growth, trade, and investment; (3) advance peace and security; and (4) promote opportunity and development. Meanwhile, it also enacted the African Growth and Opportunity Act (AGOA). While establishing the US Africa command in the name of counterterrorism, it also intensified to aid Africa democratically and divert more assistance to local people. In the US aid to Africa, the proportion of investment in the public accounted for 74% in 2012. Obama's administration rolled out a new US Strategy toward Sub-Saharan Africa that particularly emphasizes the significant role Africa plays in the US security and prosperity. With different goals in Africa,

China doesn't have to come into conflict with the US. Instead, the two may work with each other to seek common ground while reserving their difference. It is recommended that China pursue a three-pronged strategy toward Africa that attaches equal attention to politics, economy and trade, and culture (Liu 2013).

As Feng Zheying reveals in her research, given its economic interests and counterterrorism drive, the US started to value Africa's significance in geopolitics after the Cold War, by working hard to construct a network of counterterrorism based on the Horn of Africa, and shifting the focus of its aid to fight against terrorists (Feng 2010). According to researcher Hu Mei, the US regards spreading its values as part of its aid to Africa, and has formed a new pattern of democratically aiding the continent after the Cold War. In the meantime, China has adjusted its aid to aim at promoting economic and trade cooperation with Africa and realizing mutual benefits and a win-win outcome, thus generating a new aid policy which particularly advocates improving local people's livelihood. She thinks different strategies lead to different effects achieved. The US's democratic aid didn't work well while China's livelihood-oriented aid was injected with continuous momentum (Hu 2010). Unfortunately, she didn't put forth any tool to measure the actual effects of the two different patterns, let alone specific evidence or data that display the differences in these effects.

In addition to the debates over political strings discussed above, researchers also exchange their views on the policies, organizations and effects of the US's aid to Africa. For example, America tends to bind security with development together. Anderson holds that the relations between the USAID and the Department of Defense (DoD) prove to be an important factor that affects how efficient the US aid to Africa is. As Wang Lijuan and Jiang Xinru argue, the US's aid to Africa has produced positive effects on the continent. For instance, on the one hand it has created necessary conditions to African countries to develop their economies, and helped them stabilize their political situation, improve their health conditions, and lift their educational standards; but on the other hand it has also increased the inequality among these countries and their reliance on aid (Wang and Jiang 2014). In the long run, the US's aid to Africa has basically attained its goals specific for each historical period, like curbing the former Soviet Union's expansion in Africa, weakening the influence of European suzerains, and keeping a tighter rein on Africa, think (Cao and Song 2012).

Generally, a close look at the literature on aid to Africa from China and the US reveals that comparative studies are few in number, most focus on one or the other, with no more than a passing mention of the other one. The few comparative studies do, however, draw decisive conclusions. One of the reasons for which the US has changed its aid strategy toward Africa by stepping up its aid efforts is closely related to its counterterrorism initiative; and Africa's position in the US global strategy is on a rapid rise. The drastic change in China's aid policy toward Africa also occurred after the advent of the twenty-first century. After the change, China has pursued a strategy which stresses to promote cooperation and development with aid. Its cooperation-oriented investments have grown fast in Africa. Nevertheless, neither China nor the US has changed its basic standing toward aid to Africa. The US still emphasizes the importance of democratically aiding Africa, while China always advocates assisting the continent by improving local people's livelihood.

(2) Foreign aid to Africa: China vs. European countries

Some European countries have become the first donors of foreign aid to Africa, because of their colonization in the continent. After World War II, African countries gradually got rid of the colonial rule in their pursuit for national liberation and independence. As the previous suzerains, some European countries still hope to sustain their influence in Africa. To this end, they resort to foreign aid as an important policy tool.

The *Treaty of Rome* (1957) established the European Economic Community (EEC) association system, requiring the EEC member states to provide assistance for their previous colonies and overseas territories. The EEC inked four Iome Conventions with African, Caribbean and Pacific countries successively from 1975 to 1989. The Cotonou Agreement was signed in 2000, laying the institutional foundation for European countries to aid African countries.

It is worth noting that within the OECD-DAC framework, European countries offer aid to their Africa counterparts in varying methods and with divergent efforts. Germany's aid to its former colony Rwanda involves its Federal Ministry for Economic Cooperation and Development (BMZ), KfW Group (KfW), Debenham Thouard Zadelhoff (DTZ), and German Development Service (DED), among others. Priorities of aid vary throughout different historical periods. In the 1960s and 1970s, aid was usually employed as a political tool to facilitate government negotiations between two countries. In the 1980s, aid embraced a period of transformation due to the Washington Consensus. In the 1990s, the occurrence of genocide diverted more attention to emergency humanitarian assistance. Since 2000, effects of aid have drawn more importance than aid itself. Furthermore, Germany's aid to African countries also come in a rapidly expanded size (Schmidt 2003; Liu 2012), and the country is also actively exploring for more ways of aid like third-party cooperation (Chen and Zhai 2013).

The United Kingdom (the UK) is another OECD—DAC member state. With the aid provided in the colonial period counted in, the country's history of foreign aid has been more than 100 years. In 1889, Britain adopted the *Colonial Loans Act* to give its colonies GBP 3 million in aid. In 1929, the *Colonial Development Act* was enacted, which prescribed that loans and grants be channeled to colonies' agriculture and industry, so as to promote the development of its own industry and commerce in return. At the same time, the Colonial Development Fund was established to manage such aid funds. Then the *Colonial Development and Welfare Act* was promulgated in 1940. Based on the 1929 Act, it incorporated enhancing public welfare in colonies as an important objective of aid. In 1945, the act was amended, by increasing the fund aids for colonies to GBP 120 million within a decade. The *Overseas Resources Development Act* which came out in 1947 was dedicated to improving the living conditions of people in colonies through establishing companies overseas. In the following several decades, as the collapse of the colonial system, the UK introduced no laws or acts on foreign aid. Instead, it only released three white papers on the theme in 1960, 1963, and 1973 successively, in a bid to explain its basic policy and standing on this front throughout different periods of time. The year 1980 witnessed the promulgation of the *Overseas Development and Co-operation Act* by the country, which highlights that the objectives of the UK's foreign aid are to promote the economic development and people's welfare of recipient countries or regions, and sets out the statutory bodies in relation to furnishing of assistance and their powers as well as methods of aid like technical assistance, fund aid, and educational training. The UK government released two white papers as a manifestation to its standing and principles on foreign aid in 1997 and 2000. It enacted the *International Development Act* in 2002 and the *International Development Act* (Reporting and Transparency) in 2006, successively.

All of these constitute the legal framework and foundation of the UK's foreign aid. Especially the two acts introduced after 2000 set out the objectives of aid, relations between aid and its own economy, bodies furnishing of aid, and directions and fields of aid, and establish the legal status of the Department of International Development (DFID) in foreign aid (Zhang and Sun 2014).

The DFID was set up in 1997 based on the former Overseas Development Agency (ODA). As the enforcement agency of the above two acts enacted in the twenty-first century, it is responsible for realizing the UK's goals of foreign aid, which includes: tackling with extreme poverty and starvation, making primary education accessible for all, promoting gender equality and protecting women's rights and interests, safeguarding basic human health (by reducing infant mortality, raising maternal health, and fighting against HIV/AIDS, malaria and other diseases), doing better in environmental protection, and promoting global cooperation.

For the UK, aid to Africa constitutes the most important part of its foreign aid. Immediately after WWII, the UK resumed the assistance to its former African colonies, with a view to supporting the newly independent governments. Since the DFID inception, the UK's aid to Africa has been included into the overall objective of its foreign aid. The gross aid to African countries accounted for about 36% of the country's foreign aid over the period from 1994 to 1999. Interestingly, while offering aid to African countries, the UK has always given its priorities to the Commonwealth of Nations member states. Since 2000, six of the nine African countries receiving an average aid of more than RMB 100 million from the UK are the Commonwealth members.

Compared with China's aid to Africa, the UK's has been attached to stronger political strings since 2000. The country tends to raise requirements for recipient countries in terms of democracy, good governance, and even political regime. The former British Prime minister Tony Blair ever proposed the neo-interventionism (Zhang 2011). Besides, its aid has started to involve an ever-growing number of fields like military affairs, poverty reduction, and HIV/AIDS prevention and treatment. In addition to expanding the size of aid, the DFID's *Africa Directorate Operational Plan 2011–2015* makes some adjustments to recipients of aid by channeling more related resources to the countries in the direst need. Out of the 27 major recipient countries, 17 are distributed in Africa. Besides, the Operational Plan also designates the priority tasks of aid as improving health conditions and safeguarding the rights and interests of women and children. In its *Regional Program in Africa 2011–2015*, the DFID comes up with a detailed operational plan to offer aid in Africa. According to the plan, the UK support will help: 4 million peasants benefit directly from cross-border trade; 300,000 households have access to low carbon energy; avert 6000 maternal deaths; bring 17,000 malnourished people out of danger; 1 million people reach safe food with emergency food assistance; cut waiting times at border crossings (by at least 50%); invest in infrastructure along regional transport corridors; and promote regional energy development and environmental improvement with other donors.

In its bilateral assistance plans, the UK has also developed specific objectives for different recipients. For instance, as proposed by the DFID's *Burundi Operational Plan 2011–2012*, as of March 2012, the UK would ensure: more local children are in primary education (51% of whom are girls); 450,000 extra textbooks are in schools; 2000 more women have better access to justice services; and improved drug distribution, guaranteeing that none of the 263 health facilities run out of essential drugs (Li and Huang 2012).

Despite their own agenda for aid to Africa, European countries bear some resemblance in this regard since they share the same historical ties with the continent. This is especially true for the OECD-DAC member states. For example, all of them endorse the establishment of a new Europe–Africa partnership. The EU Council approved a strategic document entitled the *EU and Africa: Towards a Strategic Partnership* in December 2005. There followed the *From Cairo to Lisbon: The EU-Africa Strategic Partnership* that came out in 2007. With these two policy documents, the EU shored up its assistance to Africa, in addition to adjusting the priorities and fields of aid. By dong so, it hopes to strengthen its dialogue and cooperation with African countries, promote its democratic regimes, sustain sources of fund and markets of product, and reinforce geopolitical and military security.

Even though the EU has increased its aid efforts, expanded the scope of aid, and shifted the priorities of aid, it doesn't reduce the political strings attached to its aid for Africa. This point has been fully reflected in the aid provided by Germany and the UK and also the overall aid offered by the EU. In this sense, being attached with conditions remains a prominent hallmark of the EU's aid. All its aid agreements signed in 1992 and beyond contain conditions and terms on human rights, parallel human rights and governance, and make indiscreet remarks on recipients' political and administrative regimes (Wang 2009).

Of course, Europe is a complicated concept. We don't mean to mix up the EU, the EEC, the OECD and other related notions that involve different countries and entities. Neither do we need to distinguish them strictly for the purpose of aid to Africa. In our view, these entities, despite their different definitions, share more similarity than disparity with respect to the standing, practice and phase division of aid to Africa.

First of all, according to some existing researches, China and European countries demonstrate different features in their aid to Africa; and the fundamental difference between the two sides lies in whether political strings attached or not. Secondly, the EU's aid policy is closely linked to its other policies. Although China has completed its shift from offering grants alone to adopting a diversity of aid methods, there is a long path ahead of it before having its aid efforts integrated well. Moreover, the EU's complete set of aid policies are just what China falls short of. More importantly, when it comes to aid for Africa, China does more than it talks (Wang 2011; Li 2011). Some researchers even argue that even by putting both China and Europe in front of Africa, people won't reach consensus on China's presence in Africa. Among Chinese scholars, there may be divergent views on this front. By the same token, the discussions about the comparison between the two sides reveal a host of areas and possibilities for them to cooperate. Take anti-piracy operations in the security field as an example.

As some other researchers suggest, European countries take note of the human right issues that might exist in China's policy toward Africa, and expects China to respect the values prevailing in Africa. However, instead of caring for these aspects, China tends to focus on meeting its own needs and maintaining a dedicate balance with Europe and its countries. So it is recommended that China pay attention to the concerns of different stakeholders. This is because China and Europe may be both partners and competitors in Africa (Men and Barton 2011; Xie 2012).

The comparative study into foreign aid of China and Europe to Africa is anything but systematic, just like that in the comparison between China and the US. Furthermore, the literature involving Australia (Davis 2011), France (Cumming 1995; Rioux and Van Belle 2005; Wilson 1993), Russia (Song 2013; Parfitt 2005), and the Netherlands (Baehr 1980) proves to be a far cry from systematically expounding a country's aid to Africa or its aid to a specific field.

This situation may chiefly result from the following two factors. First, Europe is not a continent with every single part in step with each other; and as a concept, it doesn't correspond to a clear number of entities. Second, the continent as an entirety cannot share the same ground with its member states about every aspect of aid to Africa such as standing, practice, and course of evolution.

Both China and Europe want to promote the development of Africa through their aid. This is especially true for China and the UK. Even so, the two sides tend to adopt quite different methods to attain their targets. For instance, Europe's aid puts more emphasis on political strings attached and improvement in life quality, while China's tries to highlight mutual benefits and cooperation, and to narrow down its focus on survival. It is worth noting that the bilateral relations have existed long between any two of China, Europe, and Africa, and that the trilateral relations don't appear until recently. China has built deeper bilateral ties with Africa. It extends wider reach with local people and thus assumes greater risks. European countries see their bond with Africa lasting longer time, and can cement their relationship with the continent thanks to many linguistic, religious and economic conveniences. On the other side, the long history also means more burden on their shoulder. At a time when both China and Europe seek for a closer relationship with Africa, the two are quite mutually complementary there in effect. Many Europe countries seemingly have felt their influence in Africa is threatened by China. As a matter of fact, China has unconsciously become an imaginary enemy for those who play on the African arena, European countries in particular.

(3) Foreign aid to Africa: China, India and Japan

Compared with the US and European countries in terms of foreign aid, most Asian countries are either late movers or aid recipients for the past or for now. Against such a historical and practical background, we can still find some literature that discusses and compares the aid of India and Japan with that of China.

Like China, India also is one of the most populous countries in the world. It claims to own the largest number of democratic population, but it lags behind China in the spectrum of economic development. Once a colony of the UK, India is one of the first countries that received foreign aid around the world.

As its economy develops, India also does better in foreign trade, by establishing a complete set of related policies and institutions step by step. In 2003 and 2004, the Indian government spent INR 2 billion in setting up the India Development Initiatives (IDI) under the Ministry of Finance. The organization was interpreted, reformed, redefined in 2007. Besides, the India International Development Cooperation Agency (IIDCA) was founded in the same year. By then, there emerged a fairly sound organizational framework dealing with foreign aid in the country (Huang and Xie 2012). It is worth mentioning that the USAID got itself actively involved with the process, by supporting India in forming its foreign aid system.[3]

India's aid to Africa reveals its own features due to its historical and geopolitical relations with African countries.

It is before the Portuguese landed in Africa that India had maintained close trade exchanges with East Africa, thus forming the Indian Ocean trading system. In the long history of contacts, many Indian people settled down in East Africa, and intermarried with the indigenous people. There emerged Africa-Indians. As the Western countries turned African countries into their colonies, the Indian Ocean trading system declined with each passing day. Afterwards, the UK established more colonies in Africa. As a result, a torrent of Indians immigrants flowed into East Africa, and played a dominant role in its economic activities. In the meantime, plagued by the British racist policies, the immigrant Indians and local Africans rallied around to fight against the colonial ruling, and developed the African economies. From the process there even emerged the political and business leaders of Indian ancestry (Du 2011).

Over the period from India's independence to the end of the Cold War, India had always striven to become a power across the region and even the Indian Ocean. While making diplomatic exchanges with other countries, it pursued the policy of nonalignment just like China did. In June 1954, it worked with China to propose the Five Principles of Peaceful Coexistence, a basic principle for countries to handle international affairs.

Regardless before or after its independence, India has always bluntly supported Africa to abolish racial segregation policies. While African

[3]The USAID rolled out the India Country Development Cooperation Strategy (2012–2016) in 2012, aiming to support Indian's efforts to build its foreign aid system. For more details, please visit at https://www.usaid.gov/india/cdcs.

countries fought for national liberation and independence, the Indian government took a different position with them. As a result, there was something wrong with their relations in the 1950s. In the 1960s, India took the initiative to improve its ties with African countries. The Indian Technical and Economic Cooperation (ITEC) program was approved in September 1964, in a bid to provide the newly independent African countries with assistance. Indira Gandhi administration appealed for South–South cooperation under the framework of no-alignment in 1967. Since then, India has never ceased its aid for Africa, and kept supporting African countries in their political fight against racism. After the end of the Cold War, it began to change its policy toward Africa. Economic cooperation with African countries and protection of Indian people's rights and interests in Africa become the top two missions on its agenda of foreign aid. Spearheaded by the 1964 ITEC program, the country offered economic aid and technical assistance to one-fourth of African countries in the 1990s. In the meantime, the trade volume between the two sides soared by 2.8 times between 1992 and 2001 (Zhu 2005).

Since 2000, for the purpose of acquiring resources and market shares in Africa and winning its support over international affairs, India has diverted more aid to many fields concerning people's livelihood such as funding, technology, training, medical care, environmental protection, and humanism. The assistance and cooperation efforts promoted trade between India and Africa. The trade volume between the two sides stood at USD 965 million in 1991, and soared up to USD 70 billion in 2015. The *Declaration of Delhi* and the *India-Africa Framework for Strategic Cooperation* were adopted by India and Africa, which set out their cooperation plans in many fields. On the Indian front, it hoped to win over the support of African countries and become a permanent member of the UN Security Council (Qiu and Liu 2012).

Many endeavors of India in Africa highly overlap with those of China in terms of policy and practice. For instance, both of them insist no political strings attached to their aid (Wen 2014). That explains a claim held by some people that India is repeating the ways China has taken to aid Africa (Tao 2011). But a look into India's aid to African countries can awaken us to the following facts. Firstly, the assistance benefits a wide range of local people. For instance, the African Undergraduate Training program is targeted at college students from all orders of society, especially those from middle and lower classes. Secondly, the aid aimed at African countries along the Indian Ocean coasts has extended to a wider scope of projects, including the Pan African e-Network Project which commenced in 2004. Thirdly, India has possessed some edges that China doesn't have, such as the large number of overseas Indians in Africa (Xu 2015), geo-economic advantages, well-developed small and medium-sized enterprises, and special relations with regional organizations of Africa (Kang 2012). Even so, India has its own difficulties. Its economy is not strong enough to honor its commitment on aid for Africa (Tao 2011).

In the literature written in English with respect to aid to Africa, India and China are always mentioned together (Broadman et al. 2007; McCormick 2008; Cheru and Obi 2010; Santos-Paulino and Wan 2010). An exception, in this case, is a piece of literature that exclusively discusses the motivations of India's aid. Usually, aid is a game exclusive to rich countries. So this piece of literature raises a question about why a poor country like India offer assistance to other developing countries, and gives its own answer. By analyzing India's commitments that it will extend aid to 125 countries between 2008 and 2010, the researcher brings up the concept of "needy donor," claiming that the distribution of India' aid is swayed by its commercial and political interests. Compared with the OECD-DAC donors, India tends to seek for more political interests through its aid. In this sense, the countries abutting India or those with similar levels of economic development are more likely to get its project-based aid (Fuchs and Vadlamannati 2013).

Based on these discussions, we can get a glimpse into the differences in aid between India and China. China takes more regard of what recipient countries, especially their people, actually need, puts more emphasis on the construction of "hard power" exemplified by infrastructure, and gets most of its investment done by state-owned enterprises. India also stresses the importance of improving the livelihood of local people, and extends its aid to fields similar to those of China. Differently, it attaches more importance to the construction of "soft power," and most of its investment is undertaken by private companies (Biswas 2012). More importantly, even though India doesn't attach political strings to its aid bluntly as the US and European countries do, it never means that India's aid doesn't carry its appeals for political interests.

Unlike India, Japan has experienced the identity change from an aid recipient country after its defeat in WWII to a developed nation. Given the role Japan played in WWII, it is impossible for the country to get actively involved in political diplomacy as the US did, or to follow in Germany's footsteps to expand geopolitical space in the excuse of financing the development of its former colonies. Against such a backdrop, Japan resorted to foreign aid as an important form of economic diplomacy. In the 1950s–1970s, Japan's foreign aid was limited to a small size and quantity. And it commenced granting concessional loans to African countries in 1966. Among the 37 countries receiving aid from Japan, only eight came from Africa in 1968. The two oil crises in the 1970s drove Japan to realize the significance of Africa. In the 1970s, Japan's aid to Africa only accounted for 2.2% of the country's gross foreign aid. With the appearance of "Africa Fever" in the 1980s, such proportion went up to 11.9% by the end of the decade (Wang 2012). In the years from 1990 to 2005, Japan became and remained the fourth biggest donor to Africa among of the OECD-DAC state members, following France, the US and Germany (Lebovic 2005). Over the same period, Africa ascended to the biggest aid recipient of Japan, only second to Asia (Wang 2012). In 2006, Japan's aid to Africa surpassed that for Asia, and took up a 34% share of the country's total foreign aid (Wang 2012). The International Conference on African Development initiated by Japan in 1993, has been held five times by 2013 (Wang 2012).

When it comes to methods of aid, concessional loans are much more frequently employed by Japan than any other means of aid. Yen-denominated loans have always been the primary form of Japan's aid to Africa. Of Japan's bilateral aid to Africa, Yen loans accounted for 20.2, 29.9, and 43.7% (projected) in 1994, 2003 and 2013, respectively (He 2013).

With respect to fields of aid, the first Japan's Official Development Aid (ODA) Charter that came out in 1992 particularly highlights four aid principles, three of which are political democratization, economic marketization, and equal attention to environmental protection and development. At the same time, the charter also provides that the resources of aid should be concentrated in economic infrastructure and production. So manufacturing and infrastructure got aid at a share of 26.2 and 40.9%, respectively. A marked change in 2005 was that debt relief accounted for 52% of its total foreign aid. There has been another change in recent years: the topics widely talked worldwide like environment and health become the priorities to which Japan gives its foreign aid. Aid-related contents in the *Yokohama Declaration 2013* and the *Yokohama Action Plan 2013–2017* just reflect this change (Gong 2014).

As to the selection of aid recipients, Japan doesn't have any historical ties with Africa. It is different from none of the US, European countries and India. Besides, because of sharing no common course of development with Africa, it doesn't bear resemblance with China, either. In this context, choosing whom as aid recipients directly reveals the appeals of Japan's aid to Africa. The *Diplomatic Bluebook* released by the Japanese government in 2008 sets out five criteria Japan follows in choosing aid recipients, which involves strategic significance, relevance with global development, interregional balance, and other aspects. In other words, Japan intends to give its aid to the countries which bring back the resources it needs, bear strategic significance for the West, have markets that it can tap into, and won't provoke complaints among African countries. Since 1960, Japan has extended its most aid to the following two types of nations: (1) resource-rich countries like Kenya and Sudan and (2) politically influential countries like Tanzania.

So as we see, similar to India's, Japan's aid to Africa carries much more political appeals and economic pursuits. It is worth noting that the two countries both want Africa to support them in their fight for a higher position in the UN. Unlike India, Japan also hopes to promote its political values and have secure access to resources (Schraeder et al. 1998; Gong 2014; Wang 2012; Yasutomo 1989).

Generally speaking, Asia's foreign aid is more complicated than that of the US and European countries. Firstly, Asia used to be the largest aid recipient around the world. With a history of growing from poor to rich, it has actually experienced what it feels like to receive aid from others. Secondly, unlike Asia, the majority of African countries started to receive assistance from the colonial age. The Asian countries have begun doing their best to help others, while suffering from poverty and getting aid from the rest of the world. Thirdly, Asia differs from Europe in terms of internal composition. In Europe, the EEC in the past and the EU now would coordinate or arrange all member states to act uniformly with respect to their aid for Africa. However, there is no such a mechanism or an agency to do so in Asia. Instead, Asian countries each have their special interest appeals and logics, while extending aid to Africa.

For China who is located in Asia, aid donors around it are the most threatening friends. India shares a time-honored economic and ethnic bond with Africa. Japan boasts of advanced technologies and seemingly least-profit-seeking funds. Japan, India, the US, and European countries have common political views and ideologies. In the face of these partners who also extend aid in Africa, China finds itself in a situation: it has to contend with Japan's money and technology with its strength; and contest India's historical and ethnic ties with its newly built connections. What edge does China have over these countries? This is a question it seems have been solved but actually falls short of a clear answer.

5.2 China's DAH to Africa

China's aid to Africa comes as a part of foreign aid received by the continent from the international community. By the same vein, development aid for health from China to Africa also constitutes a part of all DAH that goes from the international community to the continent.

China's Foreign Aid (2011) indicates that "Medical aid plays an important role in China's foreign aid." China's DAH to Africa also forms a part of its foreign aid to the continent. The Ministerial Forum on China-Africa Health Cooperation took place in Beijing on August 16, 2013. At the meeting, the health officials on the both sides inked the *Beijing Declaration of the Ministerial Forum on China-Africa Health Cooperation* (hereinafter referred to as the *Beijing Declaration*). As undertaken by the Chinese government, given the scope and scale of mutual cooperation between the two sides, China is always geared up to share with African countries its experience in health development, and strives with them to make sure their cooperation strategies are well aligned with local priorities and pressing needs for health development. The Beijing Declaration depicts a roadmap which China and African countries can follow to solve the key health problems confronting Africa (Bai 2013).

Development aid for health from China to Africa is also set in another background of global health. Global health is basically defined as "an area for study, research, and practice that places a priority on improving health and achieving health equity for all people worldwide." It has been chiefly advocated by many international organizations such as the World Health Organization (WHO). As an important WHO member, China directly participates in the global health activities, and thus its DAH to Africa constitutes a part of all global DAH efforts. The UN's Millennium Development Goals (MDGs) sets out the guiding principles for the global health initiative since 2000, while *To Save Humanity* is a collection of essays on what ideas and practice matter for global health in recent years (Frenk and Hoffman 2015).

5.2.1 Measures

Development aid for health from China to Africa is just like a jewel in the crown of all DAH major countries and organizations worldwide extend to the continent. At the same time, it also accounts for an important part of China's foreign aid, and has been available for more than six decades (Xia and Chen 2016; Liu et al. 2014). As expounded by *China's Foreign Aid* (2011), the country develops its DAH initiative mainly by taking the following measures: building hospitals and medical care centers, establishing malaria prevention and treatment centers, dispatching medical teams, training medical workers, providing medicines, and other medical materials, and offering temporary financial assistance. Development aid for health from China to Africa also goes to these fields as well (Li 2011).

(1) Sending medical teams to recipient countries

Sending teams of medical professional to countries on the receiving end of aid is an important component of China's DAH. According to *China's Foreign Aid* (2001), China has been sending medical teams to aid recipient countries to provide them with free medical equipment and medicines. In addition to providing medical services from clinics at fixed locations, these medical teams also try to reach more of the population by traveling around countries.

By contrast, other countries have tended to adopt project-based approach to organizing and managing their Africa-bound DAH. If we regard China's dispatching medical teams to African countries as a project, it then features a flexible design. By saying so, we mean that instead of overall planning in the very beginning, the project may be adjusted in-process as needed by recipient countries. Besides, not organized on the state level, these medical teams are dispatched by China to African countries on a task-specific basis. Organized and arranged by related provincial governments, these medical teams are mainly composed of physicians, with nurses, medical technicians, translators/interpreters, and chauffeurs as important supplements. These teams usually serve two years abroad. During their service term, team members are entitled to receive housing and meal subsidies as well as extra salaries (Li 2009; Jiang 2015; Liang 2015; Chen 2014; Yang 2013; Sun 2013; Liu and Quan 2013; Jiang and Chen 2013; Fu 2013; Huang 2013; Xu 2011; Ding and Zhang 2010; Li 2011; Shen and Fan 2014).

In 1963, China dispatched the first medical team to Algeria, according to *China's Foreign Aid*. By 2009, China had altogether sent over 21,000 medical workers to 69 countries in Asia, Africa, Europe, Latin America, the Caribbean, and Oceania, treating 260 million patients in recipient countries. In 2009, 60 Chinese medical teams composed of 1324 members were still working abroad and they were distributed at 130 medical institutions in 57 developing countries. In the years from 2010 to 2013, a total of 55 Chinese medical teams were stationed to 120 places of aid, brought 3,600 medical workers to recipient countries accumulatively, and gave trainings to more than 10,000 local health personnel (Xia and Chen 2016; Harneit-Sievers et al. 2010; Wang et al. 2012).

(2) Providing medicines and medical equipment

Offering recipient countries medicines and medical equipment turns out to be another key method for China to extend its DAH abroad. As per the statistics of China's Foreign Aid, China had provided artemisinin-based antimalarial medicines worth RMB 190 million to African countries in the four years from 2006 to 2009. In the following four years from 2000 to 2013, it sent to them about 120 batches of medical equipment and medicine for free, including color Doppler ultrasound machines, CT scanners, automatic biochemical analyzers, maternal and infant monitors, critical surgical instruments, ICU monitors, and MRI scanners as well as drugs against diseases such as malaria and cholera. All of these devices and medicines totaled RMB 800 million.

(3) Building hospitals and other health facilities

Building hospitals in recipient countries is a third important means China resorts to for its DAH efforts. This means has been used for nearly ten years. According to *China's Foreign Aid*, by the end of 2009, China had aided other developing countries to build more than 100 hospitals and medical care centers; and there were over 30 hospitals under construction with its help. Between 2010 and 2012, China assisted about 80 construction projects of medical facilities, most of which were distributed in African countries, including general hospitals, mobile hospitals, health centers, specialist clinics, and traditional Chinese medicine (TCM) centers. Some typical examples in this respect are Yemen Taiz Hospital, China-African Friendship Hospital, Guinea-Bissau Cachuogo Hospital, Zimbabwe Chinoy Hospital, Chad Freedom Hospital, Uganda-China Friendship Hospital, and Zambia Mobile Hospital (Freeman and Lu 2011).

Take mobile hospitals for example. Each hospital of this kind is equipped with 12 medical vehicles, three doctors and one medical technician. In general, it only takes 20 minutes to assemble a mobile hospital which integrates the essential features of a general hospital. Composed of many departments such as internal medicine, general surgery, ENT, obstetrics, and gynaecology, mobile hospitals can furnish medical services as diverse as general surgery, emergency admissions, general radiography, testing, and intensive care. They can operate even out of water or power supply (Freeman and Lu 2011).

Some researchers further point out that after 2000, development aid for health from China to Africa has been increasing rapidly, especially in such fields as health, population, clean water, and sterilization (known as "HPWS" collectively). China has made its way to the top ten donors of DAH targeted at Africa all over the world. Among these HPWS efforts, 50% went to technical facilities, and 40% was dedicated to human resource development. At the same time, particular attention was paid to medical equipment and drugs as well as malaria prevention and treatment (Grépin et al. 2014).

(4) Engaging in malaria and HIV/AIDS prevention and treatment

Relying on artemisinin, a wonder drug against malaria, and its primary healthcare system, China also launched a large number of malaria prevention and treatment programs in Africa, which involved medical personnel trainings, field disease prevention and control, and establishment of 30 malaria prevention and treatment centers. For instance, China and Comorin rolled out a cooperation program aimed to quickly control malaria with artemisinin compounds in 2007. While consolidating the results achieved by the malaria elimination project, China also put in place a similar program on Anjouan Island of Comorin in the three years from 2010 to 2012.

In addition to DAH for Africa, China also gets itself into the global fight against HIV/AIDS, by sending medical teams to directly participate in the themed initiatives (Xu et al. 2016).

(5) Offering temporary financial resources

China provides African countries with funding aid for health purpose in a quite limited amount. Furthermore, it mainly offers its financial assistance by making donations to specific projects and to health foundations (Wang and Sun 2014). Additionally, so as to boost the development of African countries, China also announced to extend special export credit facilities and concessional loans worth USD 10 billion, of which USD 73 million was spent in raising the standards of pharmaceuticals and healthcare services across the continent (Kenyon 2010).

5.2.2 *Effects*

Compared with other countries including India, China delivers DAH to Africa with aid forms and practice unique to itself. It is worth noting that except for the information disclosed by the Chinese government, scarcely any applicable data can be found in the existing literature about China's DAH to Africa. Even though some organizations attempted to summarize the data from multiple sources, their efforts produced very limited results.

By the same token, the existing researches into China's DAH and its effects can only employee these limited data available. In the view of some researches, different from the traditional aid provided by the DAC, the Chinese practice that focuses on the healthcare system and malaria control represents that the endeavors within the framework of South–South cooperation have played a prominent role. Some other researchers hold that the medical teams dispatched by China to African countries managed to ease their severe shortage of health personnel including surgeons, urologists, and other specialist physicians (Liu et al. 2014; Yin 2006; Department of International Cooperation, Ministry of Health of China 2003), and to redress the imbalance between demand and supply of medical personnel in recipient countries to some extent.

China's Foreign Aid (2011) is quoted as saying, "These medical teams usually work in underdeveloped areas where conditions are harsh and people lack medical services and medicines; and they have cured many patients with common and frequently occurring diseases, and treated some complicated and serious diseases with acupuncture and moxibustion, medical massage and integrated use of traditional Chinese and

Western medicine, saving many critically ill patients." Besides, the team members also delivered trainings to local medical personnel through demonstrations, lectures, technical courses and academic exchanges, covering such topics as the prevention and treatment of malaria, HIV/AIDS, schistosomiasis and other infectious diseases, the patient care, the treatment of diabetes and rheumatism. There is a surprising coincidence. While sending medical teams abroad, China also dispatched other teams of professionals and construction workers to African countries (Shen and Fan 2014), so that the former could provide medical guarantee for the latter.

Observed in the big picture of all DAH received by Africa or even among all sorts of aid from China to the continent, Chinese medical teams spent less money to produce fruitful, influential results within short periods of time. What they did was not only spoken highly of by their peers in the recipient countries, but also formed sound self-evaluation and mutual recognition in these teams. For example, more than 100 medical team members were presented with medals by the recipient countries to honor their outstanding contribution in 2000–2012 alone (Wang et al. 2012).

Medicines offered by China have become wonder drugs for Africa to prevent and treat many kinds of diseases including malaria particularly (Shi 2010; Siringi 2003). On a small island of Comorin, some villages saw up to 94.4% of their population infected with malaria. After the Chinese experts guided all residents there to take medicines properly, the infection rate of this disease dropped by 98.8% remarkably. Chinese medicines are hailed so greatly that many African countries are willing to promote the Chinese practice to a wider range (Li 2011). Take Uganda as an example. Malaria claims the lives of over 80,000 local people every year, most of which are pregnant women and children. China undertook to donate antimalarial medicines to Uganda, provide local medical workers with related trainings, and establish a malaria prevention and treatment center in Kampala, the capital city of the country. In some people's view, the drugs manufactured by China feature reliable quality and high-cost efficiency. The success of Chinese pharmaceutical industry and medical equipment manufacturers in gearing to the needs of Chinese market with relatively low-cost products justifies the comparative advantage of China in this regard (Han et al. 2008; Ren and Lu 2014). Nevertheless, the traditional Chinese medicines (TCMs) provided by China for African countries become a center of debate. Some people argue that these medicines fall short of persuasively scientific evidence, and the time is not ripe to promote them extensively (Wang and Sun 2014).

The hospitals, specialist clinics, disease prevention and treatment centers, and other medical facilities built in African countries with the Chinese aid have witnessed the course of how China's DAH developed in Africa, provided a stronghold for Chinese medical teams to radiate their influence there, and eased the shortage of medical facilities in the recipient countries to some extent. For instance, the well-equipped Tappita Hospital in Liberia is operated by China, Egypt and Liberia jointly as a fruitful attempt to give medical cooperation and realize sustained operations of hospitals. At the same time, China furnishes nine provinces of Zambia with the much-wanted medical services. Of these, mobile hospitals provide essential support for the medical care undertakings of the remote and underdevelopment areas, and make vigorous contribution to enabling local people better access to healthcare services. As pointed out by some scholars who hold opposite opinions, establishing hospitals incur considerable inputs and operating costs, but generate yields less than the efforts to prevent and treat diseases and promote public health (Watson 2009).

None of the existing literature is about assessing or expounding what effects China's DAH to Africa has achieved. The possible explanation to this situation lies in that there might be a quite limited amount of related data available.

5.2.3 Controversy

Similar to China's aid to Africa, its DAH to the continent also draws the widespread attention. The new practice China has adopted after the Forum on China-Africa Cooperation (FOCAC) has also aroused suspicion, thus provoking some new controversies about China's DAH to Africa.

(1) Motivations and effects

It is generally recognized that development aid for health from China to Africa is primarily based on humanism and aimed to help Africa promote its health level and promote health equity all over the world with its unique advantages in the health sector (Browne 2012; Liu et al. 2014; Wang and Sun 2014). The medical teams dispatched by China have reached deep into African countries at the grassroots level. The work they did in terms of medical care and disease prevention has substantially improved the health situation of the places at the grassroots level including rural areas, thus making medical care more equally accessible to all people. This is an achievement unique to China's DAH efforts (Freeman and Lu 2011).

As noted by some other people, the purpose for which China renders DAH to other countries is intended to boost its own soft power, just the same as that of its other forms of aid. In other words, the country employs health assistance as a diplomatic means. By such peace-conducive actions, it attempts to guarantee and expand its national interests (Tull 2006; Zhang 2010; King 2013; Bräutigam and Tang 2012). Some people therefore arrive at a conclusion that China is second to none with respect to soft power (McGiffert 2009; Kurlantzick 2007). By furnishing DAH, China has managed to increase its political influence, acquire natural resources, ink preferential trade clauses, and build itself an image of "responsible international member" (Youde 2010).

Although China has denied repeatedly, its DAH to Africa carries its considerations for economic benefits, in the opinions of some scholars. Thanks to the free medicines brought through DAH, African countries can get the drugs in dire need, and Chinese pharmaceutical companies can create a positive image in these countries. In this way, these Chinese enterprises will become more competitive in Africa, march into local market and expand their share there, and thus reap considerable economic returns (Wang and Sun 2014; Youde 2010; Huang 2010, 2012).

Undoubtedly, China's decision to extend DAH to Africa was made based on humanitarian considerations more than six decades ago. In its over 60 years' development, China's DAH to Africa cannot be explained with one simple motivation. In the opposite, it is a complete set of responsible decisions and actions made after taking political, economic and cultural factors into comprehensive account (Liu et al. 2014; Ren and Lu 2014).

(2) Supply and demand

China delivers DAH to African countries with inspirations from its successful experience and comparative advantages. That's exactly why it has dispatched medical teams, built hospitals, and eliminated malaria with artemisinin there (Ren and Lu 2014; Fan et al. 2014). As Easterly points out, if the supplies of aid donors are not aligned with recipient countries' needs and social development, their aid won't live up to expectations (Easterly 2009; Easterly and Williamson 2011). Furthermore, all countries who offer aid to others hope to maximize their national interests. This is an extension of the Cold War thinking in a large part. The inconsistencies between supply and demand thus damper the initiative of recipient countries, and hold back the improvement of aid efficiency (Browne 2012).

In addition to the mismatch between aid and local needs, China's DAH also faces more new challenges over time. Take medical teams stationed in African countries for example. As some African countries gain a boost in their economic strength and medical standards, they start to crave for higher-level medical cooperation gradually. In some specific fields, China also falls short of health personnel and experience. However, some underdeveloped African countries exactly need a large amount of medical personnel to help tackle their basic health problems. In the ever-changing circumstances, China's DAH to Africa is expected to satisfy more complicated needs. How to continue its practice of aid on demand becomes a huge challenge facing the country (Dreher et al. 2015; Youde 2010).

(3) Sustainability

China's DAH to Africa complements with that provided by the US, European countries, Japan and India in some sense. Therefore, it produces results that other donors don't achieve and wins the worldwide recognition including that from the WHO (Ren and Lu 2014). The question about whether it can persistently furnish African countries with DAH has hence drawn attention from a wide range of parties.

Firstly, how to guarantee the sustainability of human resources. The provision of DAH in Africa has to overcome many obstacles such as unfamiliar languages, different living habits, and heavy workloads. Terrible homesickness, as well as backward health conditions and medical equipment in African countries, come as the biggest two challenges confronting the Chinese medical team members stationed there. Besides, as the pay level increases in China, the wage gap from working abroad shrinks accordingly, and people willing to do this dwindle dramatically.

These changes will render well-skilled physicians reluctant to be stationed in African countries. Or even if they are willing to do so, it means a high cost on them (Wang et al. 2012).

Secondly, how to sustain high management standards and further enhance the effects of aid turns out to be another problem that faces China's DAH to Africa. From the overall and long-term perspective, the absence of an aid strategy on the state level will lead to the divided opinions on the connotation of aid and the pursuit for interests among the related departments of the central government and provincial governments in China, thus reducing the actual effects that are supposed to get out of aid programs (Schiere et al. 2011; Liu et al. 2014; Shen and Fan 2014).

Lastly, China doesn't have a relatively independent agency responsible for coordinating and managing its foreign aid affairs as a whole. The absence is especially pressing with respect to DAH. The overlapping functions of the existing management organizations and the conflicts of interest among different departments make for the inefficient operation of and insufficient coordination among related organizations (Wang and Sun 2014).

In response to the influence of the above factors, the programs relating to development aid for Health from China to Africa cannot make timely review and summary from the perspective of knowledge or technology, much less introducing the US-style project-based management and assessment. Therefore, related personnel needs to comb through the experience and lessons learnt from the past, with a view to getting more out of aid in the future (Zou et al. 2014). According to specific researches, some tiny technical issues are likely to restrict the Chinese medical teams to play a greater role. For example, these teams are usually sent to the remote areas where local doctors won't bother to work; and with the outdated medical equipment, the dispatched medical teams can do nothing but provide some basic medical services, thus wasting their talent on petty jobs (Li 2011).

As its DAH to Africa grows larger and wider, China gets interwoven with other aid donors, and develops a close relationship with the institutions of recipient countries step by step. Against such a backdrop, China's DAH to Africa will get involved in an increasing number of topics and even disputes. So it's an opportune moment for the country to gear itself up in advance.

5.3 China's Aid to Uganda

5.3.1 China's Aid to and Cooperation with Uganda

Uganda declared its independence on October 9, 1962 (Xinhua News Agency 1962). Hereupon, China recognized it (Chen 1962), and announced to establish diplomatic relations with the country. There came out a joint communiqué approved by the two sides (State Council of China 1962).

From July 11 to 16, 1965, the former Ugandan Prime Minister Milton Obote paid a visit to China. On the last day of his trip, the governments of the two countries issued a joint communiqué. The primary purposes of it were set to condemn colonialism jointly, support the anti-colonialism fight of all African countries for national liberation and independence, denounce racial segregation, and endorse the Five Principles of Peaceful Coexistence. But it didn't mention anything about aid (State Council of China 1965).

In the subsequent four decades, seldom public literature written in Chinese language was about the contacts of the two countries. That situation lasted until June 24, 2006. On the day when the former Chinese Premier Wen Jiabao visited Uganda, the governments of the two countries released a joint communiqué again. As stated by the document, the two sides agreed that their economic cooperation had broad prospects. They expressed readiness to earnestly implement the ongoing cooperation programs and expand mutually beneficial cooperation in trade, investment, agriculture, water conservancy, telecommunications, infrastructure, energy, agro-processing, textiles as well as human resources trainings on the basis of equality, mutual benefit and common development. The two sides would increase exchange and cooperation in culture, education, health and tourism (State Council of China 2006).

The first agreement on economic and technical cooperation between China and Uganda can be traced back to as early as 1965. But in the 1960s and the 1970s, the collaboration of the two sides was mainly reflected as China's providing it with technical assistance and economic aid in the forms of grants and concessional loans. Since 1987 when China started to contract engineering projects and cooperation projects for labor services in Uganda, the two countries have scaled up their economic cooperation constantly. Following the FOCAC in 2000, China's aid to Uganda began attaching equal importance to assistance and cooperation (Li 2016; Lu 2015).

With respect to aid, Kibimba Farm was built with the help of China in 1977. Afterwards, the fields of aid extended to many sectors such as agriculture, education, health care, public facility construction, concessional loans, and debt relief. As a result of these efforts, a series of projects were constructed and put into operation, including the China-Uganda Friendship Agricultural Technology Demonstration Center, biogas digesters and middle schools in rural areas, China-Uganda Friendship Hospital, malaria prevention and treatment centers. At the same time, radio and TV programs were rolled out, and complete projects were provided for the Ugandan government office building and national stadium. Additionally, the equipment and materials China donated to Uganda include reproductive health devices (that went to the Central Hospital of the Central Region), large-sized materials and equipment, 30 small-sized farm tractors, office equipment (for the Ministry of Foreign Affairs), and malaria drugs against which China owned independent intellectual property rights (IPRs) in six batches. In the meantime, some Chinese taskforces dispatched to Uganda were listed as below: medical teams, panels of senior agricultural experts, teams of stadium technicians, and groups of experts in building agricultural technology demonstration centers (Economic and Commercial Counselor's Office, Embassy of the People's Republic of China in Uganda 2013).

With concessional loans provided by the Chinese government, Uganda has wrapped up the state backbone network and e-government affairs network projects (Phase I and Phase II), as well as the municipal engineering equipment project (Phase I). It sent 630 trainees to China where they attended courses in many fields as diverse as economic management, finance, and foreign trade, public administration, medical care, agricultural technology, information technology, education, transportation, and energy. Besides these loans, China has offered Uganda municipal engineering equipment for free, and designated China FAW Group Co., Ltd. to put related projects into operation. So far, a total of 1413 dumpers, land levelers, load trolleys, earthmovers and other vehicles have been transported from China to Uganda, which are used to maintain and repair roads and municipal facilities (Economic and Commercial Counselor's Office, Embassy of the People's Republic of China in Uganda 2013). A concessional loan worth USD 350 million has been spent in paving a six-lane, 51-km-long expressway that connects the capital of Uganda Kampala and the Entebbe International Airport (Allen and Baguma 2013).

Furthermore, the Chinese government also freed Uganda from the debts worth USD 17 million borrowed before 2005, and undertook to offer it USD 6.8 million in grants (Allen and Baguma 2013).

Some researchers try to examine these contents of aid against the economic background of Uganda and the conditions of it as a recipient country. Uganda saw its agriculture, industry, and service sectors growing unstably as a proportion of the country's GDP after 2000. For instance, the above three sectors registered a growth rate of 2.0, 11.6 and 11.6% in 2005 over 2004, respectively. The corresponding annual increase of the same three sectors stood at 2.6, 3.8 and 9.4% from 2008 to 2009, respectively. As observed by the researchers, Uganda received the gross credit aid which always accounted for around 10% of its GDP between 1998 and 2006, no matter how its economic landscape changed (Guloba et al. 2010).

Seen from the sources of aid, the gross aid that went to Uganda from 2000 to 2008 amounted to USD 6655 million. The International Development Association (IDA) offered the country aid in USD 2 billion accumulatively, and thus became the biggest donor of it, followed by the UK (with USD 830 million), the EU (USD 650 million), and the US (USD 420 million). Among the 41 countries, international organizations and private aid agencies ordered by the amount of aid, China was ranked at the 27th place with the total aid of USD 13.52 million and Japan ranked 23rd with the gross aid of USD 31 million. China's aid took up a 0.2% share of the gross aid received by Uganda. It is worth noting that the records of aid disbursements made by the top three donors (countries or organizations) in the surveyed eight years can all be retrieved except for those of the US in the fiscal year of 2008. The same went for Japan. But China's aid for three of the eight years remained unrecorded. Unlike the forms of aid adopted by other countries and organizations, China didn't grant Uganda with aid which could be directly included into its government budget scheme (Guloba et al. 2010).

China's aid to Uganda can be divided into direct aid and indirect aid. Direct aid is made up of competitive aid and supplementary aid with OECD member states, and some examples in this type are grants, loans, and trainings. Indirect aid also consists of competitive aid and supplementary aid, which goes to constructing water supply and drainage facilities and applying power transmission lines, for example. Therefore, some researchers think, China's aid to Uganda mostly takes place in the forms of technical assistance, like reception of trainees, grants, interest-free loans, subsidized loans, concessional loans, and debt relief programs. As a result, Uganda receives indirect benefits. For example, debt relief helps ease the Ugandan government's financial burden, and thus does good to local people's welfare (Guloba et al. 2010).

As to economic and trade cooperation, an intergovernmental agreement on tariff-free treatment was inked between China and Uganda in February 2010. As prescribed by the above agreement, China would firstly give tariff-free treatment to 60% of imported products from Uganda from July 1, 2010, and the percentage would be raised to 95% from January 1, 2012. This means that more than 400 types of products and materials exported from Uganda to China free of any tariff.[4]

The foreign direct investments (FDI) received by Uganda were always on the rise since 1990. It grew faster and larger after 2010 (Sam 2013). It is in 1993 that the first Chinese company was registered in Uganda. Over the period from then to 2001, China made investments totaling USD 596 million in the country, and 256 Chinese companies did business with their Ugandan counterparts, creating 28,000 jobs for local people. In 2005, the trade volume between the two countries approached USD 99.37 million. Of the goods exported from China to Uganda were mainly machinery, electronic products, textiles, garments, pharmaceuticals, and chinaware. According to the statistical data on the Chinese side, the bilateral trade volume hit USD 400 million in 2011, representing an increase of 40% from 2010 and 300% from 2005, respectively (Allen and Baguma 2013). By the end of 2011, a total of 265 companies invested by Chinese fund had been incorporated in Uganda. In 2012, China National Offshore Oil Corporation (CNOOC) invested USD 1682 million through acquisition in Uganda (Economic and Commercial Counselor's Office, Embassy of the People's Republic of China in Uganda 2013). In the 2013–2014 fiscal year, Uganda took in the FDIs in a total amount of USD 1470 million, of which USD 440 million came from China, occupying 29.9% of the total. The Chinese investment involved 53 projects, and created 21,000 job opportunities. China came out 3rd only after the UK and India by the investment volume in Uganda (Lu 2015). As of 2014, more than 400 Chinese companies had been registered in Uganda, and made investments totaling USD

[4]Paper files from Economic and Commercial Counselor's Office, Embassy of the People's Republic of China in Uganda 2013.

3634 million in many industries and fields as diverse as trade, electronics, agricultural development, leather processing, construction material production, hospitality industry, and food processing (Li 2016). As revealed by these data, the investment amount China planned to make in Uganda and the number of projects to be invested by it there ranked 1st and 2nd around the world (Fan et al. 2014).

In the field of economic and trade cooperation, there is another important category of aid: construction contracting. By the end of 2011, nearly 30 Chinese-funded project contractors had registered operations in Uganda, which included China National Machinery Industry Corporation Ltd (Sinomach), SINOHYDRO Corporation, China Railway Construction Engineering Group (CRCEG), China Communications Corporation, China Henan International Corporation Group (CHICO), Chongqing International Construction Corporation (CICO), China Jiangxi International Economic and Technical Corporation Co., Ltd., Huawei, Yanjian Group, and Guangdong Shineng Group. These Chinese companies managed to extend their business reach from the traditional fields like road and housing building, communications engineering, hydropower generation, electronic transmission and distribution circuits, and well drilling to the sectors of professional services represented by road design, factory construction, equipment installation, and geological prospecting. Chongqing International Construction Corporation (CICO) contracted a project to construct a 103 km-long road that connects Fort Portal, a western town of Uganda and the Democratic Republic of the Congo. China National Offshore Oil Corporation (CNOOC) is seeking for opportunities to build a refinery in West Uganda alongside other international firms. Besides, multiple Chinese enterprises are bidding for the construction project of Karuma Hydropower Station (Allen and Baguma 2013). As covered by some other reports, the AN Highway that starts from North Uganda to South Sudan was been completed and delivered on June 23, 2016. The project was undertaken by China Railway No.5 Engineering Group Co., Ltd. from September 2013. The 35 km-long highway involved a contract value of USD 29 million. Besides, the Chinese corporation also won the bid for two another highway construction projects which were 75 and 66 km long, respectively (Li and Li 2016). While contracting to build the Isimba Hydropower Station, China Three Gorges Corporation also paved a road that ran through Nam-pay Village in the dam areas, sponsored a soccer competition hosted by Kayunda

City, and delivered skill trainings to local employees (Zhang et al. 2015). Moreover, to seek for corporate development in Uganda, China National Offshore Oil Corporation (CNOOC) also attaches high importance to managing its relations with local communities, by respecting residents' culture and emotional bonds and making appropriate investments into community-based projects (Chai 2013).

The researches into Chinese companies registered in Uganda reveal that both Chinese state-owned enterprises (SOEs) and mixed ownership enterprises operating in the country are mostly concentrated in capital-intensive fields such as petroleum and construction. They have arrived in Uganda earlier than and come in sizes bigger than private ones. Compared with private businesses, the Chinese SOEs and mixed ownership companies show stronger interest in holistic market, and recruit more local workers to localize their workforce. Nevertheless, researchers also agree that regardless of ownership, Chinese companies go to invest in Uganda for the same purpose: tapping deep into local market. Of these companies, the SOEs and mixed ownership firms bring more Chinese government-backed projects and thus win more support from the government. In addition to capital-intensive sectors, Chinese-funded companies based in Uganda are also engaged in import/export, manufacturing, and wholesale/retail industries in a large number (Warmerdam and van Dijk 2013).

Against the backdrop where aid and cooperation are attached with equal attention, researchers have observed that compared with that of the West, China's aid to Uganda has grown rapidly in the past 10-plus years. African countries including Uganda seem to prefer China's aid over that of the West, and take the notion that China's aid directly fuels their economic development and lifts millions of local people out of poverty. In the meantime, China provides its aid based on friendship and mutual respect within the framework of South–South cooperation. Therefore, its aid is quick, simple, and effective, free of restrictions or limitations which the Western world imposes on aid recipient countries (Allen and Baguma 2013).

On this basis, some researchers have discussed how to establish relations with China with a view to boosting employment and enabling aid to benefit people persistently (Guloba et al. 2010). As a matter of fact, the discussions about the topic involve the other side of the cooperation between China and Uganda in economic, trade and many other fields. For instance, their bilateral trade faces the ever-expanding imbalance.

In 2012, the export volume from Uganda to China reached USD 40 million, up 49.5% but only accounting for one-tenth of China's export to the country. This seemingly means that more cheap, unreliable products flood into the Ugandan market to compete with its domestic products. Besides, the influx of Chinese companies into Uganda's wholesale/ retail market directly intervenes with local people's business, because the Chinese products are not only more cost-efficient but also diversified (Allen and Baguma 2013). The entry of Chinese products in a large number also has negative bearing on the local manufacturing industry. The manufacturers of the two countries reduce to vicious competition and chaotic operation (Li 2016). What's worse, the Ugandan manufacturing industry is squeezed out of the market, entailing local workers out of employment. This is largely because the Chinese companies are more willing to employee Chinese workers (Allen and Baguma 2013).

Asked about China's aid to Uganda and economic and trade cooperation between the two sides, Ugandan students who study in China prefer to give their answer from the perspective of the Chinese soft power. In their opinions, Alexander L. Vuving's theory of soft power currencies (brilliance, benignity, and beauty) (Vuving 2009) can be used to explain China's soft power in their country. China builds up its soft power from the political, economic and cultural dimensions in Uganda with the strategies and methods consistent with those in the rest of Africa (Kurlantzick 2007; Rebol 2011; Luo 2007). However, the soft power hasn't be gained all at once. Instead, it is an outcome of the hard work made by China in Uganda for many years and the attraction the Chinese revolution holds for the Ugandan leaders. Even so, China's cheap products and traditional culture indeed negatively impact its soft power (Martin 2013).

5.3.2 *China's Aid to Uganda on Agriculture*

China unveiled its aid for agriculture to Africa in 1959, by providing Guinea with food aid for free. According to the related statistics, it financed about 220 agricultural projects in Africa between 1960 and 2010, which accounted for one-fifth of all its complete projects relating to aid in Africa (Tang 2013).

The forms of aid for agriculture have also evolved over time. In the 1960s and the 1970s, building large farms and centers designed to spread agricultural technologies came as the most frequently used means for China to send its aid for agriculture to Africa. By 1980, a total of 87 agricultural projects were put in place there with the help of China, tilling farmlands in an area of 43,400 hectares. Over the same period, China also funded the construction of 16 water conservancy projects, which irrigated farmlands in 71,000 hectares. Upon completion, these projects produced remarkable results, and related business was booming. However, good times didn't last long. There emerged many issues such as production decline and business close down.

After reviewing related experience and lessons, China began shifting the focus of its agricultural assistance for African countries to technical exchanges, personnel trainings, and other aspects concerning capacity enhancement. While construing farmland facilities, it also imparts essential agricultural technologies to local farmers. But, they are not necessarily capable of taking in these well-explained techniques. In response to this situation, China adds market factors to its agricultural assistance for African countries. For example, agricultural cooperation companies are incorporated so that Chinese technicians are motivated to stay in Africa for long-term work. Besides, agricultural technology demonstration centers are established to explain how agricultural techniques are applied and train local technicians and farmers at the same time. Upon the end of the demonstration period, market factors are introduced and these centers will be operated as enterprises for the purpose of sustained development (Tang 2013; Gao et al. 2014; Zhou 2012, 2014; Li 2012).

China's aid for agriculture to Uganda came later than other forms of its aid to the country. Wrapped up in 1977, the Ugandan Kibimba Farm is the last one of the 87 complete projects China funded in Africa before 1980. In 1973, the aiding personnel dispatched by the Chinese government started to work on a patch of isolated, thatch-overgrown wetland. After several years' arduous efforts, a modernized farm rose high from the ground. With farmlands in 1000 hectares, it employed over 800 workers. In its vicinity operated rice mills, flour mills, brickfields, livestock farms, stores, bars, restaurants, schools, kindergartens, and other off-set facilities. With China's experience in developing state-owned farms flexibly applied to Uganda, this farm produced an output of 30,000-ton rice, and reaped about RMB 2 million in profit every year. But when the facility was handed over to the Ugandan government in 1982, its production and operation came across a variety of setbacks (Li 2012). The output dwindled to merely 100-plus-ton rice per *mu* in

1989, the lowest point since the foundation of the farm. Under this circumstance, the Chinese agricultural experts had to return to the farm in August 1991 (Ma 1992). After a series of reforms, it became a very good advertisement for the benefits of China's aid for agriculture to Uganda all over again (Economic and Commercial Counselor's Office, Embassy of the People's Republic of China in Uganda 2013).

Apart from Kibimba Farm, the Chinese government announced in 2006 to build 14 state-level agricultural technology demonstration centers in Africa, one typical example of which was the China-Uganda Friendship Agricultural Technology Demonstration Center (Economic and Commercial Counselor's Office, Embassy of the People's Republic of China in Uganda 2013). The construction of the demonstration center held attraction for many companies. Finally, it was constructed by Sichuan Provincial Overseas Chinese Phoenix Group. Its construction commenced in 2008 and finished in 2010. The fishery technology demonstration center integrates a host of functions such as freshwater fish breeding, marketable fish farming, feed processing, experimental research, and technical training and demonstration (Huang 2016).

At the FOCAC held in December 2015, China declared that agriculture would be high on its agenda for cooperation in the upcoming three years. Within the framework of "one Chinese province pairing with one African country" to offer targeted aid as proposed in 2012, China continues its aid for agriculture to Uganda. Specifically, the Chinese government and Ugandan government earmark USD 1.7 million and USD 800,000 respectively, for funding Chinese experts to demonstrate and promote the application of technologies in grain cultivation, fruit/vegetable production, livestock raising, and fish farming in Uganda. Sichuan-based Ke Hong Group formed a delegation along with five other local companies including Zoeve Seed. They went to Uganda to make preparations and construct the China-Uganda Modern Agriculture Demonstration Park. The project involved an investment of USD 220 million and covered an area of 380 hectares, according to its preliminary plan. Since 2016, a total of 13 projects engaged in coarse grain processing, rice planting, hen farming, and agricultural machinery service have been launched successively as parts of the demonstration park. Upon completion, the park is expected to become the largest agricultural project across Uganda (Huang 2016). Additionally, China is also funding Uganda to establish its trading organizations of organic agricultural products (Huang 2016).

China's aid for agriculture to Uganda needs to be understood within the framework of "two-sided four-tiered embeddedness." As we know, it tells a lot about the background against which China's DAH to Uganda exists, as a part of China's aid to Africa including Uganda, a part of China's aid for agriculture to Africa, and a part of all aid received by Uganda.

Therefore, we also need to know what forms of aid for agriculture the international community has extended to Uganda and other African countries from the colonial period. Over the period from 1952 to 1972, the Rockefeller Foundation used to provide a complete set of aid for agriculture which ranged from crop seeds to education on agricultural technologies in sub-Sahara African countries (Wang 2012). The extensive aid didn't begin until the 1970s, in which China played an important role (Bräutigam and Tang 2009). Or it should be said that Africa's Green Revolution was closely related to China's aid (Bräutigam 1998).

Apart from China, international organizations represent another important force behind the drive to provide aid for agriculture for Africa. Aid for agriculture from the international community to Africa almost entered a stage of stagnation in the 1980s and 1990s. During that period, China's aid for agriculture for the continent also had gone dormant, as the aiding projects started earlier were completed and handed over to the recipient countries. An example of such projects was Kibimba Farm based in Uganda. Since 1980, aid for agriculture has maintained an over 20% share of the total aid that all countries and international organizations extended to Africa. But the World Bank's market-oriented structural adjustment to the aid undertaking turned out to be a futile attempt. In the 1990s, the ratio of aid for agriculture to the total tumbled to around 10%.

However, with the advent of the twenty-first century, aid for agriculture to Africa rose again, and agriculture thus became an important impetus for the realization of MDGs. By presenting the Africa Action Plan, the World Bank recovered the role of agriculture in promoting the development of African economy. According to the OECD-DAC data, about USD 2 billion aid flows to the agriculture of Africa every year. Uganda ranks the fourth place among the African countries ordered by the total aid for agriculture received. The biggest share of such aid is contributed by multilateral organizations such as the US African Development Foundation, the International Development Association, the EU, and the International Fund for Agricultural Development.

Germany, the USA, and Japan come out top three by the number of multilateral organizations that offer the most aid. All the aid programs unfold for the common purpose of helping African countries lift their agricultural productivity. A contributing factor for the large amount of aid for agriculture may lie in that Africa is home to the most starving and populous countries and regions, which include Uganda. With respect to specific fields of aid for agriculture, the top three priorities prove to be developing strategies for agricultural development, introducing sound agricultural management systems, and enhancing agricultural management standards; the two following them are agricultural infrastructure and comprehensive land development; and the last but not least is water resource management. In recent years, the promotion of animal husbandry technologies, farming technologies, and crop production technologies has been gaining more importance gradually (Tang et al. 2011).

Examined against such a backdrop, China's aid for agriculture to Uganda also focuses its attention on practical and technical aspects and demonstrates prominent features, as other forms of aid have done.

5.3.3 *China's Aid to Uganda on Education*

Just like how we understand China's aid for agriculture to Uganda, its educational aid for the country also needs to be comprehended as part of aid in all forms it receives from the international community.

If Uganda is one of sub-Saharan African countries whose food safety is worrying, its rapidly growing population leads to a surge in the demand for not only crops but also education. According to the UN's African Statistical Yearbook, Uganda had a population of 29 million in 2006, and that number soared to 33 million in 2010 and 39 million in 2015. Its population has grown much faster in the recent five years than before (United Nations 2016).

Since the 1990s, the international community has committed the ever-growing foreign aid for education to Uganda. Over the years from 1999 to 2007, the World Bank extended the largest share of such aid to Uganda, accounting for 19% of the total educational funding received by it. Following it were the UK, the USA, the Netherlands, and Ireland. The educational aid funds tripled in 2001–2002 from 1997–1998, and accounted for 7–8% of the total aid funds received (Zheng and Sun 2012).

With the aid funds from the international community, Uganda abolished tuition fees in 1997, and made primary education accessible for all school-age children. As a result, its primary school enrollment almost doubled. The gross primary school enrolment rate of school-age children reached 132.52% during 2001–2005, and that number maintained as high as 111.13% during 2011–2015 (United Nations 2016), two figures attesting that the illiterate population at school-age leftover from the past was gradually diminishing in the country over the nearly 15 years. It should be said that Uganda developed its primary school education at the fastest speed among all sub-Saharan African countries.

The influx of educational aid funds from the international community also promoted Uganda to develop its educational policies. In 2006 when the country introduced the policy to make secondary education universally available in 2006, the expenses on secondary education grew rapidly, and as a result, the gross middle school enrolment rate increased from 18.85% during 2001–2005 to 26.83% during 2011–2015 (United Nations 2016).

The international community committed educational aid to Uganda mainly through providing it with funds. The aid funds were included into the general budget and the department-specific budget of the Ugandan government within the framework of the *Poverty Reduction Action Plan*. Of these, the large-amount fund of aid was mainly incorporated into the budget of the Ugandan government and that of its ministry of education, while the small-amount aid fund was mostly extended in a project-based manner. The *Education Strategic Investment Plan (1998–2003)* and the *Educational Sector Strategic Plan (2004–2015)* released by the Ugandan government pointed out clear directions toward which international aid funds can be allocated. They were joined by the *Uganda Joint Assistance Strategy* that came out in 2005, the *Paris Declarations* that highlighted aid effectiveness, and the *Busan Declaration* that advocated effective development. All of these policies and documents helped to get much more out of educational aid.

In the past 10-plus years, the USAID has been dedicated to improving basic education in Uganda. Specifically, it worked hard to build up the competence of primary school teachers and other education administrators; paid particular attention to HIV/AIDS control education targeted at young people; stressed to increase the involvement of parents and communities in education; and kept track of and assessed how education policies were executed actually. Ireland narrowed its focus on improving educational infrastructure, promoting curriculum reforms in teachers' education and secondary education, and reconstructing educational facilities in the remote areas of Northeast Uganda. Besides, it teamed up with Japan to develop teachers' education in the country, and turn out more competent science and math teachers for its remote and border areas. Belgium supported Uganda in developing its post-primary education and related training programs. Japan gave its priorities to enhancing the quality of post-primary education by intensifying science and math education in middle schools and underpinning the importance of vocational education and training programs (Zheng and Sun 2012; Zhang 2016).

With the increasing gross primary school enrolment ratio set aside, the improved student and teacher ratio was the most impressive achievement Uganda had made with the educational aid. The student and teacher ratio in Uganda stood at 51.88 during 2001–2005, and the rate fast dropped to 23.37 during 2011–2015 (United Nations 2016), thus indicating that the country managed to increase the number of teachers remarkably in the past 15 years. The direct outcome of educational development is the gradual fall of adult illiteracy rate, which reported 31.9% during 2001–2005 and shrank to 27.9% during 2011–2015. The female illiteracy rate decreased by 5.5% points over the past 15 years, a drop surpassing the overall level (United Nations 2016).

Compared with the efforts made by the international community, China's educational aid to Uganda mainly comes in the following four forms: delivering human resource trainings, running scholarship programs, building schools in villages, and dispatching volunteers. Examined in all the educational aid that has gone to Uganda, these aiding endeavors from China only take up a limited share, but constitute a unique force in the international aid. This is especially true for the village schools built with the help of China.

Sadly, we can hardly find any accurate data or reliable sources of data to demonstrate how many projects China has run in Uganda and how its efforts are distributed in different fields of aid. This holds true for both China's aid to Uganda and cooperation between the two sides. To clarify these questions, some researches have made field inspections in Uganda and point out that about 34% of the projects China has launched to aid Uganda still remain unreported or unpublished, and that number in South Africa even exceeds 50% (Muchapondwa et al. 2014).

References

Alden, Chris. 2005. China in Africa. *Survival* 47 (3): 147–164. https://doi.org/10.1080/00396330500248086.

Allen, Kenneth, and Eva Baguma. 2013. China-Uganda Relations: Closer Is Not Necessarily Better. China Brief 13. The Jamestown Foundation.

Angeles, Luis, and Kyriakos C. Neanidis. 2009. Aid Effectiveness: The Role of the Local Elite. *Journal of Development Economics* 90 (1): 120–134. https://doi.org/10.1016/j.jdeveco.2008.05.002.

Baehr, Peter R. 1980. The Dutch Foreign Policy Elite: A Descriptive Study of Perceptions and Attitudes. *International Studies Quarterly* 24 (2): 223–261. https://doi.org/10.2307/2600201.

Bai, Jianfeng. 2013. Beijing Declaration Issued at China-Africa Ministerial Conference on Health Cooperation and Development. *People's Daily*, August 17, P3.

Bello, Walden. 2007. China Eyes Africa: The New Imperialism? *Multinational Monitor* 28 (1): 23–26.

Biswas, Aparajita. 2012. Trade Relations Between BRICS and Low Income Countries: The Cases of China and India's Roles in Africa's Development Paradigm. *International Politics Quarterly* 3: 37–48, 184–185.

Bräutigam, Deborah. 1998. *Chinese Aid and African Development: Exporting Green Revolution*. New York: St. Martin's Press.

Bräutigam, Deborah. 2009. *The Dragon's Gift: The Real Story of China in Africa*. Oxford: Oxford University Press.

Bräutigam, Deborah. 2010. China, Africa and the Global Aid Architecture. Rochester: Social Science Research Network.

Bräutigam, Deborah. 2011. Aid 'with Chinese Characteristics': Chinese Foreign Aid and Development Finance Meet the OECD—DAC Aid Regime. *Journal of International Development* 23 (5): 752–764. https://doi.org/10.1002/jid.1798.

Bräutigam, Deborah. 2012. Is China a Challenge to the Global Aid Architecture? *Conference Papers-American Political Science Association*, 1–44.

Bräutigam, Deborah, and Kevin P. Gallagher. 2014. Bartering Globalization: China's Commodity-Backed Finance in Africa and Latin America. *Global Policy* 5 (3): 346–352. https://doi.org/10.1111/1758-5899.12138.

Bräutigam, Deborah, and Xiaoyang Tang. 2009. China's Engagement in African Agriculture: Down to the Countryside. *The China Quarterly* 199: 686–706. https://doi.org/10.1017/s0305741009990166.

Bräutigam, Deborah, and Xiaoyang Tang. 2011. African Shenzhen: China's Special Economic Zones in Africa. *The Journal of Modern African Studies* 49 (1): 27–54. https://doi.org/10.1017/S0022278X10000649.

Bräutigam, Deborah, and Xiaoyang Tang. 2012. Economic Statecraft in China's New Overseas Special Economic Zones: Soft Power, Business or

Resource Security? *International Affairs* 88 (4): 799–816. https://doi.org/10.1111/j.1468-2346.2012.01102.x.

Bräutigam, Deborah, and Haisen Zhang. 2013. Green Dreams: Myth and Reality in China's Agricultural Investment in Africa. *Third World Quarterly* 34 (9): 1676–1696. https://doi.org/10.1080/01436597.2013.843846.

Broadman, Harry G., Gozde Isik, and World Bank. 2007. *Africa's Silk Road: China and India's New Economic Frontier.* Washington, DC: World Bank.

Browne, Stephen. 2012. *Aid and Influence: Do Donors Help or Hinder?* Hoboken: Taylor & Francis.

Cao, Jinli, and Wei Song. 2012. Effectiveness Evaluation of American Policy on Aid to Africa. *Journal of International Economic Cooperation* 12: 68–72.

Chai, Wei. 2013. Community Relations Management by CNOOC in Uganda. *China WTO Tribune* 8: 56–57.

Chan-Fishel, Michelle, and Roxanne Lawson. 2007. Quid Pro Quo? China's Investment-for-Resource Swaps in Africa. *Development* 50 (3): 63–68. https://doi.org/10.1057/palgrave.development.1100403.

Chen, Yi. 1962. Foreign Minister Chen Yi's Message to Prime Minister Apollo Milton Obote of Uganda on the Decision of the Government of the People's Republic of China to Recognize Uganda's Independence. *State Council Gazette* 11: 219.

Chen, Haibo. 2014. 51 Years of China Medical Teams in Africa. *Guangming Daily*, August 14, P5.

Chen, Luqi. 2009. New Development of China's Aid to Africa in the 21st Century. Master's Thesis, China Foreign Affairs University.

Chen, Meng, and Shilei Zhai. 2013. Analysis of Comments from German Think Tanks on China-Africa Economic and Trade Relations in Recent Years. *Deutschland-Studien* 4: 62–74, 127.

Chen, Shuisheng, and Guigui Xi. 2013. People's Lives or Democracy? Analysis of China's Aid Diplomacy from the Perspective of Aid to Africa. *Fudan International Studies Review* 1: 174–191.

Cheru, Fantu, and Cyril Obi. 2010. *The Rise of China and India in Africa: Challenges, Opportunities and Critical Interventions.* London, New York, Uppsala and Sweden: Zed Books.

Chhotray, Vasudha, and David Hulme. 2009. Contrasting Visions for Aid and Governance in the 21 st Century: The White House Millennium Challenge Account and DFID's Drivers of Change. *World Development* 37 (1): 36–49. https://doi.org/10.1016/j.worlddev.2007.11.004.

Copper, John Franklin. 2016. *China's Foreign Aid and Investment Diplomacy, volume II: History and Practice in Asia, 1950–Present.* New York: Palgrave Macmillan.

Cumming, Gordon. 1995. French Development Assistance to Africa: Towards a New Agenda? *African Affairs* 94 (376): 383.

Davis, Thomas W.D. 2011. Foreign Aid in Australia's Relationship with the South: Institutional Narratives. *Round Table* 100 (415): 389–406. https://doi.org/10.1080/00358533.2011.595254.

Dent, Christopher M. 2011. *China and Africa Development Relations.* Hoboken: Taylor & Francis.

Department of International Cooperation, Ministry of Health. 2003. Strengthen the Implementation of New Strategy to Reform Health Aid to Africa—40th Anniversary of the Dispatch of Chinese Medical Teams for Foreign Aid. *West Asia & Africa* 5: 15–18.

Diana, Ntono. 2013. Chinese Multinational Enterprises in East Africa and Economic Diversification. Doctoral Dissertation, Jilin University.

Ding, Xuhong, and Daqing Zhang. 2010. Early Chinese Medical Teams in Africa (1963–1978): Among Medicine, Politics and Culture. *Medicine & Philosophy* 15: 76–78.

Dreher, Axel, Andreas Fuchs, Roland Hodler, Bradley Parks, Paul A. Raschky, and Michael J. Tierney. 2015. *Aid on Demand: African Leaders and the Geography of China's Foreign Assistance.* Rochester: Social Science Research Network.

Du, Ying. 2011. Research on the Relations Between India and East African Countries (1964–2000). Doctoral Dissertation, East China Normal University.

Easterly, William. 2009. Can the West Save Africa? *Journal of Economic Literature* 47 (2): 373–447. https://doi.org/10.2307/27739927.

Easterly, William, and Claudia R. Williamson. 2011. Rhetoric Versus Reality: The Best and Worst of Aid Agency Practices. *World Development 39* (11): 1930–1949. https://doi.org/10.1016/j.worlddev.2011.07.027.

Economic and Commercial Counsellor's Office, Chinese Embassy in Uganda. 2013. China-Uganda Economic and Trade Cooperation into New Stage. *International Business Daily*, October 22, C03.

Fan, Victoria Y., Karen A. Grepin, Gordon C. Shen, and Lucy Chen. 2014. Tracking the Flow of Health Aid from BRICS Countries. *Bulletin of the World Health Organization* 92 (6): 457–458. https://doi.org/10.1377/hlthaff.2011.1154. PMID: 22174301.

Feng, Zheying. 2010. A Comparative Study of Aid to Africa from China and the US in the Early 21st Century. Master's Thesis, China Foreign Affairs University.

Fleck, Robert K., and Christopher Kilby. 2010. Changing Aid Regimes? U.S. Foreign Aid from the Cold War to the War on Terror. *Journal of Development Economics* 91 (2): 185–197. https://doi.org/10.1016/j.jdeveco.2009.09.011.

Freeman, Charles, and Xiaoqing Boynton Lu. 2011. *China's Emerging Global Health and Foreign Aid Engagement in Africa.* Washington, DC: CSIS.

French, Howard W. 2014. *China's Second Continent: How a Million Migrants are Building a New Empire in Africa*. New York: Vintage Books.

Frenk, Julio, and Steven Hoffman. 2015. *To Save Humanity: What Matters Most for a Healthy Future*. Oxford: Oxford University Press.

Fu, Qingye. 2013. Study on Health Aid from Hunan to Africa (1973–2013). Master's Thesis, Hunan Normal University.

Fuchs, Andreas, and Krishna Chaitanya Vadlamannati. 2013. The Needy Donor: An Empirical Analysis of India's Aid Motives. *World Development* 44: 110–128. https://doi.org/10.1016/j.worlddev.2012.12.012.

Gadzala, Aleksandra W. 2010. From Formal-to Informal-Sector Employment: Examining the Chinese Presence in Zambia. *Review of African Political Economy* 37 (123): 41–59. https://doi.org/10.2307/27860746.

Gao, Guixian, Zhu Yueji, and Zhou Deyi. 2014. The difficulties, positions, and solution in Sino-Africa agriculture corporations. *China Soft Science* (1): 36–42.

Golley, Jane, and Ligang Song. 2011. *Rising China: Global Challenges and Opportunities*. Canberra: ANU Press.

Gong, Wei. 2014. Analysis of Political Functions of Japan's Development Aid to Africa. *Pacific Journal* 2: 63–75.

Grépin, Karen A., Victoria Y. Fan, Gordon C. Shen, and Lucy Chen. 2014. China's Role as a Global Health Donor in Africa: What Can We Learn from Studying Under Reported Resource Flows? *Global Health* 10 (1): 1–11. https://doi.org/10.1186/s12992-014-0084-6.

Grimm, Sven. 2008. Africa-China-Europe Trilateral Co-operation: Is Europe Naive? EDC 2020-Opinion No. 1. European Development Co-operation to 2020.

Grimm, Sven. 2011. Engaging with China in Africa Trilateral Cooperation as an Option? EDC 2020-Policy Brief No. 9. European Development Cooperation to 2020.

Grimm, Sven, John Humphrey, Erik Lundsgaarde, and Sarah-Lea John de Sousa. 2009. Challenges by New Actors in International Development. EDC 2020-Working Paper No. 4, European Development Co-operation to 2020.

Gu, Jing, and Anthony Carty. 2014. China and African Development: Partnership Not Mentoring. *IDS Bulletin* 45: 57–69. https://doi.org/10.1111/1759-5436.12093.

Guloba, Madina, Nicholas Kilimani, and Winnie Nabiddo. 2010. *Impact of China-Africa Aid Relations: A Case Study of Uganda*. Kampala: Economic Policy Research Centre (EPRC).

Hackenesch, Christine. 2011. European Good Governance Policies Meet China in Africa: Insights from Angola and Ethiopia. EDC 2020-Working Paper No. 10, European Development Co-operation to 2020.

Han, Qide, Lincoln Chen, Tim Evans, and Richard Horton. 2008. China and Global Health. *The Lancet* 372 (9648): 1439–1441. https://doi.org/10.1016/s0140-6736(08)61350-1.

Harneit-Sievers, Axel, Stephen Marks, and Sanusha Naidu. 2010. *Chinese and African Perspectives on China in Africa*. London: Fahamu and Pambazuka.

He, Xianfeng. 2011. Evolution and Characteristics of China's Aid to Africa. *Reform & Opening* 14: 23–24.

He, Wenping. 2011. China's Aid to Africa: "Teach Them to Fish". *People's Daily* (Overseas Edition), September 3, P1.

He, Tianhao. 2012. Back to ABCs: Emerging Partnerships Among Africa, Brazil, and China. *Harvard International Review* 34 (1): 30–33.

He, Dazhuo. 2013. "Expensive Aid": Tanzania-China Friendship Textile Company. *China Textile & Apparel* 5: 35.

He, Wenping. 2013. Japan's Aid to Africa: Objectives and Impacts. *Contemporary World* 8: 25–28.

Hu, Mei. 2010. A Comparative Study of China's and the US Strategies for Aid to Africa. *Journal of Hunan University of Arts and Science* 5: 30–34.

Hu, Mei. 2011. 50 Years of China's Aid to Africa and Innovation of International Aid Theory. *Socialism Study* 1: 141–146.

Hu, Angang, Yuning Gao, Yilong Yan, and Xing Wei. 2014. China's Role in the Rising of the South: Vision for 2030. *IDS Bulletin* 45: 6–21. https://doi.org/10.1111/1759-5436.12089.

Huang, Y. 2010. Pursuing Health as Foreign Policy: The Case of China. *Indiana Journal of Global Legal Studies* 17: 105–146. https://doi.org/10.2979/gls.2010.17.1.105.

Huang, Ling. 2016. Set an Example for China-Africa Agricultural Cooperation: Practice and Exploration of Sichuan-Uganda Agricultural Cooperation. *Sichuan Agriculture and Agricultural Machinery* 2: 6–7.

Huang, Jianyin. 2012. Opportunities and Challenges of Traditional Chinese Medicine in Africa. *China Medicine Daily*, May 7, P8.

Huang, Zhanhua. 2013. *Ningxia Medical Team in Benin*. Yinchuan: Ningxia People's Publishing House.

Huang, Meibo, and Jianyan Lang. 2010. China's Aid to Africa and the Challenges. *Journal of International Economic Cooperation* 6: 34–40.

Huang, Meibo, and Qi Xie. 2012. Characteristics and Trends of India's Foreign Aid. *Journal of International Economic Cooperation* 1: 63–68.

Humphrey, John. 2011. Chinese Development Cooperation and the EU. EDC 2020-Policy Brief No. 17. European Development Co-operation to 2020.

International Business Daily. 2010. Aid to Africa: Eight New and Old Initiatives. *International Business Daily*, August 14, B04.

Jakobson, Linda. 2009. China's Diplomacy Toward Africa: Drivers and Constraints. *International Relations of the Asia Pacific* 9 (3): 403–433. https://doi.org/10.1093/irap/lcp008.

Jiang, Huajie. 2015. Reexamination of the History of China's Medical Teams to Africa (1963–1983): A Discussion on Effectiveness and Sustainability of

International Aid. *Foreign Affairs Review—Journal of China Foreign Affairs University* 4: 61–81.

Jiang, Lei, and Haijun Wang. 2011. Analysis of Differences in Political Strings in Foreign Aid: A Comparative Study Based on Foreign Aid Practices of China and Western Countries. *Pacific Journal* 7: 53–62.

Jiang, Xiaoxiao, and Chen Zhang. 2013. Investigative Report on Chinese Medical Teams to the Democratic Republic of Congo. *China African Research Review* 2012: 18.

Johnson, Ken Deji. 2010. Reorienting U.S. Aid to Africa-in America's Interest. *American Foreign Policy Interests,* 32 (4), 229–236.

Ju, Zhengbo. 2010. Research on Direct Investment of Chinese Enterprises in Africa. Master's Thesis, Yunnan University.

Kang, Sheng. 2012. India's Strategy for Expanding Economic and Trade Relations with Africa and Its Inspiration for China. *Macroeconomic Research* 12: 98–105.

Kenyon, Georgina. 2010. China Offers Billions in Loans to Boost Health Research in Africa. *Nature Medicine* 16 (1): 8. https://doi.org/10.1038/nm0110-8b.

King, Kenneth. 2013. *China's Aid & Soft Power in Africa: The Case of Education & Training*. Woodbridge, Suffolk: James Currey.

Kobayashi, Takaaki. 2008. *Evolution of China's Aid Policy*, vol. 27. Tokyo: JBIC Institute.

Kurlantzick, Joshua. 2007. *Charm Offensive: How China's Soft Power is Transforming the World.* New Haven: Yale University Press.

Lebovic, James H. 2005. Donor Positioning: Development Assistance from the U. S., Japan, France, Germany, and Britain. *Political Research Quarterly* 58 (1): 119–126. https://doi.org/10.2307/3595601.

Li, Anshan. 2008a. China's Africa Strategy: National Image and Strategies. *China International Strategic Review* 2008: 14.

Li, Anshan. 2008b. In Defense of China: China's Africa Strategy and National Image. *World Economy and Politics* 4: 6–15.

Li, Anshan. 2009. History, Scale and Impact of Chinese Medical Teams for Foreign Aid. *Foreign Affairs Review—Journal of China Foreign Affairs University* 1: 25–45.

Li, Anshan. 2010. China's Aid to Africa: A Narrative by an American Scholar. *Foreign Affairs Review—Journal of China Foreign Affairs University* 5: 12–19.

Li, Anshan. 2011. *Chinese Medical Cooperation in Africa: With Special Emphasis on the Medical Teams and Anti-Malaria Campaign.* Uppsala: Nordiska Afrikainstitutet. ISBN: 9171066837.

Li, Jia. 2012. The Origin, Essence and Impact of "New Colonialism" Theory on China's Aid to Africa. Master's Thesis, East China Normal University.

Li, Wengang. 2013. "Soft Power" in China-Africa Relations. *West Asia and Africa* 5: 130–146.

Li, Xuedong. 2016. Potential and Dilemma of China-Africa Industrial Cooperation: A Case Study of Uganda. *Modern Management Science* 4: 69–71.

Li, Xiaoyun, and Jin Wu. 2009. Practical Experience and Challenges of China's Aid to Africa. *Journal of China Agricultural University* (Social Science Edition) 4: 45–54.

Li, Xiying, and Junying Huang. 2012. Adjustment to Britain's Policy on Aid to Africa. *Journal of International Economic Cooperation* 4: 82–86.

Li, Jihonh, and Jiashun Li. 2016. Ugandan AN Expressway Project Successfully Delivered by China Railway No. 5 Engineering Group. *International Project Contracting & Labor Service* 7: 93.

Liang, Wenjie. 2015. Status Quo and Development Strategy of Guangxi Medical Team to Africa. Master's Thesis, Guangxi Medical University.

Liao, Lan, and Jing Liu. 2012. Research on China's Foreign Aid from the Western Perspective. *Journal of China Agricultural University* (Social Science Edition) 4: 93–101.

Liu, Zhongwei. 2012. An Analysis of German Development Aid to Rwanda. *West Asia and Africa* 5: 144–160.

Liu, Guijin. 2013. The US Africa Strategy and Its Inspiration for China. *Party Building* 5: 62–64.

Liu, Jianhao, and Xiaoxiang Quan. 2013. The Health Status of Zanzibar and Service Effectiveness of Chinese Medical Teams to Sangzang. *Jiangsu Health Management* 5: 283–285.

Liu, Peilong, Yan Guo, Xu Qian, Shenglan Tang, Zhihui Li, and Lincoln Chen. 2014. China's Distinctive Engagement in Global Health. *The Lancet* 384 (9945): 793–804. https://doi.org/10.1016/s0140-6736(14)60725-X.

Liu, Xiangbo, Xiaomeng Zhang, and Chi-Chur Chao. 2014. Foreign Aid, Leisure Effort Choice, and Economic Growth. *Economic Modelling* 43: 435–438. https://doi.org/10.1016/j.econmod.2014.09.006.

Lo, Gourmo Abdoul. 2012. Africa and China: New Colonialism or New Strategic Partnership. *Foreign Theoretical Trends* 9: 77–82.

Lopes Sanches, Leinira. 2009. Aid to Africa: Chinese Modes. Master's Thesis, Jilin University.

Lu, Miaomiao. 2015. An Analysis of Investment and Business Environment of Chinese Enterprises in Uganda. Master's Thesis, China Foreign Affairs University.

Luo, Jianbo. 2007. Improve China's Soft Power in Africa. *Asia & Africa Review* 6: 18–24.

Ma, Jianhua. 1992. Revival of Kibimba Farm in Uganda. *Journal of International Economic Cooperation* 12: 38.

Ma, Yao. 2016. No Political Strings Ever—60 Years of China's Aid to Africa. *World Vision* 12: 22–25.

Martin, George. 2013. China's Soft Power in Africa: A Case Study in Uganda. Master's Thesis, Fudan University.

McCormick, Dorothy. 2008. China & India as Africa's New Donors: The Impact of Aid on Development. *Review of African Political Economy* 35 (115): 73–92. https://doi.org/10.2307/20406478.

McGiffert, Carola. 2009. *Chinese Soft Power and Its Implications for the United States: Competition and Cooperation in the Developing World*. Washington, DC: Center for Strategic and International Studies.

Men, Jing, and Benjamin Barton. 2011. *China and the European Union in Africa: Partners or Competitors?* Burlington, VT: Ashgate.

Moyo, Dambisa. 2012. *Winner Take All: China's Race for Resources and What It Means for Us*. London: Allen Lane.

Muchapondwa, Edwin, Daniel Nielson, Bradley Parks, Austin M. Strange, and Michael J. Tierney. 2014. 'Ground-Truthing' Chinese Development Finance in Africa. Wider Working Paper 2014/031, World Institute for Development Economics Research.

Niu, Changsong. 2014. China's Educational Cooperation with Africa: Toward New Strategic Partnerships. *Asian Education and Development Studies* 3 (1): 31–45. https://doi.org/10.1108/aeds-09-2013-0057.

OECD. 2012. *OECD Factbook* 2011: *Economic, Environmental and Social Statistics*. Paris, France and Bristol, UK: OECD.

Parfitt, Tom. 2005. Russia Clamps Down on Foreign Aid Organisations. *The Lancet* 366 (9502): 1993. https://doi.org/10.1016/S0140-6736(05)67798-7.

Pfaff, William. 1995. A New Colonialism? Europe Must Go Back into Africa. *Foreign Affairs* 74 (1): 2.

Power, Marcus, Giles Mohan, and May Tan-Mullins. 2012. *China's Resource Diplomacy in Africa: Powering Development?* Houndmills, Basingstoke and New York, NY: Palgrave Macmillan.

Qiu, Changqing, and Erwei Liu. 2012. An Analysis of India's Economic Diplomacy in Africa from the Perspective of Political Power. *South Asia Studies* 1: 30–44.

Rebol, Max. 2011. Non-interference and Practical Cooperation: An Analysis on China's Soft Power in Africa. Doctoral Dissertation, Fudan University.

Ren, Minghui and Guoping Lu. 2014. China's Global Health Strategy. *The Lancet* 384 (9945):719–721. https://doi.org/10.1016/s0140-6736(14)61317-9.

Rimmer, Douglas. 2000. Aid and Corruption. *African Affairs* 99 (394): 121–128.

Rioux, Jean-Sebastien, and Douglas A. Van Belle. 2005. The Influence of Le Monde Coverage on French Foreign Aid Allocations. *International Studies Quarterly* 49 (3): 481–502. https://doi.org/10.2307/3693604.

Rotberg, Robert I. 2009. *China into Africa: Trade, Aid, and Influence*. Washington, DC: Brookings Institution Press.

Rupp, Stephanie. 2013. China and the European Union in Africa: Partners or Competitors? *African Studies Review* 56: 190–192. https://doi.org/10.1353/arw.2013.0005.

Sam, Waigolo. 2013. Impact of FDI on Specific Interests of Established and New Firms in Uganda's Business Environment. Master's Thesis, Ningbo University.

Santos-Paulino, Amelia U., and Guanghua Wan. 2010. *The Rise of China and India*. London, UK: Palgrave Macmillan.

Sautman, Barry, and Yan Hairong. 2007. Friends and Interests: China's Distinctive Links with Africa. *African Studies Review* 50 (3): 75–114. https://doi.org/10.2307/27667241.

Schiere, Richard. 2014. The Impact of China on the Donor Landscape in African Fragile States. *IDS Bulletin* 45: 46–56. https://doi.org/10.111/1759-5436.12092.

Schiere, Richard, Leonce Ndikumana, and Peter Walkenhorst. 2011. *China and Africa: An Emerging Partnership for Development?* ed. R. Schiere, L. Ndikumana and P. Walkenhorst. Abidjan: African Development Bank Group.

Schmidt, Heide-Irene. 2003. Pushed to the Front: The Foreign Assistance Policy of the Federal Republic of Germany, 1958–1971. *Contemporary European History* 12 (4): 473–507. https://doi.org/10.2307/20081179.

Schraeder, Peter J., Steven W. Hook, and Bruce Taylor. 1998. Clarifying the Foreign Aid Puzzle: A Comparison of American, Japanese, French, and Swedish Aid Flows. *World Politics* 50 (2): 294–323. https://doi.org/10.2307/25054039.

Shen, Gordon C., and Victoria Y. Fan. 2014. China's Provincial Diplomacy to Africa: Applications to Health Cooperation. *Contemporary Politics* 20: 182–208. https://doi.org/10.1080/13569775.2014.907993.

Shi, Yunyu. 2010. Medicine in China's Foreign Health Aid. *Strait Pharmaceutical Journal* 8: 275–277.

Shu, Yunguo. 2010. China's Aid to Africa: History, Theory and Characteristics. *Journal of Shanghai Normal University* (Philosophy & Social Sciences Edition) 5: 83–89.

Siringi, S. 2003. Africa and China Join Forces to Combat Malaria. *The Lancet* 362. https://doi.org/10.1016/s0140-6736(03)14105-0.

Smith, Nicholas T. 2010. Africa's Freedom Railway: How a Chinese Development Project Changed Lives and Livelihoods in Tanzania. *African Studies Quarterly* 11 (2/3): 174–176.

Song, Yanmei. 2013. Characteristics of Russian Development Aid: Comparison with the Soviet Union Period. *Russian Studies* 4: 150–171.

Song, Wei. 2014. China in Africa: Innovative Mechanisms to Meet Challenges. *International Business Daily*, April 7, A07.

Stein, Howard. 2002. Chinese Aid and African Development: Exporting Green Revolution. *Africa: Journal of the International African Institute* 72 (1): 164–166.

Strauss, Julia C. 2009. The Past in the Present: Historical and Rhetorical Lineages in China's Relations with Africa. *The China Quarterly* 199: 777–795. https://doi.org/10.1017/s0305741009990208.

Strauss, Julia C., and Martha Saavedra. 2009. *China and Africa: Emerging Patterns in Globalization and Development*, No. 9. Cambridge: Cambridge University Press.

Sun, Xian. 2013. Research on Medical Aid from Shandong to Africa. Master's Thesis, Shandong University.

Sun, Yun. 2014. Africa in China's Foreign Policy. Washington, DC: Brookings Institution Press.

Tang, Xioayang. 2013. Evolution and Effect of China's Agricultural Aid to Africa. *World Economy and Politics* 5: 55–69.

Tang, Lixia, Jin Wu, and Xiaoyun Li. 2011. International Aid for Agricultural Development in Africa. *World Agriculture* 7: 51–56.

Tao, Duanfang. 2011. India Follow China's Path in Africa. *World Vision* 12: 22–23.

The State Council. 1962. Joint Bulletin of the People's Republic of China and Uganda on the Establishment of Diplomatic Relations. *State Council Gazette* 11: 218.

The State Council. 1965. Joint Communique of China and Uganda. *State Council Gazette* 9: 144–146.

The State Council. 2006. China and Uganda Issued Joint Communique. *People's Daily*, June 25, P3.

Tull, Denis M. 2006. China's Engagement in Africa: Scope, Significance and Consequences. *The Journal of Modern African Studies* 44 (3): 459–479. https://doi.org/10.2307/3876304.

United Nations. 2016. *African Statistical Yearbook 2016*. Scanprint, Denmark.

Vuving, Alexander. 2009. *How Soft Power Works*. Rochester, NY: Social Science Research Network. SSRN: 1466220.

van de Walle, Nicolas. 2010. Us Policy Towards Africa: The Bush Legacy and the Obama Administration. *African Affairs* 109 (434): 1–21. https://doi.org/10.2307/40388444.

Wang, Xinying. 2009. Adjustment of EU's Policy on Aid to Africa. *Asia & Africa Review* 4: 45–49.

Wang, Xinying. 2011. A Comparative Study of EU and China's Policy on Aid to Africa. *Asia & Africa Review* 1: 50–54.

Wang, Liang. 2012. Research on Rockefeller Foundation's Agricultural Aid to Black Africa (1952–1972). Master's Thesis, East China Normal University.

Wang, Ping. 2012. Review of Japan's Development Aid to Non-Governmental Organizations: From the Perspective of Diplomatic Strategy. *Foreign Affairs Review—Journal of China Foreign Affairs University* 6: 113–126.

Wang, Qingqing. 2012. A Comparative Study of Aid to Africa from China and Japan Since the 21st Century. Master's Thesis, Huazhong Normal University.

Wang, Yuhong. 2012. Cooperation and Development: A Study on China's Aid to Africa. Doctoral Dissertation, Jilin University.

Wang, Xinying. 2013. Achievements and Challenges of China's Aid to Africa. *International Study Reference* 7: 23–28.

Wang, Chao, and Shanggang Liang. 2010. China's Aid to Africa: Improving People's Lives through Practical Work. *Outlook Weekly* 48: 28–30.

Wang, Lijuan, and Xinru Jiang. 2014. The Influence and Essential Evaluation of the United States' Aid to Africa. *Pacific Journal* 2: 52–62.

Wang, Xiangcheng, and Tao Sun. 2014. China's Engagement in Global Health Governance: A Critical Analysis of China's Assistance to the Health Sector of Africa. *Journal of Global Health* 4 (1): 010301. https://doi.org/10.7189/jogh.04.010301.

Wang, K., S. Gimbel, E. Malik, S. Hassen, and A. Hagopian. 2012. The Experience of Chinese Physicians in the National Health Diplomacy Programme Deployed to Sudan. Global Public Health 7 (2): 196–211. https://doi.org/10.1080/17441692.2011.594450.

Warmerdam, Ward, and Meine Pieter van Dijk. 2013. Chinese Stateowned Enterprise Investments in Uganda: Findings from a Recent Survey of Chinese Firms in Kampala. *Journal of Chinese Political Science* 18 (3): 281–301. https://doi.org/10.1007/s11366-013-9250-6.

Watson, Helena. 2009. Aid, Aid Everywhere but Still Not a Drop in the Sink. *British Medical Journal* 338 (7688): 239. https://doi.org/10.2307/20511889.

Wei, Xuemei. 2011. China's Aid to Africa and Improvement of China's Soft Power. *Journal of University of International Relations* 1: 31–36.

Wen, Cuiping. 2014. A Comparative Study of Aid to Africa from China and India in the 21st Century. Master's Thesis, China Foreign Affairs University.

Wilson III, Ernest J. 1993. French Support for Structural Adjustment Programs in Africa. *World Development* 21 (3): 331–347. https://doi.org/10.1016/0305-750x(93)90148-3.

Woods, Ngaire. 2008. Whose Aid? Whose Influence? China, Emerging Donors and the Silent Revolution in Development Assistance. *International Affairs (Royal Institute of International Affairs 1944–)* 84 (6): 1205–1221. https://doi.org/10.2307/25144989.

Xia, Qingjie, and Yujiang Chen. 2016. Models of Health Aid to Africa in the World and China's Investment in Health Aid to Africa. *International Aid* 2: 18–32.

Xiao, Yang. 2013. Reputation and Rights: Strategies for Improving China's National Image in North Africa. *Contemporary World* 3: 65–67.

Xie, Qiang. 2012. Aid from China and EU to Africa: Seeking Cooperation in Differences. Master's Thesis, Fudan University.

Xie, Qi, Tian Feng, and Meibo Huang. 2012. Clarify Misunderstandings about China's Foreign Aid. *International Economic Review* 4: 147–157.

Xinhua News Agency. 1962. Uganda, a New African Country. *World Knowledge* 21: 2.

Xu, Guoqing. 2015. An Analysis of New Situation of India-Africa Relations Under Modi. *South Asia Studies* 2: 62–80.

Xu, Wenying. 2011. Research on Medical Team from Shanghai to Morocco (1975–1985). Master's Thesis, East China Normal University.

Xu, Qianlei, Xu Xiangqian, Shiping Xie, Huijun Guo, and Liran Xu. 2016. AIDS Prevention and Treatment with Traditional Chinese Medicine: Practice and Reflection. *Chinese Journal of Traditional Chinese Medicine* 4: 1368–1370.

Yang, Xinjian. 2013. *Forty Years of Dedication: A Collection of Commemorative Essays on the 40th Anniversary of Hebei's Foreign Medical Aid*. Lagos: Academy Press.

Yasutomo, Dennis T. 1989. Why Aid? Japan as an Aid Great Power. *Pacific Affairs* 62 (4): 490–503. https://doi.org/10.2307/2759672.

Yin, Hongwei. 2006. Charm of Chinese Medical Teams to Africa. *South Reviews* 22: 38–41.

Youde, Jeremy. 2010. China's Health Diplomacy in Africa. *China: An International Journal* 8: 151–163.

Yu, Weibin. 2014. Research on China's Cultural Soft Power in Non-foreign Policy. Doctoral Dissertation, Wuhan University.

Zafar, Ali. 2007. The Growing Relationship Between China and Sub-Saharan Africa: Macroeconomic, Trade, Investment and Aid Links. *The World Bank Research Observer* 22 (1): 103–130. https://doi.org/10.2307/40282338.

Zhang, Yuhui. 2006. Research on China's Foreign Aid. Doctoral Dissertation, Central Party School.

Zhang, Xiangdong. 2007. Western Misunderstanding of China's Africa Policy and Practice. *Peace and Development* 1: 52–54.

Zhang, Chun. 2010. Medical Diplomacy and Cultivation of Soft Power: A Case Study of Chinese Medical Teams to Africa. *Modern International Relations* 3: 49–53.

Zhang, Guangrong. 2011. UK Aid to Africa: Overview, Characteristics and Influencing Factors. *Journal of International Economic Cooperation* 5: 38–42.

Zhang, Haibing. 2012. Development-Oriented Aid: A Study of China's Model of Aid to Africa. *World Economic Research* 12: 78–83.

Zhang, Zhen. 2016. Teacher Education in Uganda Under Effective Aid Agenda. *Asia-Pacific Education* 4: 270.

Zhang, Xioamin, and Tongquan Sun. 2014. Research one Regulatory System of Britain's Foreign Aid. *Journal of International Economic Cooperation* 5: 50–55.

Zhang, Xiaohua, Yi Yang, and Haipeng Guo. 2015. Social Responsibility in Going Global. *Chinese and Foreign Company Culture* 12: 30.

Zheng, Song, and Xiaochen Sun. 2012. International Aid for Education in Uganda: Structure and Effect. *Comparative Education Review* 12: 10–14.

Zhou, Haichuan. 2012. Sustainable Development of China-Africa Agricultural Technology Demonstration Centers: Problems and Countermeasures. *China Soft Science* 9: 45–54.

Zhou, Quanfa. 2014. Reflection on Ways towards Sustainable Development of China-Africa Agricultural Technology Demonstration Center. *China Journal of Tropical Agriculture* 10: 101–104.

Zhu, Mingzhong. 2005. India and Africa (1947–2004). *South Asia Studies* 1: 20–26.

Zou, Guanyang, Barbara McPake, and Xiaolin Wei. 2014. Chinese Health Foreign Aid and Policy: Beyond Medical Aid. *The Lancet* 383 (9927): 1461–1462. https://doi.org/10.1016/S0140-6736(14)60713-3.

CHAPTER 6

Development Aid for Health from China to Uganda

6.1 Uganda and Its Healthcare System

In international affairs, the Sahara Desert is often used as a dividing line between the African regions south of the Sahara Desert and north of the Sahara Desert. The African continent south of the Sahara Desert, also known as the sub-Saharan Africa or sub-Saharan region, is home to black people or Nile Valley peoples. It is also the world's most impoverished region with the most complex spectrum of diseases. Communicable diseases such as AIDS, Ebola virus disease, and malaria all have complicated relations with this region.

Uganda is located in eastern Africa, and belongs to the East African Community (EAC) together with Kenya, Tanzania, Burundi, Rwanda and South Sultan, all in sub-Saharan Africa. Uganda covers an area of 241,000 km^2,[1] close to the 243,400 km^2 in 1956, equivalent to the size of the British mainland. Although it is a landlocked country, there are many lakes in Uganda, including Lake Victoria, Lake Albert, Lake Edward, and Lake George. Situated on the plateau in East Africa, Uganda has an average altitude of 900 m, and most of the country has a tropical, mild climate. The average annual temperature is 22 °C, with the highest temperature of 35.8 °C and the lowest of 8.5 °C. It has

[1]The number varies in different documents. For example, in Table 6.3, the area is only 20.46 km^2.

Z. Qiu, *When Friendship Comes First*, China and Globalization 2.0,
https://doi.org/10.1007/978-981-32-9308-3_6

abundant rainfall, with an annual rainfall of about 1000–1200 mm, most concentrated in April, May, September, and October (see Fig. 6.1).

It is said that as early as in the eleventh century, the people of southern Buganda, had established their kingdom near Lake Victoria. Lake Victoria, also called Victoria Nyanza, is the world's largest plateau-based lake, with an area of 69,400 km^2. It is also the world's second-largest freshwater lake, from which the Nile River originates. By the second half of the nineteenth century, the Kingdom of Buganda had already become the largest and most powerful kingdom in the region of Lake Victoria, and had resisted British invasions many times. In the end, however, it still became a British protectorate. The British stirred up internal strife between the kingdoms including Buganda by sending missionaries and other religious measures. Over the more than 20 years, the British basically disintegrated Buganda and its surrounding kingdoms including Tooro, Ankole, and Bunyoro-Kitara, and signed an agreement with Germany in 1890 to carve up East Africa. In 1894, Kingdom of Buganda became a British protectorate. The Uganda Agreement of 1900 confirmed that Buganda was part of Uganda; from 1907, London started to send a commissioner to administer the country.

During the colonial era of Uganda, Britain launched reforms in the colonial areas, proclaiming support for their development. In the late 1920s, the resistance in Uganda compelled Britain to carry out reforms, including the constitutional reform. By March 1961, when the elections were held, three major political parties had been formed: the Ugandan People's Congress (UPC), the Democratic Party (DP), and Kabaka Yekka. On October 9, 1962, Uganda declared independence, but it remained a member of the Commonwealth.

More than three decades of its independence, Uganda shifted from the federal system to republic. According to the 1942 colonial constitution, the country adopted federalism in the wake of its independence in 1956, when Milton Obote, head of the UPC, was elected as Prime Minister, and Frederick Mutesa II, head of Kabaka Yekka and the Kabaka (King) of Buganda, became the ceremonial President. In 1964, the bipartisan coalition collapsed; in 1966, the central government captured the Kabaka Palace, and Frederick Mutesa II to fled Britain.

In 1967, Uganda adopted a new constitution, and became a republic, outlawing all kingdoms and kings. Ugandan President Milton Obote published the *Common Man's Charter* in 1969 and the *Nakivubo*

Fig. 6.1 Administrative map of Uganda (*Source* http://www.nationsonline.org/oneworld/map/uganda-administrative-map.htm, retrieved on August 18, 2016)

Pronouncement in 1970, condemning feudalism and reiterating one nation and one government.

On January 25, 1971, General Idi Amin Dada led a military coup that overthrew Obote, who then fled to Tanzania. In March 1979, more than 20 exiled political groups opposed to the rule of Idi Amin formed the Uganda National Liberation Front (UPLF) and the Uganda National Liberation Army (UPLA) in Moshi, Tanzania. On 10 April, the UPLA occupied Kampala with the support of the Tanzanian army, and Amin fled.

On April 11, a new government was formed under Yusuf Lule, who was replaced by Godfrey Binaisa only two months later. Binaisa ruled for less than one year before being ousted in May 1980, and Paulo Muwanga then formed a new cabinet. At this time, the military infighting came to a halt. In December 1980, the founding Prime Minister Milton Obote of the UPC won the general election, and resumed power nine years later. In 1981, however, Yoweri Museveni, believing that the elections were manipulated, led the National Resistance Army to wage a guerrilla war against Obote's regime. In July 1985, Obote was overthrown by the coup of Bazilio Olara-Okello, who was soon defeated by Tito Okello. A few months later, in January 1986, the second Okello was overthrown by Yoweri Museveni, who then took office as President.

The five years witnessed tremendous political turbulence, when Godfrey Binaisa, Paulo Muwanga, Milton Obote, Bazilio Olara-Okello and Tito Okello successively seized power and were replaced. It was not until January 29, 1986, when Yoweri Museveni, organizer of the National Resistance Movement, was inaugurated that Uganda finally found a path to political stability. Since 1986, although Uganda held a multi-party referendum in 2005, Museveni has remained as president, and he won the presidential election for the fifth time in 2016.

The administrative divisions of Uganda have undergone changes. In the late 1970s, under the rule of Idi Amin, Uganda was divided into six levels: provinces, regions (cities), counties, districts, towns, and villages; there were 10 provinces, 39 regions, four cities, and 122 counties.[2] In 1980, provinces were abolished, and the number of regions was reduced to 33. These were followed by further changes.[3]

[2]Investigative team to Uganda. 1978. *Investigative Report on Health in Uganda*. Kunming: Yunnan Provincial Archives. File No.: 131: 3: 28: 6.

[3]http://www.statoids.com/uug.html.

Table 6.1 Number of administrative areas in Uganda, 1969–2014

Level of administrative units	*1969*	*1980*	*1991*	*2002*	*2014*
Regions	21	33	38	56	112
Counties	111	140	163	163	181
Sub-counties	594	668	884	958	1382
Parishes	3141	3478	4636	5238	7241

Source Statistics (2016)

The latest administrative divisions vary in different sources of data, which may have different definitions and serve different purposes. According to the Ministry of Local Government of the Government of Uganda,[4] Uganda is divided into four administrative regions, namely, the eastern region (32 districts), the central region (23 districts and one city), the western region (26 districts), and the northern region (30 districts). The 111 districts are sub-divided into counties and municipalities. Under counties and municipalities are towns, parishes, and villages.

The administrative divisions in Uganda's census are different. Under the counties are sub-counties, and then parishes, and there are no "towns" (Statistics 2016). Since 1969, the number of administrative units at all levels except township has changed drastically. For example, the number of districts rose five times, and the number of sub-counties and parishes more than doubled (Table 6.1).

In 1956, Uganda had a population of 5.3 million, but there were 65 ethnic groups. The main ethnic groups were the Bantu living in the central and western regions, Nilotic in the Nile Valley and the northwest, and Half-hamite in the east, and the Bantu made up the majority. Uganda has always been a melting pot with five distinct linguistic systems and more than 30 indigenous languages (Sekidde 2013). Luganda is a universal language in the country. Christianity is the most widely professed religion, and hundreds of thousands believe in Islam (Zhou 1956; Zhu 1959).

Uganda's census data (Table 6.2) show that its population has been growing fast since its independence, almost doubling every 20 years. According to the UN data, Uganda's population increased to 39 million in 2015 (United Nations 2016), an increase of about five million over the previous year.

[4]http://www.uganda-sds.org/local-governments. Uganda passed the *Local Government Act* in 1997, giving local governments relative autonomy.

Table 6.2 Changes in population size

Census year	*Male*	*Female*	*Total*	*Annual growth rate (%)*
1911	1,116,903	1,349,422	2,466,325	
1921	1,320,286	1,534,322	2,854,608	1.5
1931	1,707,437	1,834,844	3,542,281	2.2
1948	2,481,394	2,477,126	4,958,520	2.0
1959	3,236,902	3,212,656	6,449,558	2.5
1969	4,812,447	4,722,604	9,535,051	3.9
1980	6,259,837	6,376,342	12,636,179	2.7
1991	8,185,747	8,485,558	16,671,705	2.5
2002	11,824,273	12,403,024	24,227,297	3.2
2014	17,060,832	17,573,818	34,634,650	3.0

Source Uganda Bureau of Statistics (2016)

Table 6.3 Changes in population size and density by region

		Total	*Central*	*Eastern*	*Northern*	*Western*
Area (km^2)		204,633	39,899	29,962	83,967	50,805
Size	2002	24,227,297	6,575,425	6,204,915	5,148,882	6,298,075
	2014	34,634,650	9,529,227	9,042,422	7,188,139	8,874,862
Density	2002	118	165	207	61	124
	2014	169	239	302	86	175
Growth rate (%)		43.2	44.8	45.9	41.0	41.1

Source http://www.statoids.com/uug.html

In addition, the increase in population density varies by region (Table 6.3). According to available data, the eastern and central regions are among the top two in population size and population density, and also population growth rate. In 2014, the population density of the eastern region was 3.5 times that of the northern region, and 1.7 times that of the western region. Kampala, capital city of Uganda, belongs to the central region, and Jinja, where Chinese medical teams worked, is located in the eastern region.

According to the data published by the United States Central Intelligence Agency (CIA),[5] the median age of Uganda was 15.6 in

[5] https://www.cia.gov/librnry/publications/the-world-factbook/geos/ug.html.

2015, ranking 228th among the 229 countries and regions in the world, making it the youngest country second only to Niger by 0.4 years. In its population pyramid, 48.47% of the Ugandan population was in the 0–14 age bracket, and only 2.04% aged 65 or above (Fig. 6.2). In 2015, Uganda was among the world's top five countries and regions by population growth, with a population growth rate of 3.24%; its birth rate was 43.79%, ranking second in the world; the mortality rate was 10.69, ranking 36th; the average age of first-time mothers was 19.3; and a country with net emigration, Uganda had a net migration rate of 0.74.

Uganda registered a GDP of EUR11 million in 2006, and EUR23.7 million in 2015. Its GDP grew 8.1% in 2007, 10.4% in 2008, 7.7% in 2010, and 5.3% in 2015. Although there was no negative growth, the growth rates were quite unstable, with the lowest rate of only 2.6% in 2012. Per capita GDP was on the rise, growing from EUR380 in 2006 to EUR607 in 2015. Urban population made up 12% of its total population in 2000, and the ratio grew to 13% in 2005 and to 16% in 2015. Urbanization is advancing gradually. Uganda had an economically active population of 13.5 million in 2010, and 16.1 million in 2015 (United Nations 2016), and a working-age population of 18.58 million, of which

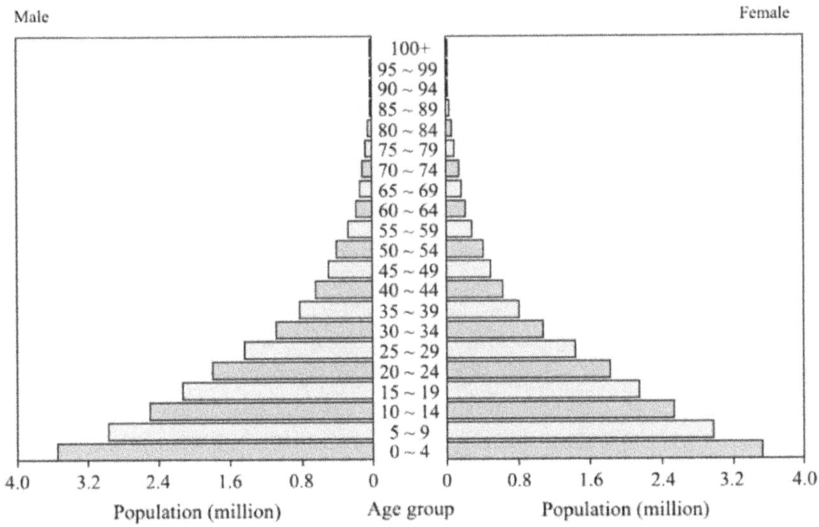

Fig. 6.2 Population structure of Uganda, 2015 (*Source* https://www.cia.gov/librnry/publications/the-world-factbook/geos/ug.html)

the population working in agriculture, industry and services accounted for 40, 10, and 50%, respectively.[6] The proportion of people living below the poverty line was estimated at 19.7% in 2013.

The CIA's data are different from those of the UN. According to the CIA, Uganda's GDP at purchasing power parity totaled USD 72.48 billion in 2013, USD 724.8 billion in 2013, USD 76.05 billion in 2014, and USD 79.88 billion in 2015, with a growth rate of 4 to 5% for three consecutive years; its GDP per capita was USD 1,900 in 2013, and around USD 2000 in 2014 and 2015. In terms of sector composition, agriculture contributed 26.3% to its GDP, industry 21.3%, and services 52.4%. As to final consumption expenditure, housing consumption accounted for 72.6% of the GDP, government spending 8.9%, fixed assets investment 29.7%, goods and services exports 22.5%, and goods and services imports 33.9%. From 2013 to 2015, the savings rate stayed within the range of 17–21%, and the inflation rate based on consumer prices ranged from 4.5 to 6.0%.

In order to better coordinate foreign-assisted resources, the Ugandan government developed the *Uganda Joint Assistance Strategy* (UJAS) (Uganda et al. 2005) in 2005 on the basis of consultation with major donors. This represents a milestone in Uganda's assistance strategy and management, promoting the coordinated and best use of assistance from all sides. In 2006, the African Development Bank (ADB) evaluated the strategy and commended it as a very effective aid coordination strategy (Puetz 2006).

In brief, Uganda has a relatively stable political environment, an evenly distributed, fast-growing young population, and a large economically active population. Its economic growth is basically slow and unstable; its industry is underdeveloped, the urbanization rate is low, the bulk of consumption is on housing, its imports exceed exports, the savings rate is not high, and prices are relatively stable.

China started to learn about Uganda as early as in the 1950s. Shortly after Uganda became independent on October 9, 1962, China established formal diplomatic relations with it, and maintained friendly relations with the Ugandan government despite the political turmoil in the 1980s. China decided to send its first medical team to Uganda when the African country was beset by its worst ever political chaos, and didn't bring the team back even during the Ugandan Bush War.

[6] https://www.cia.gov/librnry/publications/the-world-factbook/geos/ug.html.

Uganda's healthcare system is a typical hierarchical structure with two management levels and five service levels. The management and service institutions all come under the jurisdiction of the Ministry of Health. Among them, the National Referral Hospitals and the Regional Referral Hospitals are directly under the administration of the Ministry of Health, while service agencies at other levels are under the Regional Healthcare service Headquarter (Fig. 6.3).

In this structure, health resources and service capabilities of healthcare organizations decrease from top to bottom. Jinja Hospital, where Chinese Medical Team had worked for 30 years, is a Regional Referral Hospital at the second service level, and also the largest hospital in the eastern region.

In Uganda, healthcare services are delivered through public institutions, PNFP (private, non-for-profit) institutions, private medical practice, traditional and complementary practices (such as herbal medicine,

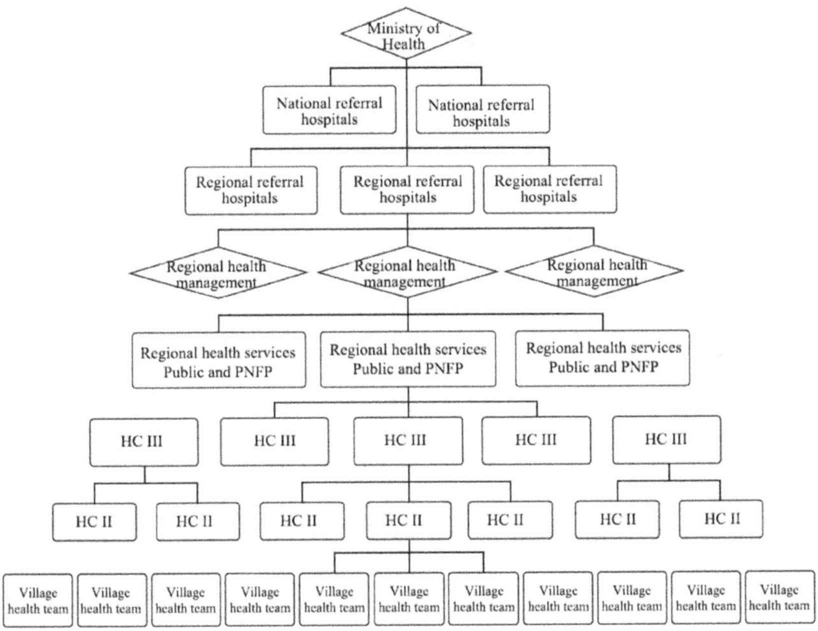

Fig. 6.3 Uganda's healthcare system, 2016 (*Note* Drawn by the author based on different sources of data)

Table 6.4 Health facilities by region (Public and PNFP), 2015

Type	*Central region*	*Eastern region*	*Northern region*	*Western region*	*Total*
Administrative unit	263	428	332	407	1430
Clinic	645	34	32	120	831
General hospital	53	30	27	34	144
HC II	1065	618	484	774	2941
HC III	318	324	271	376	1289
HC IV	51	48	31	67	197
National Referral Hospital	2	0	0	0	2
Regional Referral Hospital	3	3	4	4	14

Source Ministry of Health. 2015. Healthcare workers Bi-Annual Report. Kampala: Ministry of Health, Uganda, p. 8

traditional birth attendants, bonesetters, and spiritual healers), as well as community health workers, promoters, and drug peddlers. As can be seen from Table 6.4, the number and distribution of management and service institutions at different levels, from National Referral Hospital to Health Center II (HC II), forms a typical hierarchical structure.

In the healthcare system, staff of public institutions accounted for 52%, PNFP institutions 12%, and others 36% (Ministry of Health 2015). The proportion of approved posts filled at different levels of institutions varies greatly, which is 64% for National Referral Hospitals, 79% for Regional Referral Hospitals, and 69% for local health institutions. The number and proportion of posts filled at public health institutions are shown in Table 6.5.

According to the CIA's data[7] and data from other sources[8] (some data included in Table 6.6), the basic health indicators of Uganda can be summarized as: high maternal mortality rate (ranking 37th in the world), high infant mortality rate (ranking 21st), and short life expectancy (ranking 211th). Moreover, Uganda ranked 10th with a high HIV prevalence among adults, and had an "extremely high" risk grade in major

[7]The mortality rates of the countries and regions are ranked from high to low; the higher the ranking, the higher the mortality rate, and the worse the health status. See https://www.cia.gov/library/publications/the-world-factbook/geos/ug.html.

[8]Mutiatina, Boniface. 2016. Uganda Healthcare System. *A Presentation at McMaster Health Forum*, McMaster University, May 27.

Table 6.5 Total filled positions by staff in public health institutions

Category	*Norm*	*Filled position*	*Percent filled*
Doctors	1296	936	72
Nurses	19,946	16,584	83
Midwives	6061	4607	76
Clinical officers	2758	2780	101
Laboratory staff	2737	2379	87
Anesthesiologists	725	215	30
Pharmacists	370	31	8
Dispensers	420	232	55
Other allied health staff	1177	820	70
Cold chain technicians	284	115	40
Consultants	305	107	35
General administrative staff	1337	1356	101
Health administrative staff	374	124	33
Support staff	8622	4573	53
Others	6055	3330	55
Total	52,467	38,189	73

Source Ministry of Health. 2015. Healthcare Workers Bi-Annual Report. Kampala: Ministry of Health, Uganda, p. 11

Table 6.6 Health status statistics of Uganda and its East African neighbors, 2015

	Uganda	*Rwanda*	*Tanzania*	*Kenya*
Total population	37,101,745	45,925,301	51,045,882	12,661,733
Median age (year)	15.6	19.3	17.5	18.8
Population growth rate (%)	3.24	1.93	2.79	2.56
Birth rate (per 1000 people)	43.79	26.4	36.39	33.75
Maternal mortality rate (per 100,000 live births)	343	510	398	290
Infant mortality rate (per 1000 live births)	45.0	39.4	42.4	58.2
Life expectancy	54.9	63.8	61.7	59.7
% of health expenditure in GDP	9.8	4.5	7.3	11.1
HIV prevalence (%)	7.3	5.3	5.34	2.82

Source Mutiatina, Boniface. 2016. Uganda Healthcare system. *A Presentation at McMaster Health Forum*, McMaster University, May 27, 2016

communicable diseases. In 2011, the contraceptive prevalence rate was about 30%.

According to the CIA's data,[9] Uganda ranked 58th in the world by the proportion of health spending in GDP in 2014. With regards to the ratio of health workers to the population, in 2015, the ratio of doctors, nurses, dentists, and lab technicians to the population was 1:24,000, 1:11,000, 1:77,000, and 1:16,000, respectively. In 2010, there was one hospital bed per 2000 people in the country. In 2015, the proportion of sanitary toilets was 28.4% in urban areas, and 17.3% in rural areas; 14.1% of children under the age of five were underweight, ranking 51st in the world.

To sum up, against the background of the rapid population growth, Uganda's health management and service system, though structured, faces a lot of challenges. Due to the serious shortage of health workers, brain drain of senior medical professionals, and other factors, communicable diseases cannot be treated effectively; child malnutrition rate, maternal mortality rate, infant mortality rate and total mortality rate are high; and people have a relatively short life expectancy. At the same time, compared to the approximately USD 15 health expenditure per capita (Okwero et al. 2010),[10] the share of total national health expenditure in GDP is disproportionately high.

In short, compared to its rapid population growth and people's needs for healthcare services, Uganda is facing a serious shortage of health resources, especially basic healthcare resources.

6.2 Chinese Medical Professionals Going to Uganda

6.2.1 Situation Faced by China's First Medical Team to Uganda

In 1978, the Chinese government set up an investigative group preceding the Chinese medical teams in order to learn about Uganda's needs for DAH. No data are available as to the composition of the investigative

[9] https://www.cia.gov/library/publications/the-world-factbook/geos/ug_html.

[10] Mutiatina pointed out that Uganda's health expenditure per capita was USD 27, and the number suggested by a consulting agency was USD 44.

group, and the purpose, time, methods, and process of the investigations. Fortunately, the investigative report[11] developed by the group gives us a glimpse of the situation China's first medical team to Uganda was going to face.

When the investigative group was in Uganda, the country was ruled by Idi Amin. As the investigative report states,

> Since he took office more than seven years ago, Amin has been relying on the army to maintain power and suppress the opposition, and taking advantage of Islam and small tribal forces in the region to exclude and attack other religions and ethical groups that make up the majority of the population. Due to Amin's political oppression, economic deterioration, and high prices, people live a hard life. The contradictions between classes, ethnical groups, and religions and within the leadership are intensifying, and people's complaints are heard everywhere, aggravating its political turmoil. To change the situation and stay in power, Amin in 1977 announced a three-year action plan for restoring the national economy to mitigate discontent among the public.
>
> … Amin had fabricated lies against China many times. After September 1972, he expressed willingness to improve relations with China. Recently, Amin has repeatedly praised China for not interfering in the internal affairs of other countries and for supporting the National Liberation Movement. He also expresses thanks for our assistance to Uganda,[12] speaks highly of our expatriates for their frugality and amiableness, and says he is willing to strength friendship and cooperation between China and Uganda.

The report also points out that the common diseases in Uganda are malaria, venereal diseases, measles in children (and pneumonia), trauma, hernia, premature delivery, and tuberculosis.

Before China sent medical teams, Uganda's DAH came mainly from the UN agencies. The World Health Organization (WHO) provided emergency aid and training resources; the United Nations Children's Fund (UNICEF) provided food, vaccines and equipment; and the United Nations Development Programme (UNDP) supported the construction of training schools and technical schools with personnel

[11] Investigative team to Uganda. 1978. *Investigative Report on Health in Uganda*. Kunming: Yunnan Provincial Archives. File No.: 131: 3: 28: 6.

[12] Referring to the Kibimba Farm China helped build from 1973.

training and related facilities and equipment. In addition, the government of Liberia helped Uganda build a hospital with 100 beds and had 20 nurses study in Liberia for six months. No further information is available. Therefore, it can be said that China is one of the first few countries to assist Uganda.

At that time, Uganda's health management system was quite different from it is today. At present, there are only two levels of management (Fig. 6.3), namely, the Ministry of Health and the Regional Healthcare service Headquarter. Back then, there were four levels: the state, provincial, regional, and county (Fig. 6.4). The healthcare system was also different from it is now. Currently, the healthcare system has six levels, extending to the communities; at that time, there were only four levels, and at the lowest level were villages (Table 6.7).

The differences in health resources are even more striking. In 1978, Uganda had a total of 62 hospitals, with about 10,000 beds. The ratio of beds to its population was 1:1200, the ratio of doctors was 1:30,000, and the ratio of nurses was 1:4000. While the country still faces a shortage of health resources today, its health resources were even scarcer at that time, especially doctors.

In addition, medical facilities and equipment were in extreme shortage, as the investigative report points out:

> There are no pharmaceutical and medical equipment companies in Uganda. Drugs are mainly imported from France, Britain, West Germany, Yugoslavia, India, the Soviet Union, Denmark, China, and Switzerland. Medical equipment is mainly imported from Britain, the Netherlands, and West Germany…The types of drugs are limited, and some hospitals are seriously short of drugs. The quantity of medical equipment is also insufficient.

Against this background, the Chinese government designated the government of Yunnan Province (then Yunnan Provincial Revolutionary Committee) to dispatch medical teams to Uganda. After five years of preparation, the health authorities of China and Uganda officially signed an agreement in 1982, agreeing that in the 10 years from 1983 to 1993, China would send five batches of medical teams to Uganda.

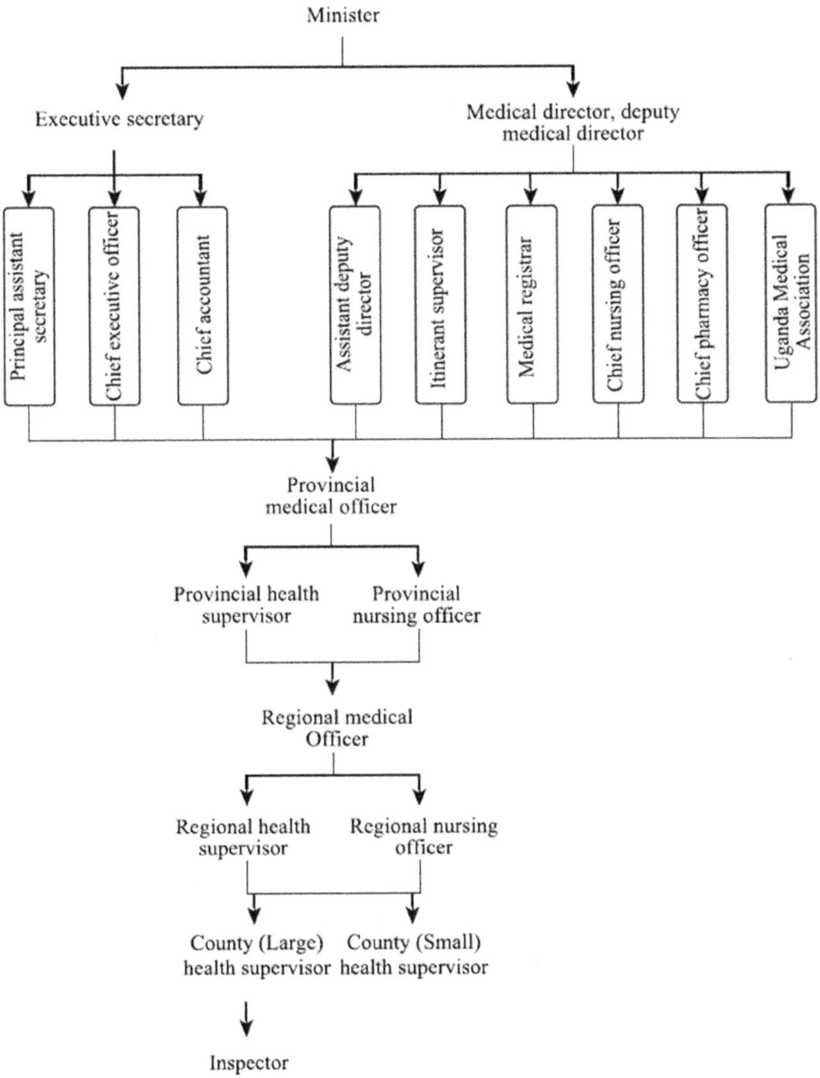

Fig. 6.4 Uganda's health management system, 1978 (*Source* Investigative team to Uganda. 1978. *Investigative Report on Health in Uganda*. Kunming: Yunnan Provincial Archives. File No.: 131: 3: 28: 6)

Table 6.7 Government-funded health facilities in Uganda

		Central hospital (1)	*Provincial hospital (8)*	*Regional hospital (32)*	*Rural hospital (21)*
Beds		1500	150–1000	87–300	100
Outpatients per day		3000	600–1000	300–900	200–300
Staff	Total	4000	450–1050 ±	200–250 ±	150 ±
	Doctors	121	6–36 ±	6–9 ±	2–3 ±
	Physician assistants	46	11–45 ±	6–11 ±	3–6 ±
	Nurses	400	46–150 ±	30–60 ±	40–45 ±
Departments		Internal medicine, surgery, gynecology and obstetrics, pediatrics, ophthalmology, ENT, urology, chest, tuberculosis, stomatology, psychiatry, pharmacy, radiology, physical therapy, laboratory	Internal medicine, surgery, gynecology and obstetrics, tuberculosis, laboratory, pharmacy, radiology	Internal medicine, surgery, gynecology and obstetrics, pediatrics, radiology, stomatology, tuberculosis, pharmacy	Andrology, gynecology, pediatrics, and obstetrics; radiology and pharmacy at clinics
Medical equipment		Two 500 mA X-ray machines with TV; monitors and defibrillated pacemakers in the emergency room; electronic blood cell counters, rapid blood potassium and sodium test instruments, and cardiac catheter examination equipment in the laboratory; well-equipped operating rooms	2–4 X-ray machines (100–200 mA); devices for biochemical testing and bacterial culture in laboratories; only small surgeries can be conducted in operating rooms due to lack of devices	1 or 2 X-ray machines (25–100 mA), large infusion equipment, and old equipment in operating rooms	The same as regional hospitals, with relatively new devices

(continued)

Table 6.7 (continued)

	Central hospital (1)	*Provincial hospital (8)*	*Regional hospital (32)*	*Rural hospital (21)*
Technical level	Capable of X-ray inspection and laboratory tests; equivalent to provincial hospitals in China	Equivalent to local hospitals in China	Equivalent to county-level hospitals in China	Equivalent to commune-level hospitals in China
Notes	Teaching hospital affiliated to Makerere University, and affiliated radiology school	Affiliated nursing and midwifery schools		

Source Investigative team to Uganda. 1978. ***Investigative Report on Health in Uganda***. Kunming: Yunnan Provincial Archives. File No.: 131: 3: 28: 6

6.2.2 "A Useless Move": Dispatch of China's First Medical Team to Uganda

The following is quoted from the *Yunnan Foreign Aid Newsletter*[13] issued by Yunnan Provincial Revolutionary Committee on November 26, 1979.

> The medical team was set up by Yunnan Provincial Health Department in the beginning of the year, and has been approved by the Ministry of Health. It is now on standby to go to Uganda.
>
> The 13-member medical team is composed of 11 doctors from Yunnan Provincial No. 1 People's Hospital, No. 1 Hospital and No. 2 Hospital Affiliated to Kunming Medical Institute, and Affiliated Hospital to Yunnan TCM Hospital, an interpreter selected by Yunnan Foreign Affairs Office, and a cook selected by Xiguan Municipal Department of Commerce. The team is highly competent…11 people hold an associate degree and above, and one graduated from secondary technical school…In terms of medical skills, the team consists of two associate chief physicians (internal medicine and surgery), two senior physicians (ophthalmology and radiology), and seven physicians (testing, stomatology, orthopedics, gynecology and obstetrics, pediatrics, anesthesia, and TCM). They mostly have more than one or two decades of clinical experience.

The medical team was originally scheduled to arrive in Uganda before 1980, but was delayed due to the political turmoil in Uganda. From March to April 1979, more than 20 Tanzania-based political groups overthrew Idi Amin, who then fled after having been in power for nine years. From 1981 to 1985, the political situation was basically stable despite the internal turbulences under the rule of Obote. Against this backdrop, the medical team stood ready. A document[14] released by Yunnan Provincial Health Department on September 16, 1981, states,

> According to the letter on the medical team to Uganda from the Ministry of Health ([81] No. 528) and the regulations by the State Council Foreign Affairs Office ([78] No. 1588), our province set up a medical

[13]Yunnan Provincial Revolutionary Committee. 1979. Medical Team Stands by for Uganda. *Yunnan Foreign Aid Newsletter*, Issue 18. Kunming: Yunnan Provincial Archives.

[14]Political Division of Yunnan Provincial Health Department. 1981. *Letter on the Medical Team to Uganda and Name List of the Medical Team.* Kunming: Yunnan Provincial Archives. File No.: 131: 4794: 30.

> team to assist Uganda in 1979. The team has received off-job foreign language training for eight months, and is now on standby due to the political unrest in Uganda.

On January 18, 1983, ahead of the arrival of the inaugural medical team from China to Uganda, a preparatory team traveled to Kampala, capital of Uganda. Then Chinese ambassador to Uganda Li Shi held a banquet to entertain the minister, vice minister and executive secretary general of Uganda's Ministry of Health and the Chinese medical team. Accompanied by the personnel with the Economic and Commercial Counselor's Office of the Chinese Embassy in Uganda, the medical team paid a visit to the vice minister and executive secretary general of Uganda's Ministry of Health, health commissioner of Jinja, and president of Jinja Hospital.

According to the report submitted by the preparatory team,[15] the government of Uganda held very high expectations of the Chinese medical team, and hoped the team could work in two places. But the preparatory team believed that considering the resources available, the medical team had better work in one place. Moreover, given the poor medical conditions of Jinja Hospital, the Chinese medical team had to bring common and emergency drugs that could be used for one or two months. The following quote from the report describes how poor the working environment is at Jinja Hospital.

> Only three kinds of routine tests can be done in the laboratory...No reagents are available for bacterial culture and biochemical tests...There are two X-ray machines...They lie idle for four years because no one can use them...Contrast agents are insufficient...The pharmacy has a quite limited amount of drugs, and common drugs are in short supply...There are few varieties of drugs on the shelves of the drug storehouse, which are basically empty...
>
> In the operating rooms, there are two...and no surgical drapes. They badly lack small surgical towels, large surgical towels, and surgical gowns.
>
> There are two ambulances, one unusable due to the lack of wheels...

Two months after the preparatory team arrived, the first Chinese medical team got to Jinja Hospital in Uganda's second-largest city of Jinja.

[15] Advance group of medical team to Uganda. 1983. *Report on the Situation*. Kunming: Yunnan Provincial Archives. File No.: 131: 16: 439: 35.

It is the first time China has sent a medical team to Uganda 20 years after it set up its first medical team in 1963 and sent it to Algeria on the request of its government 20 years ago. Despite the political turmoil in Uganda, China responded to the country's needs for DAH by sending the medical team without any other purpose, which seemed "a useless move" in China's diplomacy and foreign aid.

6.2.3 *"A Sincere Heart": Practice of China's First Medical Team to Uganda*

Before the dispatch of the medical team, China only helped Uganda to build the Kibimba Farm. The construction was started in 1973 shortly after Amin took power, and was completed in 1977, when Amin remained in power. In 1978, when the Chinese government sent an investigative group to learn about Uganda's DAH needs, Amin's regime was still stable.

The situation became quite different when China handed over the Kibimba Farm to Uganda in 1982, and sent the first medical team in 1983. At that time, Obote, the first Ugandan head of government China recognized, resumed power. Later, the three regime changes from Obote to Museveni testified China's sincerity—China did not abandon its "useless move" in Uganda. Up to now, China has sent 17 batches of medical teams to Uganda, one batch every two years. During the past more than 30 years, the medical teams had stayed at Jinja Hospital for 30 years.

To help readers understand the Chinese medical teams' aid to Uganda, the following is an introduction to the town of Jinja and Jinja Hospital.

According to the present administrative divisions, Jinja is in Jinja District in the Eastern Region of Uganda. Its population grew from 289,500 in 1991 to 501,300 in 2012, with a population density of 745 persons per km^2. Jinja District covers an area of 673 km^2 (equivalent to half of Changping District in Beijing), and the headquarters is Buwenge. The district is highly reliant on agriculture. The food crops include beans, peanuts, sorghum, millet, cassava, potatoes, and cash crops include coffee and cotton.

Jinja is also the second largest city of Uganda, approximately 80 km from Kampala, the capital of Uganda, and its urban area covers about 81 km^2. It had a population of 71,213 in 2002, and increased slightly to 72,931 in 2014. The majority of the population is Bantu, and speaks

Lusoga. There are 15 universities and colleges in Jinja, including the Eastern Campus of Makerere University, Jinja Campus of Busoga University, Jinja Campus of Kampala University, and Nsaka University.

Jinja Hospital, whose full name is Jinja Regional Referral Hospital, was established in 1926. With 600 beds, it is one of the 14 regional hospitals in Uganda, one of the three largest regional hospitals in the Eastern Region, and one of the 16 teaching hospitals in Uganda. Its 20-bed ICU was built in 2009 with funds from the government of the United States, Uganda, and Jinja.

When China's first medical team arrived at Jinja Hospital in 1983, Jinja Hospital was quite different from it is today. The medical team wrote in a summary,[16]

> (Jinja hospital) is one of the three teaching hospitals in Uganda. There are 400 beds and nearly 1000 staff members (including about 200 teachers and students of the affiliated nursing and midwifery school)...Its clinical departments include internal medicine, surgery, obstetrics and gynecology, pediatrics, ophthalmology, stomatology, and others. There are two consultant physicians (equivalent to chief physicians in China) in surgery... one consultant physician in internal medicine, and one in obstetrics and gynecology...There are not enough reagents and equipment for tests, most of the devices are damaged and cannot be updated...As to technical levels, the hospital on the whole is equivalent to a general county-level hospital in China.
>
> Due to years of war and other reasons, the hospital is dilapidated and poorly equipped, and lacks medicines and other materials, and there are only empty bedsteads in wards. When the team arrived, not a single thermometer could be found in the whole hospital, and there were only two or three blood pressure meters. Patients were only cleaned with cold boiled water before their operation. There were no disinfectant towels or surgical gowns in operating rooms. Without aspirators, blood could surge out during operations, with flies buzzing around...

As can be seen from the file, in the first half of the 1980s, Jinja Hospital, as a teaching hospital, had a very high position in Uganda's healthcare system, but its medical conditions were terrible, reflecting the serious shortage of health resources in Uganda at that time.

[16]Chinese medical teams to Uganda. 1985. *Work Summary of First Chinese Medical Team to Uganda*. Kunming: Yunnan Provincial Archives. File No.: 131: 3: 377: 1.

In addition to the harsh environment, the team members were also faced with distrust and doubt from the staff of Jinja Hospital. It was not because their peers were narrow-minded or because they used to work with doctors from Britain, Italy, the Netherlands, India, the Soviet Union, Bangladesh, South Korea, and other countries before the arrival of the Chinese medical team; but it was because they really knew little about China. The medical team described what they observed in the summary,

> Uganda was deeply influenced by the West. At the beginning, local staff had reservations about the Chinese medical team. Because of local bias against women, a Ugandan doctor even asked me if I, an obstetrician, could perform operations. Upon hearing this, everyone got angry and anxious: angry that they knew so little about us, and anxious about how to carry out our work (especially surgery) under such conditions.

Still, the medical team put saving people first, and successfully operated on a patient with uterine rupture, removing all distrust in the obstetrician. The medical team members did all they could to help. They were not only doctors, but also worked as carpenters, mechanics, electricians, and so on. They also asked other teams from China to give a hand.

> They refitted surgical footstools with packing boxes and asked other experts from China to help repair exhaust fans and operating beds in operating rooms, install the doors of the drug storehouse, and repair other devices. The radiographer repaired X-ray machines.
>
> … On the Christmas Eve of 1984, two traffic accidents happened in Jinja, causing more than 20 deaths and injuries. Those injured were sent to the hospital. Chinese doctors came with drugs and medical equipment as soon as possible.

At that time, their Ugandan colleagues were on holiday!

In addition to their dedication, Chinese doctors also stood out with their expertise. For example, urinary fistula repair surgeries were once canceled at the National Referral Hospitals because of the less-than-expected effects; to meet the urgent needs of Ugandan patients, the gynecologist and surgeon of the medical team worked together to perform such surgeries, and their surgical skills won high acclaim. As a result, patients from all corners of the country went to Chinese doctors for help.

The medical team knew well that the cooperation with the Ugandan side was of vital importance.

> Cooperation with the Ugandan side holds key to success in our work. We are here for friendship.

It can be seen that the Chinese government offered aid to Uganda sincerely by sending the first batch of medical teams, and the medical team members kept in mind that their mission was to convey such sincerity to Uganda with their medical ethics and skills. For them, abilities and skills are not a stepping stone to higher social status or greater wealth, but a bridge to solidify friendships. The Ugandan side felt China's sincerity. The president of Jinja Hospital is quoted in the summary, "At the most difficult moment when Uganda is struggling to revitalize the economy, you Chinese doctors are here to help us. This is true friendship. The Chinese medical team is most cooperative in all aspects."

In the summary, the medical team comes up with recommendations on how to better strengthen the friendship between China and other countries.

> Medical teams should be set up according to the specific situations of the recipient countries or regions, to strengthen the areas of weakness or fill up the gap.

Chinese medical teams are precisely set up to meet the needs of the recipients. Perhaps this is why medical teams have become a symbol of DAHCU, and the embodiment of China's sincerity in foreign aid.

6.2.4 *A Mission: Dedication of the Chinese Medical Team Under War and AIDS Threat*

The most worrying thing was not the poor medical conditions, but the political turmoil in Uganda. In July 1985, the handover to the second batch of Chinese medical teams coincided with Uganda's political turbulence. Milton Obote was overthrown, different factions within the military fought for power, and Yoweri Museveni led the National Resistance Army to wage a guerrilla war. It is no exaggeration that the second batch of Chinese medical teams worked in Uganda defying a rain of bullets. The following is an example.[17]

[17] Chinese medical teams to Uganda. 1986. *Update on the Chinese Medical Teams to Uganda in Wartime (January 13–29, 1986)*. Kunming: Yunnan Provincial Archives. File No.: 131: 3: 393: 1.

> On January 23, the medical team went to the hospital as usual, only to find that there were few patients and almost all Ugandan staff members of the hospital were absent...The situation in Jinja was tense, with gunshots from time to time. However, the medical team held on until they finished the emergency caesarean section (pelvic stenosis, dystocia) and mandible fracture traction more than two hours later than they were supposed to leave. On that afternoon, almost only Chinese physicians performed operations. The members of the medical team also checked out the wards and treated the patients.
>
> Since the evening of January 24, Jinja had been under intensive gunfire for two days. The artillery thundered amid gunshots day and night... We moved the patients to safe places. We also prepared for emergencies so that we would not panic even some soldiers broke in. On the night when gunfire was most intense, we took turns on night shifts in case something went wrong.
>
> Within the six months in Uganda, the medical team has witnessed two coups. Already aware of the risk of working abroad in complicated situations, we kept calm even in wartime... And whenever it was possible, we overcame difficulties to provide any medical assistance.

During the civil war, local Ugandan medical staff hardly dared to come to work. They even told the medical team not to come because it was too dangerous.[18] But Chinese doctors remained at their posts. During that period, there were almost only Chinese doctors working at Jinja Hospital.

Although the political situation stabilized after Museveni came to power, price hikes made life difficult for the people, and the morale of Ugandan medical staff was affected. In this situation, the Chinese medical team stayed committed to its duties. From January to May 1986, the medical team served 9998 outpatients and 1408 inpatients, performed 179 operations, and rescued 83 emergency patients, or an average of 56 outpatients, eight inpatients, one operation, and 0.5 emergency patient per day.[19] During the two years in Uganda, the second batch of medical teams received 58,662 patients and performed 778 major operations.

[18] Yunnan Provincial Health Department. 1987. *Chinese Medical Teams in Uganda—Materials for the Selection of Outstanding Members of the Second Batch of Medical Teams.* Kunming: Yunnan Provincial Archives. File No.: 131: 3: 416: 1.

[19] Chinese medical teams to Uganda. 1986. *Job Briefing of the Chinese Medical Teams to Uganda for Q2 of 1986.* Kunming: Yunnan Provincial Archives. File No.: 131: 3: 394: 15.

With the end of the war came another threat—AIDS. Uganda has been one of the world's top five countries in terms of HIV infection rate. As shown in Table 6.6, the prevalence rate of AIDS in Uganda is as high as 7.3% even today, much higher than in other East African countries. 20 years ago, China still had very limited knowledge of the disease. In the face of HIV/AIDS threat and with China's imposition of an entry ban on people with HIV/AIDS, it was natural that the members of the medical team felt fear, especially after Tian Xinghua, an otolaryngologist, got a 4–5-cm cut on his left palm by a puncture needle when performing a surgery on an AIDS patient.[20] In a letter to China's Ministry of Health in 1988,[21] Li Ming, leader of the third-batch medical team, wrote,

> Since August 1987, our team has tested 300 inpatients and outpatients, and 192 (64%) of them were positive… The occupational HIV risk among medical staff is quite high. In the gynecology and obstetrics department of Munogo Hospital in Kampala, seven staff members were infected. At Jinja Hospital, two have died of AIDS since July last year, and another three are critically ill, including one at the gynecology and obstetrics department, the head nurse of the ophthalmology department, and a nurse of internal medicine). It is unknown whether there are more cases. Currently, Jinja Hospital is short of peracetic acid and gloves. The outpatient department and the inpatient department are not separated, and there are no isolation measures. It is not rare for doctors to get their hands stabbed or cut during operations, so there is much chance of infection.
>
> We came to know via China National Radio that China has prohibited people with HIV from entering the territory. For the safety of the team members, we hereby outline the questions for your consideration.
>
> (1) Could special funds be allocated to Yunnan Provincial Health Department to ensure sufficient supply of disinfectants, latex gloves and film-type disposable gloves, as well as vaccines, sulfamethoxazole, nystatin, cyclosporine, etc.?
>
> (2) If any team member is infected with HIV, will they be allowed to return to China? If yes, how will they be isolated and treated? Can they get together with their family? Is it likely that they will be isolated in remote, desolate areas like lepers?

[20] Investigative group of the Ministry of Health to Uganda. 1991. *Investigative Report of the Ministry of Health on Uganda*. Kunming: Yunnan Provincial Archives. File No.: 131: 3: 590: 11.

[21] Chinese medical teams to Uganda. 1988. *Report of the Chinese Medical Teams to Uganda on the First Serious Case Under AIDS Threat*. Kunming: Yunnan Provincial Archives. File No.: 131: 3: 436: 28.

(3) Could any health insurance against occupational HIV affection be provided for the medical team?

(4) Will a team member infected with HIV be advised or forced to emigrate to Uganda?

(5) If their family member is also infected and thus unable to work, how to support their young children and the elderly?

(6) If a country with a high prevalence rate of AIDS fails to take isolation measures despite repeated suggestions, will China bring back the medical team to that country?

During the two years in Uganda, this medical team, despite their fear of AIDS, received more than 60,000 patients, performed 1766 operations, rescued 521 emergency patients, treated 13,807 patients with acupuncture and moxibustion, carried out 338 new operations, and treatments of 38 types, including partial replantation of palms and thumbs, and treated 30 rare and special cases of 20 types. On average, the team served 83 patients, performed 2.5 operations, and treated 20 patients with acupuncture every day. It is found that a doctor at Jinja Hospital who serves 10 patients a day is "super busy." Based on this criterion, the members of the medical team were "super busy" almost every day.

Soon the Chinese medical teams overcame their fear of AIDS, and began to explore new ways to treat AIDS together with local doctors. For example, Wu Yunchao, a doctor of internal medicine in the fourth batch, worked at the specialist clinic every week, and treated 1257 AIDS patients during the two years in Uganda.[22] The fifth batch, entrusted by the president of Jinja Hospital, treated 98 patients using garlic therapy, with an effective rate of 68%. This had an influence beyond Uganda. The medical team received visits and phone calls from Kenya and Hong Kong, and got close attention from the American Dehydrated Onion & Garlic Association. *New Vision*, Uganda's state newspaper, also made a special report.

6.2.5 *"A Silver Needle": 30-Plus Years in Uganda*

DAHCU, originally planned for 10 years, has by now lasted for more than 30 years. The best representative of the 30-plus years of medical service is acupuncture. Starting with acupuncturist Zhou Youmin of

[22] Chinese medical teams to Uganda. 1991. *Making Friends with Uganda—Yunnan Provincial People's Hospital on the Fourth Batch of Chinese Medical Teams to Uganda*. Kunming: Yunnan Provincial Archives. File No.: 131: 3: 509: 19.

the first batch, acupuncturists are almost "a standard component" of the Chinese medical teams to Uganda. The following is quoted from a report of the second batch.[23]

> The acupuncturist is busy with body acupuncture, auricular acupuncture, massage and other treatments for five or six hours a day. A lot of chronic patients suffering from low back and leg pain, limb numbness, paralysis, asthma, and intractable hiccups, come to ask the team for help. Among them is the director general of Uganda's Ministry of Agriculture. He had to use a walking stick due to traumatic low back pain in the previous three years, and has recovered just after one course of acupuncture.
>
> ... There are senior officials and ordinary people who come for acupuncture...A patient who suffered from a lumbar fracture and was unable to move writes in his letter to the medical team,"... I was brought to the hospital on a bicycle. Thanks to your careful treatment and help, I can now ride a bicycle myself.

On September 25, 1986, a Ugandan TV station conducted an interview on acupuncture. The president of Jinja Hospital proposed several times to establish an acupuncture center in Uganda. Noting that Europe and the United States were learning and studying the traditional technique of acupuncture, Uganda's Ministry of Health hoped Chinese acupuncturists could pass on the skills to benefit Ugandan people.

When the investigative group of China's Ministry of Health visited Uganda in 1991, the Ugandan side even hoped that the Chinese government could send acupuncturist proficient in foreign languages to teach and train Uganda medical staff in Kampala.[24] We find that among the numerous cases of DAH from China to Africa, one of the most popular services is acupuncture.[25] For many Ugandan people, acupuncture may be the final option. Once effective, it will undoubtedly bring them great joy. Acupuncture is therefore considered a magic.

[23]Yunnan Provincial Health Department. 1987. *Chinese Medical Teams in Uganda—Materials for the Selection of Outstanding Members of the Second Batch of Medical Teams.* Kunming: Yunnan Provincial Archives. File No.: 131: 3: 416: 1.

[24]Investigative group of the Ministry of Health to Uganda. 1991. *Investigative Report of the Ministry of Health on Uganda.* Kunming: Yunnan Provincial Archives. File No.: 131: 3: 590: 11.

[25]In the ethnography titled "Hosts and Guests: Jinja Hospital and Chinese Medical Teams", there is a section depicting the process and stories about how acupuncture was included into Uganda's healthcare system.

Soon after, acupuncture took root at Jinja Hospital. The acupuncture department was set up, and the hospital arranged for its staff to learn the procedures. Over the more than 30 years, the service of Chinese medical teams might have made some departments at the hospital redundant, but the acupuncture department has been among those having been operating continually. It is no surprise that every batch of medical teams has left legendary stories about acupuncture.

Although the Chinese medical teams left Jinja Hospital in 2012, the acupuncture department is still in operation, and is one of the most popular departments. In 2014 and 2015, we visited Jinja Hospital, and found that the acupuncture department already had no Chinese doctors, and it is local nurses and medical assistants that carried out acupuncture. We leafed through the treatment records, and saw that there were at least 20 patients a day.

In DAHCU, the medical teams are like a silver needle, inserted into the "acupuncture point" of cooperation between China and Uganda. "I think what we have benefited most is that acupuncture, a technique of traditional Chinese medicine, has become part of Jinja Hospital. And the hospital is known for the Chinese medical teams and the acupuncture department. The medical teams also taught some locals to give acupuncture treatment. It can be said that acupuncture is a name card for the Chinese medical teams,"[26] said Chrisine Ondoa, former president of Jinja Hospital and Uganda's Minister of Health.

What's more, for the hospital, which had a high turnover of local medical staff and much to improve, the Chinese medical teams had filled up the gap in many aspects, and every batch of the medical teams had brought about new changes to the hospital.

6.3 China-Uganda Friendship Hospital

Another milestone in DAHCU is the establishment of China-Uganda Friendship Hospital.

Based on full communication and consultation with the Ugandan government, China invested about USD 8 million, along with some USD 2.5 million from Uganda, to set up China-Uganda Friendship

[26] Interview with Christine Ondoa, Director General, Uganda Aids Commission, at 8:15 a.m., August 26, 2015. Interviewer: Rehema Bavuma.

Hospital in Nagum, Kampala. The construction was started in December 2009, and completed in November 2011. On January 7, 2012, Chinese Ambassador to Uganda Zhao Yali, on behalf of the Chinese Government, and Uganda's Minister of Health Christine Ondoa, on behalf of the Ugandan Government, signed the handover certificate. The handover ceremony was covered by a number of Ugandan TV stations such as NTV and newspapers such as *New Vision*.

China-Uganda Friendship Hospital is a large regional general hospital, covering an area of 17,993 m^2. It consists of eight buildings, including the two-story emergency and outpatient building (on the first floor are the outpatient hall, registration and payment room, pharmacy and emergency, surgery, and pediatrics clinics; and on the second floor are internal medicine clinic, malaria prevention and control center, and gynecology, obstetrics, and stomatology clinics); the two-story medical technology building (the first floor includes the laboratory, pathology, functional examination and radiology rooms, and central supply room; the second floor includes the surgery department and administrative office); the two-story inpatient building (each floor has two nursing units; on the first floor are internal medicine and pediatric wards, and on the second floor are surgery, gynecology and obstetrics wards, and ICU), as well as the logistic support building, youth activity center, morgue, and gatehouse.

The hospital, with a style of Ugandan architecture, features a patient-friendly design. The rotary stairs are convenient for patients to go up and down, and especially for stretchers and trolleys in the case of power failure. There are corridors connecting different buildings. In the buildings are standard and neat rooms, such as the internal medicine, surgery, gynecological and pediatric clinics, operating rooms, outpatient clinics, wards, and treatment rooms. Compared with the poorly equipped Jinja Hospital, China-Uganda Friendship Hospital can remind one of a top hospital in China.

The hospital has a designed capacity of 100 beds (including emergency beds). It now has a medical staff of 245, including 10 local doctors. The medical equipment provided by the Chinese government mainly include mobile X-ray machines, automatic biochemical analyzers, CT machines, ultrasound diagnostic devices (desktop), electrocardiograph, anesthesia machines, electric operating tables, and multi-functional anesthesia monitors. But it is a regret that the important lighted signs inside the hospital and the medical equipment and equipment imported from China are only in Chinese.

Uganda's Ministry of Health regards China-Uganda Friendship Hospital as an important part of Uganda's healthcare service provision, hoping that the hospital, together with Mulago National Referral Hospital, can help give the capital city's three million people better access to healthcare service.

In the field survey in 2014, we conducted an in-depth interview with the president of the hospital,[27] an orthopedist with several decades of working experience at Mulago National Referral Hospital. In Uganda, high-level medical staff is still in short supply, with nearly half of the doctors from China. Moreover, medical equipment fell short of what was needed. Almost all equipment of China-Uganda Friendship Hospital is imported from China. Therefore, "China" is a key word in the president's work.

When asked "What would happen if Chinese doctors were away," the president replied,

> We would encounter many difficulties, especially in terms of equipment supply. Our equipment comes from China.
>
> We want to have more equipment, which makes us more competitive than our peers. Our laboratory, X-ray rooms and operating rooms all have very good equipment. We hope to get more equipment to increase our competitive edge.

The subtext of what the president talked about is "Chinese doctors." In the process of hospital management, the president often asks the Chinese medical teams for advice.

On the part of the Chinese government, the establishment of China-Uganda Friendship Hospital is a milestone in the development aid for health from China to Uganda. It not only pools together health aid resources from China for the purpose of pursuing a single project, but it also constitutes a solid demonstration of what DAHCU is and can do, thereby improving it DAHCU with respect to the

[27] Interview with Dr. E. K. Naddumba, president of China-Uganda Friendship Hospital, on July 22, 2014. Place: China-Uganda Friendship Hospital; interviewers: Qiu Zeqi, Zhang Tuohong, Xie Zheng, Ma Yumin, and Zhang Huaxin.

delivery of aid. An official with the Chinese Embassy in Uganda pointed out,[28]

> The first thing we considered is to bring into play the combined effect. We pulled together all drugs and medical equipment available. The medical team planned to come here, but the conditions (in the capital) did not permit. Then the hospital was established, with good hardware, but it still lacked experienced medical staff. After the medical team came, the hospital now has sound hardware and software. The medical team also can play a better role here. Second, compared to the capital, Jinja is a small town after all. It covers a smaller population, and has less impact. If the hospital is based in the capital, patients across the country will come.

As a milestone in DAHCU, China-Uganda Friendship Hospital has drawn high attention from the governments of the two countries. Its completion ceremony was attended by Zhao Yali, Chinese Ambassador to Uganda, Zou Xiaoming, Counselor of the Economic and Commercial Counselor's Office of Chinese Embassy in Uganda, representatives of the Chinese medical team to Uganda, Christine Ondoa, Uganda's Minister of Health, Dr. Luwago Asuman, Executive Secretary of Uganda's Ministry of Health, Erias Lukwago, Mayor of Kampala, and Dr. Edward Naddumba, the inaugural president of the hospital. After the hospital came into operation, Han Qide, special envoy of Chinese President Hu Jintao and Vice Chairman of the Standing Committee of the National People's Congress, paid a visit to the hospital when he was in Uganda to attend the celebrations for the 50th anniversary of Uganda's independence. Ugandan Vice President Edward Ssekaudi and Minister of State Vincent Nyanzi also inspected the hospital. On the hospital's first anniversary, Dr. Lukwago Asuman, Executive Secretary of Uganda's Ministry of Health, and Dr. Amandua Jacinto, director of the Department of Clinical Medicine, attended the ceremony.

In field surveys, we found that China-Uganda Friendship Hospital had developed rapidly, with about 1000 visits per day in 2014.

Before the establishment of China-Uganda Friendship Hospital, China tentatively provided USD 400,000 to help build the Malaria

[28] Interview with Ouyang Daobing, counselor of Economic and Commercial Counselor's Office of Chinese Embassy in Uganda, at 10:00 a.m., August 4, 2015. Place: Economic and Commercial Counselor's Office; interviewers: Qiu Zeqi, Ma Yumin, and Zhuang Yu. Dai Zheng, head of the 16th batch of Chinese medical teams to Uganda, was also present.

Consortium at Mulago National Referral Hospital, in an effort to help Uganda fight malaria. Regrettably, the Malaria Consortium didn't live up to expectations. The Chinese government even considered relocating the Malaria Consortium to China-Uganda Friendship Hospital.

6.4 Data from Other Sources

As the Chinese government has not released detailed data on foreign aid, we try to collect data on DAHCU from other sources in addition to data on the cases.

First, we obtain and sort out relevant information from China. AidData.org,[29] a website that warehouses datasets on information about China's foreign aid.[30]

Second, we collect information about China's aid to Africa from the Chinese media, and then process the information.

The following is mainly based on data from the two sources.

To create a basic landscape of China's foreign aid, we use the visual tools on China.AidData.org to illustrate the general situation of China's foreign aid and China's DAH to Africa. Figure 6.5 shows the distribution of 2762 foreign aid programs among 5044 geographical locations. Clearly, most of China's foreign aid in 2000-2015 went to the African continent.

By extrapolating from the layout of China's foreign aid we were then able to arrive at an overall picture of China's DAH to Africa. Figure 6.6 shows the 348 DAH programs distributed among 628 geographical locations. These programs fall within three broad categories: health, population policies/programs and reproductive health, and water supply and sanitation, and most of them are in the African continent.

It should be noted that programs marked on the map only include geocoded programs, excluding those without geographic information. We looked up relevant data in the database on China.AidData.org.

According to the database, from 2000 to 2015, the total number of China's foreign aid programs was 12,197, of which there were 7113 official aid programs, and 6032 included in the dataset; data

[29] The accuracy of the data released on the website is to be verified. We refer to the site only in order to present a rough overall picture of China's foreign aid.

[30] [According to its website, China.AidData.org is a research lab at William & Mary, which is an American university in Williamsburg, VA.—Trans.].

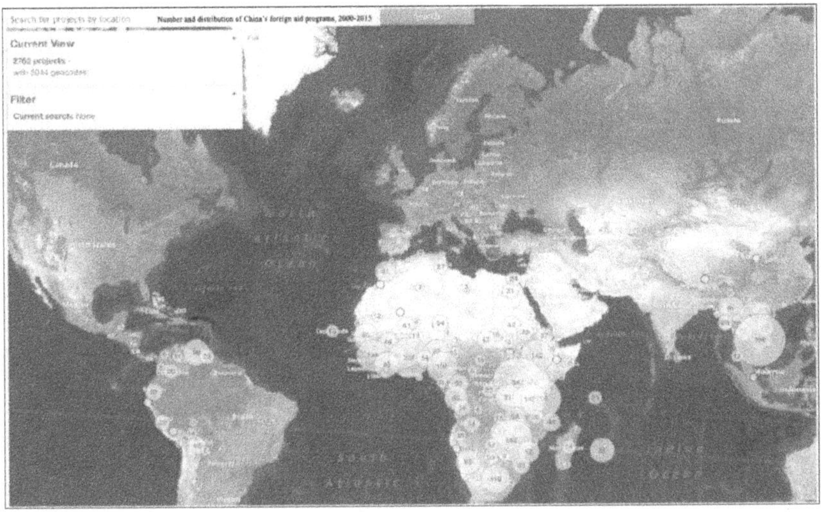

Fig. 6.5 Number and distribution of China's foreign aid programs, 2000–2015 (*Note* The number of programs marked on the map only includes those in the countries shown there. *Source* http://china.aiddata.org/geospatial_dashboard, retrieved on September 8, 2016)

on funds of only 2953 programs were available, which totaled USD 604,689,287,464.

Among the official aid programs, 1061 were DAH programs and 877 included in the dataset; data on funds of 285 programs were available, totaling USD 6,919,292,441. Due to the massive data and lack of regional sub-category information in the dataset, we were unable to sort out specific data on China's aid and DAH to Africa. If calculated based on the above data, DAH funds accounted for just 1.2% of total foreign aid funds.

To make up for the deficiency, we gathered data from Chinese publications, but they generally contained no information on program-related aid expenditure. So we had to sort out data on "foreign aid cases." From 2000 to 2014, there were 1690 cases of China's aid to Africa, covering agriculture, education, sports, health, economy, construction and maintenance, donations and other fields. Among them, 304 cases were DAH to Africa, accounting for 18%.

It must be noted that data from the two sources are incomplete. In particular, there are many missing values in the record of program funds.

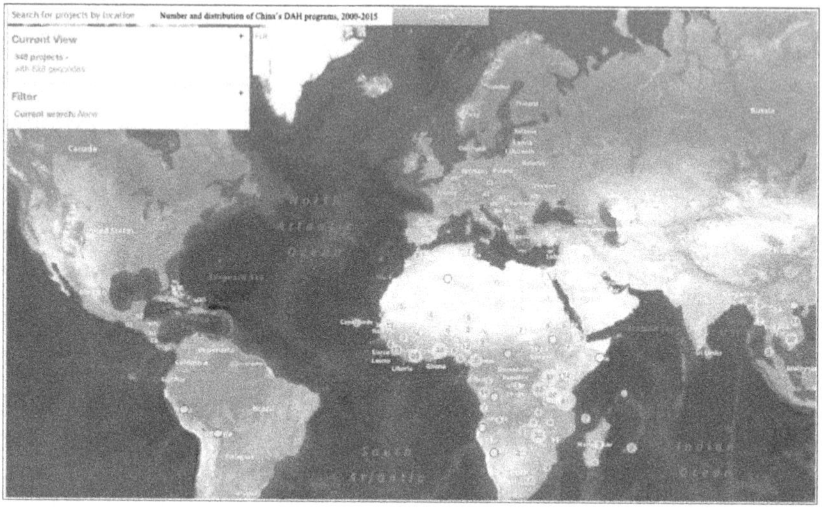

Fig. 6.6 Number and distribution of China's DAH programs, 2000–2015 (*Note* The number of programs marked on the map only includes those in the countries shown there. *Source* http://china.aiddata.org/geospatial_dashboard, retrieved on September 8, 2016)

Funding data are available for only 40% of foreign aid programs, and 27% of DAH programs. Nevertheless, something is better than nothing. At least they allow us to get the big picture. For example, since 2000, China has spent at least USD 604.7 billion in foreign aid, of which at least USD 6.9 billion is used for DAH, mainly in Africa.

There were 51 cases of China's aid to Uganda, accounting for 3.0% of its aid to Africa. In addition to the seven batches of Chinese medical teams to Uganda, there were 18 other cases of DAHCU, accounting for 8.2% of China's DAH to Africa and 49% of China's aid to Uganda. It can be seen that while China's aid and DAH to Uganda made up a small part of its aid to Africa, DAH accounted for a high proportion of China's aid to Uganda.

The 18 other cases of DAHCU basically include the provision of anti-malarial drugs, provision of training, support for the construction of the Malaria Consortium and its devices and equipment, and assistance with the establishment of China-Ugandan Friendship Hospital and support for its devices and equipment.

According to China.AidData.org, from 2000 to 2015, China carried out 102 aid programs in Uganda, and there were data for 98 of them;

funding data were available for 54 programs, which totaled USD 963,251,028; there were visualized data for 90 programs distributed in 188 locations (Fig. 6.7). Of the 102 aid programs for Uganda, 32 were DAH programs, and 31 were included in the dataset; funding data were available for only 14 programs, which totaled USD 143,532,837; DAH accounted for 14.8% of total aid; and the programs were geographically dispersed (Fig. 6.8).

Further analysis on the 31 DAH programs included in the dataset shows that in addition to sending medical teams, China's aid to Uganda

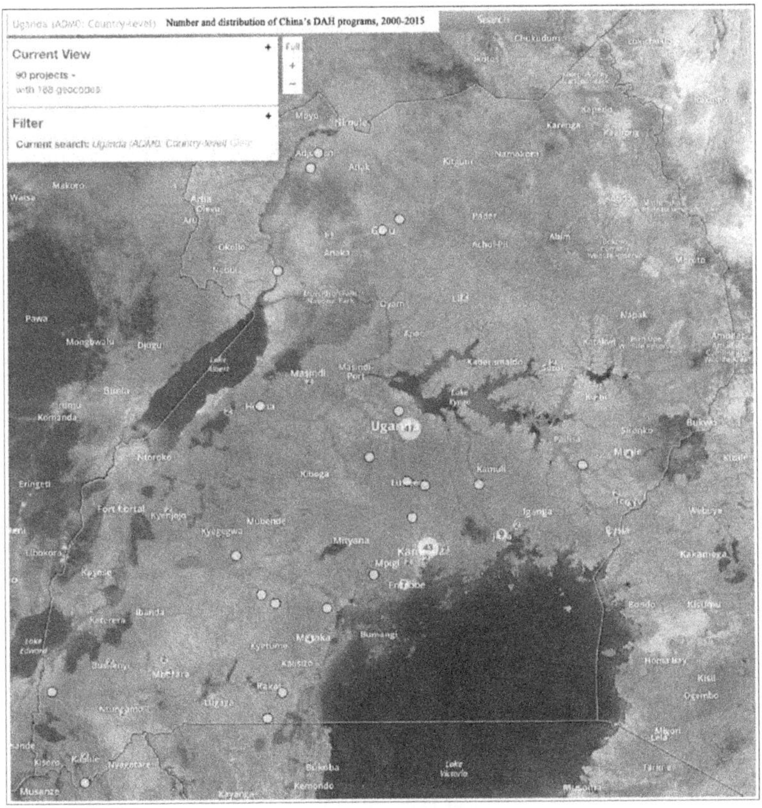

Fig. 6.7 Number and distribution of China's aid and DAH programs in Uganda, 2000–2015 (*Note* The number of programs marked on the map only includes those in the countries shown there. *Source* http://china.aiddata.org/geospatial_dashboard, retrieved on September 8, 2016)

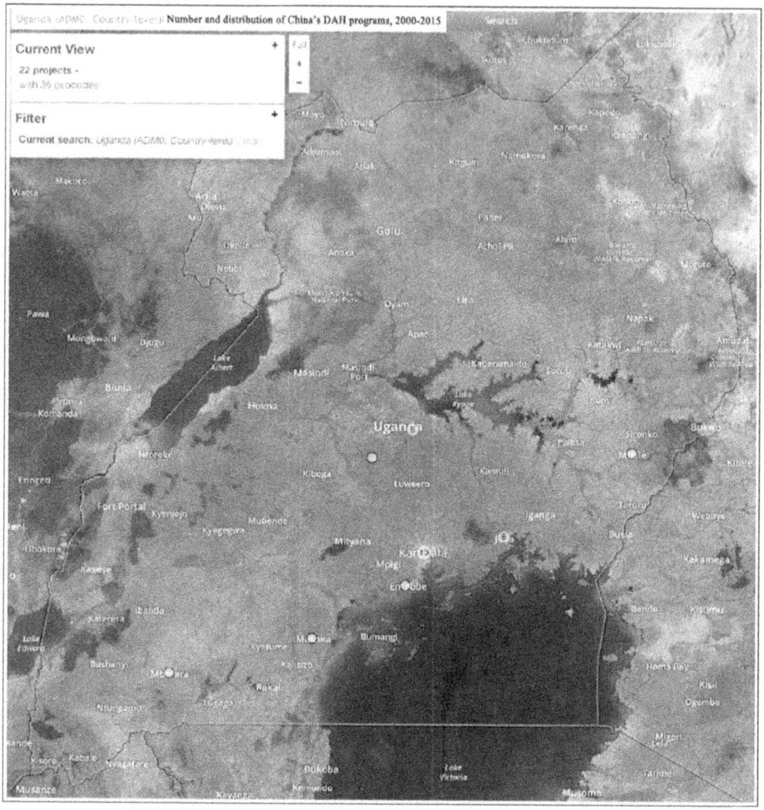

Fig. 6.8 Number and distribution of DAHCU programs, 2000–2015 (*Note* The number of programs marked on the map only includes those in the countries shown there. *Source* http://china.aiddata.org/geospatial_dashboard, retrieved on September 8, 2016)

included providing antimalarial drugs, helping fight Ebola viruses, providing training, helping build the Malaria Consortium and China-Ugandan Friendship Hospital and providing devices and equipment, as well as donating medical computers, devices used for AIDS prevention and control, and devices for reproductive health.

To sum up, other types of aid in DAHCU except the dispatch of medical teams fall within the categories as we observed in field surveys, that is, assisting in the establishment of hospitals and malaria facilities, donating drugs and medical equipment, and providing training. Among these types of aid, Chinese medicines always go hand in hand with Chinese medical teams, and the provision of drugs against malaria and AIDS has been an extended aid in recent years, especially since the Forum on China–Africa Cooperation; China-Uganda Friendship Hospital, though put into operation not long ago, has produced good results.

References

Ministry of Health. 2015. *Healthcare Workers Bi-Annual Report.* Kampala: Ministey of Health.

Okwero, Peter, Ajay Tandon, Susan Sparkes, Julie McLaughlin, and Johannes G. Hoogeveen. 2010. *Fiscal Space for Health in Uganda*, vol. 186. Washington, DC: The World Bank.

Puetz, Detlev. 2006. *Uganda Joint Assistance Strategy: A Review of the Harmonization Process in Five Countries.* Abidjan: African Development Bank Group.

Sekidde, Serufusa. 2013. A Record of Aid to Uganda. *China Healthcare Workforce* (10): 33–34.

Uganda, African Development Bank, Australia, Germany, The Netherlands, Norway, Sweden, United Kingdom and The World Bank. 2005. *The Uganda Joint Assistance Strategy.* Kampala.

Uganda Bureau of Statistics. 2016. *The National Population and Housing Census 2014—Main Report.* Kampala, Uganda.

United Nations. 2016. *African Statistical Yearbook 2016.* Scanprint, Denmark.

Zhou, D. 1956. Uganda. *World Knowledge* 10: 23.

Zhu, Shan. 1959. Uganda. *World Knowledge* 14: 18–19.

CHAPTER 7

Effectiveness of the Development Aid for Health from China to Uganda

In 1983, China sent the first medical teams to Uganda, marking the beginning of development aid for health from China to Uganda (DAHCU). Between then and the beginning of the twenty-first century, DAHCU was carried out primarily in two ways, i.e., Chinese medical team, going to Uganda and Chinese government donating medicines and medical equipment to the country. The medical teams did provide service in cases of medical emergencies, but only occasionally. China did not begin to help Uganda build hospitals and malaria facilities until at most a decade ago. This chapter focuses more on the medical teams than the other two forms of aid mainly because more time is still needed to ascertain the effects of the latter.

7.1 China's Aid to Africa Against the Backdrop of Changing Landscape of International Aid

Moyo's statement about China's influence in Africa since 2000 seems to only touch on the actual influence in African settings. Perhaps data can speak more.

According to the World Bank, a total of USD 2852.4 billion in international aid has been provided since 1960, of which USD 835.4 billion has been delivered to countries across sub-Saharan Africa, and as much as USD 30.6 billion to Uganda. Since 2000, the total amount of international aid has reached USD 1647.4 billion, of which about USD 523.7

Z. Qiu, *When Friendship Comes First*, China and Globalization 2.0,
https://doi.org/10.1007/978-981-32-9308-3_7

billion has gone to sub-Saharan Africa, and USD 20.8 billion to Uganda. International aid offered since 2000 accounts for 58% of total aid since 1960, and aid to sub-Saharan Africa since 2000 accounts for 62.7% of total aid to the region since 1960. This implies that a majority of the increase in aid since 2000 has been directed toward sub-Saharan African countries; for Uganda, the ratio is 68%, the highest among sub-Saharan African countries. It can be concluded that since 2000, a higher proportion of international aid has been channeled to low-income countries in Africa and sub-Saharan Africa.

The amount of DAH has also expanded. Data from the World Bank show that DAH rose from USD 2.805 billion in 2000 to USD 11.6 billion in 2014. But it should be noted that the proportion of DAH in total aid has not changed much, with the lowest of 4.4% and the highest of 6.8%, basically within the same range as that of the previous 40 years.

Assuming that the data on China.AidData.org can be used for reference, the share of DAH in China's total aid is only 1.2%, far below the average of the international community. In aid to Uganda, DAH accounts for 14.8%, much higher than the international average. Although it is uncertain whether the data are accurate, the trend they reflect is acceptable, that is, DAHCU has undergone some special changes in recent years. In fact, judging from the characteristics of DAH, this is indeed the case. In DAH, the types of aid have been enriched from dispatching medical teams to helping build hospitals and disease prevention and control centers, providing personnel training, and donating medicine and equipment. This is actually a general trend in Uganda and in Africa at large since the Forum on China–Africa Cooperation in 2000.

Assuming that the World Bank' statistics include China and using the data of China.AidData.org as a reference, it can be estimated that China's foreign aid has made up 36.7% of total international aid since 2000. China has provided more than USD 300 billion in aid to Africa, accounting for 57% of the international aid to sub-Saharan Africa. In fact, based on the analysis of data on China.AidData.org, it can be inferred that the World Bank' data do not incorporate China' data in full; otherwise, the two ratios would fall to 26.9 and 36.4%. Even so, the proportions still seem exaggerated, much higher than China's official data, although it is a fact that China's aid in Africa has grown rapidly.

Data from the World Bank and OECD clearly show that China is not among the top 10 donors of DAH to Uganda.

Against this backdrop, it is apparently unrealistic to use USAID or OECD project evaluation methods and tools (USAID 2015; OECD 1991) to assess DAHCU, especially its efficacy, because China does not have a project managed system for DAHCU at all.

Moreover, because the Malaria Consortium and China-Uganda Friendship Hospital came into operation not long ago, it is still too early to evaluate their effectiveness, especially their impact. It is also not time to conduct effectiveness studies on the donation of medicines and medical equipment and equipment. Therefore, DAHCU effectiveness evaluation should justifiably be focused on the medical teams, which also involves other types of DAH.

As mentioned earlier, DAHCU produces notable outcome on each level corresponding to the four tiers in our framework of "two-side four-tiered embeddedness." The following discussions will be based on this idea. (1) At the practical level, whether it is the medical teams or facilities such as the China-Uganda Friendship Hospital these are all provided at the request of the Ugandan government, and meant to supplement and strengthen Uganda's own healthcare resources. (2) In terms of DAH received by Uganda, while the Chinese medical teams not only help ease Uganda's acute shortage of healthcare workers but also provide medical services on the frontline at places such as the Jinja Hospital, they do not overlap with any other DAH Uganda receives. In fact, they complement them, thereby optimizing the overall structure of DAH in Uganda. (3) The of DAHCU depends on that of overall DAH a country receives. Despite its distinctive nature, DAHCU accounts for a very small share of DAH Uganda receives, and mostly takes the form of practical actions on the ground. So its impact on the effectiveness of [international] aid in general to Uganda is yet difficult to gauge. (4) In terms of diplomacy, even though its scale is quite limited against what Uganda receives in DAH, insofar as DAHCU plays an important role in facilitating connections between the two countries, it is effective as a diplomatic instrument. (5) With the rapid development of China–Uganda economic relations, the number of Chinese investors and traders in Uganda has also increased significantly. Given the shortage of healthcare resources in the country, DAHCU undoubtedly offers these Chinese expats something of a healthcare safety net, a natural extension of the program's original objective.

7.2 Improving Resource Supply

The arrival of the Chinese medical teams literally doubles the size of the staff at the Jinja Hospital and the newly opened China-Uganda Friendship Hospital. This made DAHCU in its earliest days a form of emergency aid to a healthcare system in critical condition. Though it continues to play that role as far as the hospitals are concerned, DAHCU has evolved in terms of how it fits in with Uganda's healthcare system and overall DAH received by the country. This is not because DAHCU has itself changed, but because of changes to its background, environment and parameters in which it is embedded.

The concept of "emergency aid," or "lifeline," has its roots in traditional Chinese culture. As a Chinese saying goes, aid is to be used for alleviating emergency, but not as a remedy for poverty. In other words, if what is needed is the opportunity for the needy to create greater values for themselves, they must not be denied this kind of help. In economic jargon, this kind of assistance generates maximum marginal utility. For sociologists, such assistance is something that brings equality of opportunity. Of the different kinds of emergency situations, those in which people's lives are at risk have the greatest urgency. There is an idea in Buddhism that says "Better saving one life than building a seven-story pagoda." Emergency health aid is essentially a lifesaver.

By contrast, chronic need for assistance suggests the possibility of dependency on aid, which should therefore not be given. In Chinese culture, it is considered wrong to do what would encourage dependency and laziness. In economic parlance, this kind of assistance produces zero marginal utility; in sociology, this would be considered a form of social inequality, that is, given the scarcity of resources, they should be optimally allocated, i.e., priority should be given to those with the most dire needs. Therefore, the idea that alleviating emergency is wiser than remedying poverty amounts to a philosophy of emergency assistance.

Another Chinese adage also aptly captures the effectiveness of emergency aid—"to those shivering in cold snowy weather pieces of coal are a lifeline." The line is from a poem by Fan Chengda, of the Song dynasty, in which Fan depicts how giving those on the verge of dying from hypothermia the means to stay warm can be a life-saving act.

The arrival of the first Chinese medical teams at Jinja Hospital in April 1983 was just such a "lifeline" to Uganda's healthcare system at that time.

Crude estimates based on a general reckoning of the health management system of Uganda and the ranking structure of government-funded hospitals in 1978 suggest that the country had about 280 doctors at central and provincial hospitals. The first Chinese medical teams consisted of two support staff and 13 doctors. Those 13 doctors accounted for 5% of all doctors at Uganda's central and provincial hospitals.

The impact of Chinese medical teams on Uganda goes far beyond enlarging the rank of the medical staff. With their skills and specialties, Chinese medical teams carried a big weight in Uganda's healthcare workers. At that time, Jinja Hospital, one of the three teaching hospitals in Uganda, only had three chief physicians. We estimate that there would be no more than 12 chief physicians in the whole country. The first batch of Chinese medical teams alone consisted of six chief physicians, accounting for half of the national total.

In addition, Chinese medical teams brought more and better technologies to Jinja Hospital, and mitigated staff shortages at the hospital, in areas ranging from otorhinolaryngology to anesthesia. Most notably, acupuncture was introduced to Uganda's healthcare sector.

It may be for these reasons that members of the first Chinese medical teams were invited by Ugandan presidents, whether before the 1986 civil war or during the early stage of Museveni's reign, as guests of honor.

After more than 30 years, the role of Chinese medical teams in Uganda has weakened notably because of three major factors.

The first is the development of Uganda's healthcare system. In 1983, Uganda had eight central and provincial hospitals and 32 regional hospitals. By 2015, there were 16 national and regional referral hospitals, and as many as 144 general hospitals (Table 6.4), with nearly 1300 doctors at public hospitals. Against this background, Chinese medical teams are no longer as important as they used to be.

The second factor is the healthcare service systems. In Uganda, doctors employed at public hospitals can set up private clinics, or leave their jobs in these hospitals on their own accord. Chinese medical teams felt the impact of such regulations when they first arrived in the country. Many Ugandan doctors and nurses trained by Chinese medical teams would quit their jobs at public hospitals, take part-time jobs, or set up their own clinics to increase their earning. In our survey, we found that doctors of Uganda's public hospitals have two basic career aspirations: to move up the managerial rank in the healthcare system, or to start their own practice. In this case, the "emergency aid" to Uganda was not used to improve the services at the public hospitals, which was the expected social benefit, but instead afforded individuals the opportunity to pursue their own interests. While local doctors were pursuing their own interests, Chinese doctors had to deal with the daily work that should have been done by the local staff.

The third factor is the development of DAH in Uganda. Until the first Chinese medical team arrived in 1983, Uganda only received bilateral DAH from Libya, and such aid was not directly incorporated into Uganda's health budget. Except for the aid programs of international organizations, there were no other bilateral or multilateral programs aimed at promoting the development of Uganda's healthcare system, improving its healthcare services, or dealing with serious diseases. As mentioned earlier, into the twenty-first century, DAHCU, despite its growth in absolute terms, has seen its relative share decrease. To be specific, the total sum of DAHCU over the past 30 years or so maybe less than the annual average of what the US has provided in DAH to the country since 2000.

In this changing landscape, although the skills and specialties of Chinese medical teams are still valuable and Chinese medicines and medical equipment still important, once a "lifeline," DAHCU's importance within Uganda's healthcare system has significantly diminished.

Still, the establishment of China-Uganda Friendship Hospital, not an emergency aid, offers an opportunity for DAHCU to maximize its effectiveness, although it is effectiveness from the perspective of the donor rather than the recipient. By integrating aid resources, China-Uganda Friendship Hospital will enable DAHCU to consolidate its effectiveness in not only resources but also in intelligence and governance.

For the recipient, China-Uganda Friendship Hospital is a new regional general hospital in Uganda, set to relieve the pressure of healthcare service provision in the greater Kampala metropolitan area. Although this also seems to be resource effectiveness, it provides an opportunity for integrating DAHCU to help improve healthcare services in Uganda.

In short, from the perspective of both the donor and the recipient, DAHCU has gradually turned from emergency aid to a supplement in the rapidly growing DAH received by Uganda, but China-Uganda Friendship Hospital provides an opportunity for integrating DAHCU to make the most of its small share.

7.3 Optimizing DAH Structure

DAHCU, with a history of more than 30 years, is a health resource for Uganda, and as one type of DAH received by Uganda does not overlap with other parts of DAH. It holds a unique place in Uganda's healthcare system. The effectiveness of DAHCU in the structures of Uganda's healthcare system and DAH to Uganda derives from its practical modality: Chinese medical teams, as well Chinese medicines and medical equipment.

With the changes in the DAH landscape, the effectiveness of DAHCU in the two structures has also evolved, from fulcrum effect to proximity effect and potentially to demonstration effect.

Archimedes, the ancient Greek mathematician, wrote in a letter to King Hiero that "Give me a place to stand, and a lever long enough, and I will move the world." In the 1980s, DAHCU was exactly such a fulcrum in the two structures. It was an important part of Uganda's healthcare system and also the only bilateral sector in DAH to Uganda, thereby helping to optimize the structure of both.

With the expansion of DAH received by Uganda, especially the enormous aid from the US, DAHCU has maintained its unique position and remained independent of other DAH, but it is no longer at a fulcrum point.

The challenges facing Uganda's healthcare system today include funding shortage, prevention and control of major infectious diseases, and improvement of basic health care. In this context, huge funding and the capacity to cope with major infectious diseases have become the new fulcrum.

DAHCU apparently does not have the two features, so its position in the two structures retreats to efficacy in local structure, i.e., efficacy in the human resources structure of Jinja Hospital. In fact, the efficacy in local structure always exists, but was concealed when DAHCU was at a fulcrum point.

Chinese medical teams, as healthcare workers in coordination with other parts of DAHCU, have initiative and conscious activity, thus capable of reproduction. By disseminating skills, Chinese medical teams have a positive influence on healthcare workforce in the proximity, thus achieving reproduction of techniques and skills. The scope of influence or efficiency of reproduction is closely linked to posts or the size of the stage they have.

It can be seen from DAHCU practices that Chinese medical teams have not become part of Uganda's health education, or health management system, but instead have long stayed at a regional hospital. This position determines that Chinese medical teams cannot exert influence by training health staff or helping improve health policy and management system, but only providing services at their posts at Jinja Hospital.

The "proximity effect" from the "Three Degrees of Influence" theory (Christakis and Fowler 2009) is an applicable concept to describe such influence or efficacy. The "proximity effect" means that no matter for what people come together, there will be social influence, that is, people have influence on each other. The "Three Degrees of Influence" theory emphasizes that people's influence on other people or things around them gradually dissipates and ceases to have a noticeable effect on people beyond the social frontier that lies at three degrees of separation.

For doctors, they have the greatest influence on the nearest group, and the scope of influence does not exceed three degrees of separation, including: (1) the hospital's medical and managerial personnel, and patients; (2) residents in the community where the hospital is located; and (3) the local healthcare system.

Data from field surveys show that Chinese medical team members have a direct influence on their Ugandan colleagues. Actions with proximity effect include: teaching and guiding Ugandan medical professionals, holding workshops, and setting an example.

When the first Chinese medical team arrived, Jinja Hospital was the second-largest teaching hospital in Uganda; by 2016, it was still one of the 14 teaching hospitals. At a teaching hospital, teaching is a duty of doctors, where the proximity effect occurs. Available data show that each batch of Chinese medical teams teaches about 50 interns per year. During their stay at Jinja Hospital from 1983 to 2012, Chinese medical teams trained at least 1500 people, exceeding the total number of doctors at public hospitals. If all of them worked at public hospitals, Uganda should not have been short of doctors at all.

In addition to teaching, Chinese medical teams also provided guidance for residents, and communicated with outpatient care doctors. As shown in the work logs filed by Chinese medical teams and in the interviews with doctors who worked at Jinja Hospital, it is common for Chinese medical teams to instruct local doctors and nurses through specific diagnosis and treatment activities. Such stories can be found, and abound, for every Chinese medical team. The guidance ranges from western medicine including internal medicine, surgery, gynecology, pediatrics, stomatology, otolaryngology, urology, anesthesiology, to traditional Chinese medicine including acupuncture, and from diagnoses to operations; even plasterers could get advice from Chinese medical teams.[1] Based on relevant data, it is reasonable to assume that Chinese medical teams instruct an average of 20 doctors and nurses per year, and over the past more than 30 years, the total number exceeds 600, which is apparently a large number for Jinja Hospital.

Instructing Ugandan doctors and holding workshops are the most direct way for Chinese medical teams to help their Ugandan colleagues, but regrettably, the effects may be compromised due to language barriers. In field surveys at Jinja Hospital, we found that the first challenge for Chinese medical teams providing medical services in Uganda is language.

"In the first few months, almost all of them needed interpreters to help them communicate; but after some time, they can speak a little English. Our nurses live with them, and will also help translate for them (other local languages)."[2]

Language barriers would undoubtedly affect the abovementioned three forms of interaction. They weaken closeness between individuals, and thus affect efficiency at the first degree of separation. It remains uncertain whether language barriers can be made up for with behaviors.

Setting examples is a basic mission of the Chinese medical teams. Over the past 30 years, the conduct of the team members, wherever they may be, at the Jinja Hospital, the China-Uganda Friendship Hospital, or in the presence of risks of HIV infection, has been exemplary.

The dedication and selflessness of Chinese doctors are deeply engraved on the minds of Ugandan people. The work ethics and professionalism of Chinese medical teams have won praise from the Ugandan government and Ugandan people. When Chinese medical teams were stationed at Jinja Hospital, it soon became a hospital that served not only people within the region, but patients from around the country, especially people suffering from tricky diseases. Now, China-Uganda Friendship Hospital is also attracting patients across the country.

[1]Chinese medical teams to Uganda. 1985. *Two-Year Work Summary of 3rd Batch of Chinese Medical Teams to Uganda*. Kunming: Yunnan Provincial Archives. File No. 131: 3: 458: 7.

[2]Interview with Anyori Margaret, nurse of Jinja Hospital, at Jinja Hospital on October 22, 2015. Interviewer: Rehema.

In this sense, the "proximity effect" of Chinese medical teams directly reaches Ugandan patients and their families at all levels, from presidents, vice presidents, and ministers to common people. Anyone who has contact with Chinese medical teams gives the thumbs up to the medical ethics and skills of Chinese medical teams. It goes without saying that every batch of Chinese medical teams has created many touching and admirable stories.

Chinese medicines are an integral part of Chinese medical teams. Since the first Chinese medical team arrived in Uganda, Chinese medicines have gained a foothold in the country's healthcare system. As mentioned before, the first team brought with them medicines that could be used for several months. Since then, Chinese medicines have never been absent.

It would be fair to say that Chinese medical teams have created many firsts with their extraordinary medical ethics and skills, in which Chinese medicines, medical equipment, devices and facilities play an indispensable role. Using these familiar medical supplies and instruments has increased the confidence of the team members.

The mutual effect between doctors and medicines and medical equipment constitutes effective healthcare services, which in turn enhance the reputation of not only the doctors but also the medicines and medical equipment used by them. In this sense, Chinese medicines and medical equipment have long left a good impression on proximal actors, and become an organic part of the proximity effect of Chinese medical teams.

China-Uganda Friendship Hospital and the Malaria Consortium have received a great deal of attention from the Ugandan government. In the two structures of Ugandan's healthcare system and DAH received by Uganda, however, they are not at a strategic position as Chinese medical teams used to be. China-Uganda Friendship Hospital is indeed the only regional hospital built through bilateral cooperation, but is just one of the 14 regional hospitals in Uganda,[3] so it does not occupy a unique

[3]The 14th batch of Chinese medical teams working at Jinja Hospital, served 22,593 hospital visitors and 3400 hospitalized patients, and the 16th batch working at China-Uganda Friendship Hospital served 20,584 hospital visitors and 3459 hospitalized patients. It can be seen that the numbers of the two batches are close, suggesting that the Chinese medical teams didn't have greater effect with better facilities. See Work Summary of the 14th Batch of Chinese Medical Teams to Uganda (July 16, 2011), and Work Summary of the 16th Batch of Chinese Medical Teams to Uganda (August 8, 2015).

position. The Malaria Consortium, dwarfed by the US's assistance to Uganda in malaria prevention and control, is simply another institution in the two structures.

As to Chinese medicines and medical equipment, they were brought with Chinese medical teams at the beginning, and gained high reputation thanks to the teams' efforts. With the development of bilateral trade, more and more Chinese medicines and medical equipment have entered Uganda through other channels; at this time, fake or shoddy goods produced in China have appeared in Ugandan market, posing a direct threat to the reputation of Chinese medicines and medical equipment (Yuan et al. 2013; Yuan 2013) and also the structure of DAH.

Against this background, it occurred to us during our field surveys that the integration of DAHCU with the China-Uganda Friendship Hospital is probably another way to help optimize the structure of both the country's domestic healthcare services and its DAH. In other words, China-Uganda Friendship Hospital can serve to demonstrate China's healthcare service model, especially the supply of basic healthcare, thus helping to improve the structural effectiveness of DAHCU.

7.4 Strengthening Connections

Although health is a common concern of mankind, the people medical professionals deal with are not only organisms but also social beings, and medicines and medical equipment are not only physical objects but also have national attributes. If such premise is acknowledged, it means that DAH is not only aid from one country to another, but also builds connections between the countries. If the relations between countries are conveyed and reflected by government leaders, the relations DAH connects can simplified into the relations between people of different nationalities and social-economic status, and DAHCU is at the junction of the relations.

In the history of China–Uganda relations, DAHCU used to be one of the few junction points, which can be called "structural holes," but now it is one of the many junction points, or "nodes."

"Structural holes" is a concept originally developed by Ronald Stuart Burt to study social structures in competitive societies (Burt 2008). Like embeddedness, it is also an analytical instrument.

If aid from China, aid received by Uganda, and international DAH are seen as three social networks, then the relations between them can be illustrated in Fig. 7.1. In the figure, the network where node A is located represents all kinds of aid received by Uganda, the network where node B is located illustrates international DAH, and the network E is located illustrates aid from China; E represents DAHCU, A represents Uganda's healthcare system, and B represents DAH from other donors; the positions of A, B, and E are very subtle, which are called "structural holes" by Burt. For example, E connects China to Uganda's healthcare system and even Uganda, and also connects China to international DAH. Without E, the connections between aid from China and the other two networks would be cut off. This is the effect of node E in the whole relations, i.e., "structural hole effect."

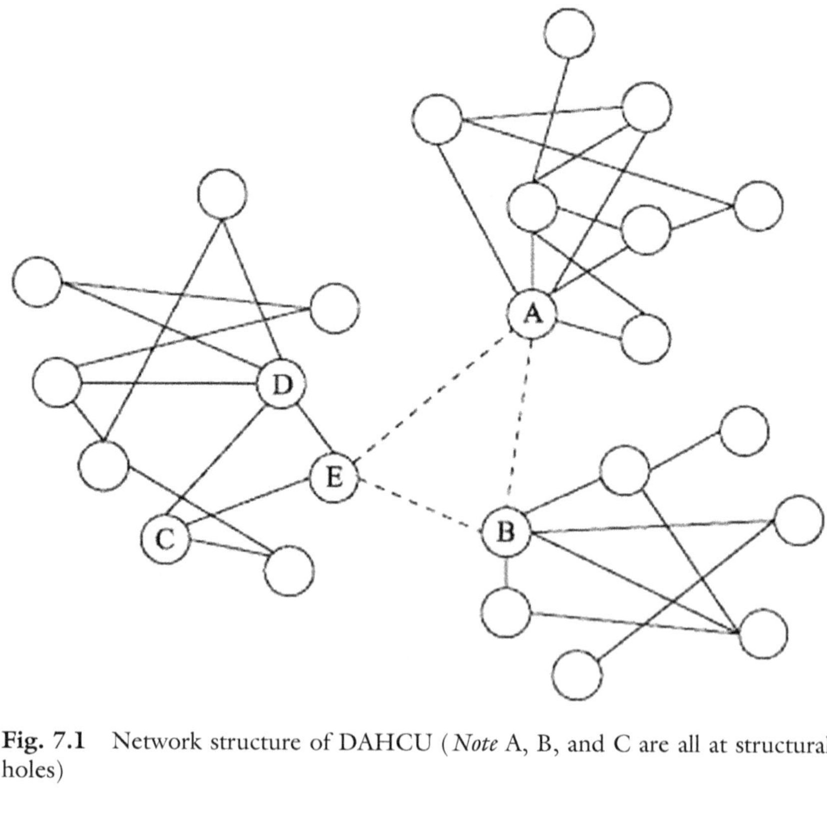

Fig. 7.1 Network structure of DAHCU (*Note* A, B, and C are all at structural holes)

DAHCU had "structural hole effect" in China–Uganda relations at the early stage. Chinese medical teams and Chinese medicines and medical equipment used to be among the few structural holes. Given the biological characteristics of mankind, they were not politically sensitive structural holes. On the grounds of health needs and supply, Chinese medical teams and Chinese medicines and medical equipment could reach out to any person in need, whether they are president or common people.

Such "structural hole effect" enabled DAHCU to help cement existing connection between China and Uganda. In field surveys we learned that in every Chinese medical teams there were members who have been invited as guests of honor to meet with Ugandan presidents. The relation network of DAHCU ranged from Uganda's government leaders and their families to the remote villages of Masinya and Dabani in eastern Uganda, the hometown of the doorkeepers for Chinese medical teams. The fact that Chinese medical teams were welcomed and appreciated by the whole city of Jinja suggests that DAHCU was within the community network of Jinja.

With the diversification of China–Uganda ties, the structural hole position of DAHCU has been "diluted" by other "connections." Although healthcare needs will never disappear, DAHCU could no longer maintain the structural hole position in China–Uganda relations, with its constructive role in connection-building in some aspects reduced from national level to individual level. For instance, a single doctor of Chinese medical teams once represented DAHCU in the network structure, but this is not the case now—they no longer represent DAHCU, or even the Chinese medical team; instead, their relation with a Ugandan senior official is just personal connection. Likewise, Chinese medicines and medical equipment no longer represent China or DAHCU, but simply their brands.

With the diversification of China–Uganda relations and aid received by Uganda, changes to the role of DAHCU in connecting the two countries seem irreversible. This is determined by the very nature of relational connections, and also explains why some people believe that international aid has turned from a form of "philanthropy" to what is essentially a "market."

7.5 Benefiting the Expat Community

China's understanding of Uganda has further evolved since 2000. Before that, relations between the two countries were mostly played out through activities by the two governments. Since 2000, with the inception of the Forum on China–Africa Cooperation (FOCAC) and other initiatives, the two countries have seen more interactions of different types and at various levels. It was reckoned that in 2010, about 7000 Chinese people worked in Uganda[4]; by 2016, that number grew to 10,000–50,000.[5]

With the increase in interactions, China's engagement with Uganda has expanded to a greater number of areas, including investment, trade, assistance, construction, wholesale, and retail. In 2012, China overtook the UK to become the largest trade partner of Uganda.[6]

What this development means is China is no longer just a donor but has become a multifaceted partner. It is a notable trend that there will be more Chinese people in Uganda, and the frequency of their visit will also grow.

Health is a common issue for human beings. Starting with the first Chinese medical batch, there was a tacit understanding that in addition to what was in their official job description, the teams would be expected to provide healthcare services to the best of their abilities to Chinese expats, including not just Chinese citizens but all ethnic Chinese.

Every Chinese medical team has stories about helping Chinese aid workers, traders and entrepreneurs, business people from Hong Kong, people from Taiwan, and many more. As the number of Chinese working and living in Uganda continues to rise, the importance of the medical dispatch to the expats has become ever more prominent even though both their workload and utilization of their medicine and medical equipment supply have seen only a slight increase.

[4]Jaramogi, Pattrick, 2013. Uganda: Chinese Investments in Uganda Now at Sh1.5 Trillion, in allafrica, February 20, 2013. http://allafrica.com/stories/201302190354.html.

[5]Leong, Trinna, 2016. China's Small Traders Seek Their Fortune in Uganda, in *Straits Times*, February 22, 2016. http://www.straitstimes.com/world/africa/chinas-small-traders-seek-their-fortune-in-uganda.

[6]Ghosh, Palash, 2012. Chinese in Uganda: Exploiters or Economic Partners? In *International Business Times*, August 8, 2012. http://www.ibtimes.com/chinese-uganda-exploiters-or-economic-partners-742398.

These jobs are not included in DAHCU agenda or the agreements between China and Uganda, so we call them the spillover effectiveness of DAHCU.

References

Burt, Ronald. 2008. *Structural Hole: The Social Structure of Competition*, trans. Min Ren, Lu Li, and Hong Lin. Shanghai People's Publishing House.

Christakis, Nicholas A. and James H. Fowler. 2009. *Connected: The Surprising Power of Our Social Networks and How They Shape Our Lives.* New York: Little, Brown & Company.

OECD. 1991. *DAC Principles for Evaluation of Development Assistance.* Paris: Development Assistance Committee.

USAID. 2015. *Evaluation Toolkit.* Washington, DC: USAID.

Yuan, Qing. 2013. Chinese Anti-malarial Drugs Are All Reliable. *Xinhua Daily Telegraph*, January 5, P3.

Yuan, Jirong, Pengfei Shi, Zimei Fu, Ke Wang, and Hui Cheng. 2013. Chinese Anti-malarial Drugs into Africa Are Not Fake Drugs. *People's Daily*, January 8, P4.

CHAPTER 8

A Deeper Understanding of Development Aid for Health from China to Uganda

It was thought that DAHCU was only a matter between China and Uganda, and was embedded in a holistic international aid system, and in Uganda's social, economic and cultural fabric, and governance system, but this is not the case. Through literature review and field research, we arrive at the following conclusions.

8.1 A More Nuanced Analysis: Going Beyond the Donor and the Recipient Countries

At the beginning of this book, we try to construe the DAHCU framework based on relational logic, believing that DAHCU is part of bilateral relations, embedded in the systems of both the donor and the recipient. The analytical framework in Fig. 2.1 is established hence.

This framework turns out to be well-grounded, compatible with the existing literature. In the process of sorting through the literature, however, we got a grip on the implication: DAHCU is indeed embedded in bilateral relations, but on either part, there are four tiers of embeddedness.

Z. Qiu, *When Friendship Comes First*, China and Globalization 2.0,
https://doi.org/10.1007/978-981-32-9308-3_8

Aid is a process, in which not every link features four-tiered embeddedness at the same time or all the time. Take China-Uganda Friendship Hospital as an example. In the process of negotiations, China would take into account the overall aid landscape and the pattern of aid to Africa, and take China-Uganda Friendship Hospital as a "whole project"—it is one of the more than 100 hospitals that China has helped build in Africa, and also the only one in Uganda. Uganda would also consider the hospital's position and role in its healthcare system.

Once an agreement is reached between the two sides, it would extend from the bilateral political, economic and social spheres to a multilateral environment. This multilateral environment includes the relations between the hospital and aid to Africa, aid to Uganda, DAH to Africa, and DAH to Uganda.

Once completed, the hospital, as an established fact, would divorce itself from the previous multilateral relations, and directly enter into the relations with aid Uganda received from all donors, with Uganda's layout and adjustment of health resources, and follow-up relations with the provincial aid agencies in China, and relations involving the operation and maintenance of facilities, equipment, instruments, medicines, and so on.

Therefore, we find that DAHCU not just features two-sided four-tiered embeddedness, but structured, process-based bilateral, and multilateral multi-tiered embeddedness. In these processes, there are effectiveness issues in every link; and the evaluation of effectiveness of DAH from China to Africa health aid also entails the choice of "effectiveness" dimensions.

If aid is considered a long process starting from negotiation, then aid underway has, to some extent, diverted away from the previous process to the recipient's system; even if the donor needs feedback or is given feedback, it is just a domestic political process of the donor, which has little impact on aid (Mwenda and Tangri 2005). Therefore, we can put aside the four-tiered embeddedness of the donor who decides whether to provide aid, and turn the "two-sided four-tiered embeddedness" framework into a comprehensive framework, a unilateral four-tiered embeddedness framework for China in particular. It must be noted that when it comes to specific fields of aid, multilateral relations are embedded in the unilateral framework, as is the case with DAHCU, which is embedded in the overall DAH from all donors to Uganda.

8.2 A Drop in the Ocean: Development Aid for Health from China to Uganda and China's Growing Economic Might

Aid received by Uganda accounted for around 10% of its GDP from 1998 to 2006 (Guloba et al. 2010), and its proportion in gross national income (GNI) peaked at 26.1% in 1992, and was 14% in 2000, 16.4% in 2006, and 6.19% in 2014.[1] In other words, aid plays an important role in Uganda's economy. According to the data of the World Bank and OECD, while the share of DAH in total international aid stayed at 4.5–7.0% after 2000, the proportion remained as high as 25% in Uganda after 1995.

Uganda's health expenditure is highly dependent on foreign aid, as government funding accounts for only about 10% of health expenditure (Stierman et al. 2013; Juliet et al. 2009). It can be seen that that although DAH makes up only one-fourth of total aid received by Uganda, it is crucial to health expenditure, equivalent to a lever for health policy.

China provided RMB 89.34 billion in foreign aid from 2010 to 2012, accounting for merely 0.06% of its GDP (RMB 139,040.9 billion) over the same period. If China contributed USD 8 million to China-Uganda Friendship Hospital, and other DAH expenditures were a variable, say, USD 12 million in total,[2] then the annual average during the three years was about RMB 26 million, accounting for 0.78% of China's foreign aid.

From 2010 to 2012, Uganda received about USD 1.69 billion in DAH, of which DAH from China accounted for only 0.7% (Fig. 8.1). China's spending on China-Uganda Friendship Hospital is the largest amount of aid ever in the history of DAHCU. Even so, DAHCU only accounts for a very proportion of DAH received by Uganda. Then, why is China considered to play such an important role in DAH to Africa and to Uganda (Grépin et al. 2014)?

It must be noted that although aid accounts for just about 10% of Uganda's GDP, the share of DAH in its health expenditure is very high, as shown in Fig. 8.1. Therefore, aid carries heavy weight in Uganda's

[1] World Bank. http://data.worldbank.org.cn/indicator/DT.ODA.ODAT.GN.ZS?locations=UG&view=chart.

[2] Such a big share seems unlikely.

Fig. 8.1 DAHCU in Uganda's health expenditure (*Note* The proportional relationship of different parts in the figure is determined based on the available data)

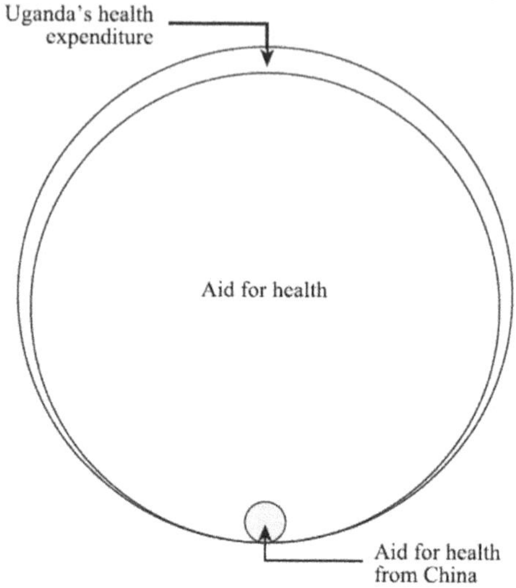

healthcare system. In terms of the amount of aid, DAHCU is like a drop in the ocean in DAH received by Uganda.

It is fair to say that the cooperative relationship between China and Africa and between China and Uganda is not achieved overnight, but the result of efforts over decades. The influence of "a drop in the ocean" is attributed to China's consistent efforts, in which the most important is a fundamental principle in Chinese culture—relating to each other with heart. China hopes the cooperative relationship can last, but that obviously requires efforts from both sides.

References

Grépin, Karen A., Victoria Y. Fan, Gordon C. Shen, and Lucy Chen. 2014. China's Role as a Global Health Donor in Africa: What Can We Learn from Studying Under Reported Resource Flows? *Global Health* 10 (1): 1–11. https://doi.org/10.1186/s12992-014-0084-6.

Guloba, Madina, Nicholas Kilimani, and Winnie Nabiddo. 2010. *Impact of China-Africa Aid Relations: A Case Study of Uganda*. Kampala: Economic Policy Research Centre (EPRC).

Juliet, Nabyonga Orem, Ssengooba Freddie, and Sam Okuonzi. 2009. Can Donor Aid for Health Be Effective in a Poor Country? Assessment of Prerequisites for Aid Effectiveness in Uganda. *The Pan African Medical Journal* 3 (9): 9.

Mwenda, Andrew M., and Roger Tangri. 2005. Patronage Politics, Donor Reforms, and Regime Consolidation in Uganda. *African Affairs* 104 (416): 449–467. https://doi.org/10.2307/3518724.

Stierman, E., F. Ssengooba, and S. Bennett. 2013. Aid Alignment: A Longer Term Lens on Trends in Development Assistance for Health in Uganda. *Global Health* 9 (1): 7. https://doi.org/10.1186/1744-8603-9-7.

CHAPTER 9

Conclusion

9.1 From Aid to Cooperation: New Opportunities

9.1.1 *Providing Aid Is Only the Beginning*

In the field of development aid, aid effectiveness draws high attention from the international community. From the five principles of the *Paris Declaration on Aid Effectiveness* to the introduction of South–South cooperation and people-to-people cooperation into the *Accra Agenda for Action*, and to the advocacy for promoting partnership with assistance as a catalyst to enhance effectiveness in the *Busan Partnership for Effective Development Cooperation*, the international community's understanding of aid effectiveness has constantly evolved and deepened.

Literature research shows that the international community's understanding of aid has fundamentally changed, from giving, help, aid, and assistance to seeing aid as an area of competition. Nevertheless, the problems about DAH effectiveness have remained unsolved. For example, first, the donors, though their number is growing rapidly, still work separately, lacking a sound coordination mechanism; second, the donors tend to focus on their areas of interest, while giving short shrift to the healthcare system of the recipients; third, an enormous amount of aid funds have been transferred to institutions in developed countries (such as pharmaceutical factories, consulting firms, and auditing firms) rather than be directly injected into recipient countries.

Z. Qiu, *When Friendship Comes First*, China and Globalization 2.0,
https://doi.org/10.1007/978-981-32-9308-3_9

Based on this, some studies think that to direct funds toward researchers and organizations in developing countries is more economical, and better for capacity building (Winters 2010), because these researchers and organizations know better how to combine intervention projects with local healthcare systems.

Perhaps the insignificant share of China's early aid had made China's proposals routinely ignored. In fact, from the Eight Principles for Economic Aid and Technical Assistance to Other Countries, China has taken aid as a way to provide emergency, and developed aid plans based on the demands and development of the recipients. Aid effectiveness or development effectiveness has never been a problem for aid China, or DAH from China.

The aid landscape is undergoing major changes. International aid has increased rapidly since 2000, and the growth in aid over the past 15 years has exceeded total aid of the 1950s. The share of DAH, however, has changed little compared with that before the twenty-first century; in other words, DAH has indeed increased, but only proportionally to total aid. Moreover, people's views on aid are also changing. Aid, once a means of making the recipients submissive or cooperative, is now becoming a tool for donors to vie for spheres of influence.

Against this backdrop, China, a former recipient, has now turned into a donor, whose foreign aid has risen rapidly. In its aid, aid to Africa has always accounted for the largest share, growing from 46 to 52%. Whether China is joining the donor competition for spheres of influence is controversial, and is beyond the scope of this report, so it will not be discussed here. What can be discussed is that in tandem with the international trends, China's DAH is also growing. Regrettably, we have not obtained the detailed data.

For Uganda, a recipient country, the amount of aid and the types of aid received are also increasing rapidly. Since 1995, aid received by Uganda has tripled, covered almost all fields, of which DAH has increased 4.5 times. Nevertheless, funds directly at the disposal of Uganda's healthcare system are still meagre, with a shortage of funds in important areas, especially basic health care, because a majority of funds go to basic healthcare data and major diseases that the donors are concerned about, such as AIDS, malaria, and tuberculosis. Simply put, the funds are still in the hands of donors.

In this case, the evaluation of Development aid for health from China to Uganda (DAHCU) effectiveness cannot be separated from the changing historical and developmental backgrounds. From the perspective of both the donor and the recipient, the following conclusions can be drawn within the analytical framework of two-sided four-tiered embeddedness.

On the part of the recipient, DAHCU, despite its small share, reached Uganda when the country was most in need of help of this kind. DAHCU was once a prominent component of Uganda's healthcare workforce human resources and DAH, and had important influence on the postwar recovery of Uganda. It was a lifeline Uganda's healthcare workforce, the "leverage to move the earth" at the tiers of Uganda's healthcare system and DAH, and the "structural hole" in China–Uganda relations.

With Uganda's political stability, the change in demands for healthcare services, and the dramatic expansion of DAH received by Uganda, DAHCU is still unique as a resource type, a structural component, or a medium of China–Uganda relations, but its effectiveness is declining quickly.

As a resource, its share in Uganda's healthcare system and DAH has dropped rapidly. According to a rough calculation, DAHCU now accounts for only 0.7% of DAH received by Uganda, becoming the "icing on the cake."

As a structural component, its importance in Uganda's healthcare system and DAH structures has declined rapidly. Although DAHCU does not overlap with any other types of DAH, it is no longer so important, changing from the very one to one of the many options.

As a diplomatic medium, its uniqueness in China–Uganda relations is declining rapidly. Apart from DAHCU, there are many types of aid and cooperation between China and Uganda. With the diversification of exchanges with China, the types of diplomatic media Uganda can choose are also growing fast. Therefore, DAHCU could no longer maintain its structural hole position in bilateral relations.

From the perspective of the donor, DAHCU is a kind of aid on demand, without been endowed with any specific purpose. In this sense, the effectiveness of the recipient is the effectiveness of the donor. This is true of effectiveness in bilateral relations. In addition, China has gained another effect from the spillover effects of DAHCU, i.e., providing healthcare service support for Chinese people living in Uganda.

Like the recipient, China also faces the decline in DAHCU effectiveness. The establishment of China-Uganda Friendship Hospital may be a turning point in multiple senses. The aid modalities have changed from discrete aid such as the dispatch of medical teams and provision of free medicines, equipment, and facilities to cooperative and integrated aid like co-establishment of disease prevention and control centers and general hospitals. With regard to the use of aid resources, the originally scattered DAHCU resources have been integrated; although their combined share is still small, they are expected to have aggregation effects, and thus have demonstration effects in healthcare services and utilization in Uganda's healthcare system and DAH structures.

Looking at the development of DAHCU over the past more than 30 years, we can see that at the beginning, China provided aid to the best of its ability to meet the urgent needs of Uganda, hoping to make friends with a sincere heart, and did it. At the time, DAHCU played a unique role in Uganda' healthcare system, reflecting that China was a friend of Uganda in adversity. Things have now changed. Whether friendship in adversity can flourish in prosperity depends on too many factors. More importantly, aid has become an area of competition, and a market. Whether the two countries can maintain their friendship is a test of the wisdom and capability of China's aid, including DAHCU.

9.1.2 Towards More Cooperation: Future Outlook for Development Aid and Development Aid for Health

As we know from the literature, international aid originates from humanitarianism. After World War II, the concept of "development" was added to humanitarianism, so the terms of "humanitarian aid" and "development aid" coexisted. No matter what it is called, assistance or aid is different from "giving," in that underlying aid are always the intentions of the donors, from political strings, such as support in the United Nations votes, to economic resources. Thus, the recipients, in whole or in part, become a market for the donors to realize their intentions (Sumner and Mallett 2013). In the field of aid, the competition between donors involves not only economic interests but also political and even moral interests—some donors always try to judge other participants, including the recipients, from the moral high ground. Perhaps in a human society, the only thing that the winner takes at all is moral interests!

In this case, if the donor is the seller, then the recipient is the buyer. The seller has scarce products in their hands, while the buyer wants to buy products that are suitable and affordable. In the process of development, however, neither the buyer nor the seller knows what is suitable for the buyer. Based on their own experience, some of the sellers think it is important to focus on the long term, while others believe ideal is not practical; the buyers also have no idea about what is really suitable because they have never had any experience in that respect. Therefore, only in practice can the buyers and the sellers have the opportunity to reach a consensus, that is, to "cross the river by touching the stones" (Jones 2015).

Whether in humanitarian aid or development aid, the donors and the recipients have made explorations for more than 60 years, and gradually accumulated some experience. For the recipients, although long-term thinking is better, the key is to meet the immediate needs. This is understandable. If a family only has enough food for one week, finding food that they can eat after that week is certainly more important than anything that comes a month later, a year later, three years later, and beyond. For the donors, they often lack empathy for others' situations, and make demands on the recipients according to their own experience. China received aid from others not long ago, so it fully understands the recipients' feelings and experience, and would like to share its experience with the recipients. Perhaps it is for this reason that China's aid has unique advantages in the intense competition of development aid, and the friendship forged with the recipient through decades of efforts, though the amount of aid is relatively small, has strong competitive advantages, which have rewritten the traditional rules of development aid, that is, aid is more about "cooperation" than "assistance" or "giving."

Unlike in assistance and giving, in cooperation, all parties not only have equal status but also equal rights. The interests, rules, and demands of both the donors and the recipients are emphasized. Most importantly, the donors and the recipients are involved in aid activities all the time. They participate in, face and share the successes and failures, experiences, and lessons, and interests and risks in all links and stages of aid; the recipients are not only given support but also allowed to make explorations on their own, and grow through trial and error. We believe that this is probably the main factor that makes China's aid more popular in developing countries in Africa and elsewhere, and also the main dimension where traditional donors feel challenged.

DAH shares the commonality of development aid, and also has its particularity. Its particularity lies in that due to the mobility of human beings, diseases and health concerns such as AIDS, atypical pneumonia, and Ebola may have a global impact. Therefore, DAH is provided not only for the recipients, but also for donors themselves. In this case, DAH has the attributes and characteristics of "cooperation," requiring the donors and the recipients to cooperate based on sincerity,, mutual understanding, and practicality. These are exactly the principles China has followed in its DAH to Africa and Uganda, and why it has won the respect, trust and gratitude from the recipients, thus promoting bilateral and multilateral ties.

With regard to Moyo's questions, there are mainly two reasons why China's recent efforts and the building up of China's influence over Africa have made traditional donors feel challenged. On one hand, China has increased aid to Africa, and made cooperation an effective backup and sustainable mechanism for aid, which suits the needs of African countries for aid, development and better lives. On the other hand, by the time China increased its efforts in the process of Africa's development, China has already been an old friend of African people and African governments, which is indebted to China's long-term presence in Africa. In particular, DAH, once "a useless move," has gained a foothold in the cooperation opportunities between China and Africa, just like a silver needle injected into "an acupuncture point." It is the silver needle of DAH that has contributed to the wide consensus between China and Africa, and China's influence over Africa and Uganda.

9.1.3 Opportunities for China

When looking ahead to the future development of DAHCU, we should, in addition to the general trends of international aid, take into account the landscape of China–Uganda relations and the broader China–Africa relations.

Into the twenty-first century, cooperation and trade between China and Africa have grown rapidly. According to the white paper on China–Africa economic and trade cooperation issued by the Chinese government (2010, 2013), the total volume of trade between China and Africa increased from only USD 12.14 million in 1950 to USD 100 million in 1960, and exceeded USD 1 billion in 1980; and it passed the USD 10 billion mark in 2000, it surged to more than USD 100 billion in 2008, and was close to USD 200 billion in 2012. Bilateral trade surpluses and deficits alternated. In 2012, exports from Africa to China far exceeded

China's exports to Africa. In addition, the proportion of trade with Africa in China's foreign trade increased from 2.23% in 2000 to 5.13% in 2012, and the proportion of trade with China in Africa's foreign trade rose from 3.82% in 2000 to 16.13% in 2012. This indicates that China–Africa trade has a more important impact on Africa than on China.

Cooperation and trade between China and Uganda deserve special attention. Since the first Chinese-funded enterprise was registered in Uganda in 1993, China over the past more than 20 years has overtaken India and Britain, the traditional trade partners of Uganda, to become the country's largest trade partner, and ranked the third following Britain and India in the field of investment (Lu 2015). China is even considered to have the largest planned investment in Uganda, and the second most planned investment projects (Yuan 2014).

In other words, in addition to aid, investment, trade and cooperation are also significant to China–Uganda relations. In particular, China-Uganda Friendship Hospital has unprecedentedly adopted the mode of economic cooperation, the first in the history of DAHCU and in the field of aid.

Having observed such trends and facts, we believe that there may still be room to improve the effectiveness of China's aid to Uganda and DAHCU.

First, the Eight Principles for Economic Aid and Technical Assistance to Other Countries are in the interests of both China and the recipients. Combining aid and cooperation on the premise of adhering to the principles is good experience China has accumulated in foreign aid since the reform and opening-up by "crossing the river by feeling the stones," and is also a successful practice of transferring China's own experience as a recipient to the provision of aid. China can and should expand its practices and sum up experiences to provide theoretical and practical guidance for further transforming the concepts of international aid.

Second, DAHCU is now at a turning point. The establishment of China-Uganda Friendship Hospital is the herald of this turning point, and the direction of future development needs to be clarified. In the short term, China is unlikely to overtake the United States by increasing aid, but this does not mean that the effectiveness of China's aid, including DAHCU, will always be dwarfed. A country's healthcare system is not a mechanical system, but an ecological system, in which all links and components are interdependent and promote each other. With a small share of 0.7%, DAHCU still has effectiveness in Uganda's healthcare system and DAH, which means that DAHCU still occupies the right niche, though its importance is declining.

The key to reviving the importance, just as how DAHCU gained in importance, lies in identifying the pain point in Uganda's healthcare system. We believe that this pain point is the provision of basic healthcare services. For DAHCU, it is impossible to help Uganda improve the provision of basic healthcare services by burning money to raise the country's medical expenditure per capita from USD 15 to USD 35, but it can work together with Uganda to explore the model of effective provision of basic healthcare services through demonstration.

As the world's most populous country, China has ensured people's access to basic healthcare services with quite limited resources, and formed a set of effective systems. China's experience is obviously an inspiration to other countries lacking resources. Uganda has a healthcare service provision system similar to that of China, which extends from metropolitan areas to remote communities. The problem facing Uganda is how to use the limited resources to make the existing system work effectively. In brief, what Uganda needs is what China has, a solution without spending massively.

Based on this, we propose that China-Uganda Friendship Hospital be developed into a training and demonstration platform for healthcare service provision in Uganda. Via this platform, China's approaches and best practices in the provision and utilization of basic healthcare services can be transplanted to Uganda, and different levels of service agencies can be engaged to build a vertical demonstration "line" that extends from Health Center III to village health teams.

If so, Chinese medical teams will no longer be "long-term workers," but "mentors" and "teachers." The scope of their effectiveness will be directly extended from their colleagues and patients to the field of basic healthcare service provision along the line. In this way, Chinese medical teams can reach out to more patients and even have an influence on Uganda's healthcare system.

Chinese medicine and medical equipment, equipment and facilities are no longer exclusive to Chinese medical teams, but will be available to Ugandan people as part of basic healthcare services. To this end, the "cooperative development" model initiated by China can be adopted, setting a clear direction for Chinese investment. In this way, DAHCU is no longer just aid, but a "trigger" promoting mutually beneficial and win-win cooperation between China and Uganda.

This will not only cultivate for the recipient a local medical team that "will never leave," to quote Premier Zhou Enlai, but also form a sound and sustainable mechanism that can improve basic healthcare service provision for the people of Uganda, and promote the development of Uganda's healthcare system.

If "relating to each other with heart" is the way of making friends in Chinese culture, then "getting the knack" is the way of doing things. After all, strength, important as it is, can be rivaled by wisdom and "knack." To meet the interests of the peoples of the two countries and to serve China's own interests by promoting the development of Uganda is exactly the "knack" that China's aid, especially DAHCU, should try to get.

If this is what DAHCU aspires to do, then China-Uganda Friendship Hospital has provided the best opportunity. How to make full use of this opportunity requires careful planning and active action by DAHCU.

We believe that three points need to be emphasized.

First, take the rules and the dynamics of the market seriously. Even though we are unwilling to admit that "aid" is becoming a market, we cannot ignore the trend of marketization. In such an environment, China's principles and experience are important, but turning them into the principles and experience of the market is even more important. In recent years, China has made explorations in this regard, including the attempt to combine aid and cooperative development. Yet how to make such attempts a consensus in the field of international aid remains an issue to be addressed; and how to make the market protect the interests of China rather than erode the reputation and prestige China has built over decades in aid and DAH is an even more important policy issue.

Second, take into consideration the impact of recipient countries' institutional maladies on aid effectiveness. In this report, we have shown many drawbacks in Uganda's health management system and service system. For example, the healthcare workforce system of Uganda not only affects the effectiveness of health aid in Uganda, but also the effectiveness of DAHCU. Although non-interference in the internal affairs of other countries is one of China's basic principles for foreign aid, we cannot ignore the impact of their internal affairs on China's interests. Therefore, adjusting the strategy of DAHCU needs to be put on the agenda.

Third, make the most of the power of data. With the rapid development of Internet technology and data technology, data has increasingly become the basis for decision-making, and the basis for influence dissemination. The philosophy of treating others with honesty and respect is important, but it is more important to use data-based facts to prove its importance, and the importance of Chinese values and Chinese experience. When not only the Chinese side but also science proves it, that will be more convincing. Therefore, efforts should be increased in the fundamental work of collecting and integrating data for China's foreign aid.

Even if we don't take action, we cannot stop others from doing that. China.AidData.org is a case in point. If we think that the data on that platform is incomplete or even wrong, we have to be able to show that by present another set of data. Otherwise, people would continue to use those data, even if we think they are problematic.

In short, much remains to be done to improve the quality of data collection, which is fundamental to the successful execution of China's foreign aid in general and DAH in particular.

References

Jones, Sam. 2015. Aid Supplies over Time: Addressing Heterogeneity, Trends, and Dynamics. *World Development* 69: 31–43. https://doi.org/10.1016/j.worlddev.2013.12.014.

Lu, Miaomiao. 2015. An Analysis of Investment and Business Environment of Chinese Enterprises in Uganda. Master's Thesis, China Foreign Affairs University.

Sumner, Andrew, and Richard Mallett. 2013. *The Future of Foreign Aid: Development Cooperation and the New Geography of Global Poverty*. New York: Palgrave Macmillan.

Winters, Matthew S. 2010. Accountability, Participation and Foreign Aid Effectiveness. *International Studies Review* 12 (2): 218–243. https://doi.org/10.1111/j.1468-2486.2010.00929.x.

Yuan, Jirong. 2014. Chinese Investment Boosts Uganda's Manufacturing Industry. *People's Daily*, November 23, P21.

Afterword

To examine international aid from the perspective of social anthropology is an academic adventure, in that international aid is a research area of international relations, in which social anthropology rarely set foot.

Ever since the colonial period, international aid has been a kind of relationship between countries, involving political, economic, military and other bilateral and multilateral activities. After World War II, with the rising status of economic activities in national development, international aid became mainly the economic aid from rich countries to poor countries. The occasional health aid was also manifested as humanitarian emergency aid. China's health aid to African countries in the 1950s was among the earliest of regular bilateral health aid.

Understanding of international aid is usually considered to belong to the international relations arena. In addition to project-based evaluation, some studies have explored the effectiveness of international aid from the economic angle. It was not until the beginning of the twenty-first century that some monographs on international aid turned their focus to "aid effectiveness" and the relationship between aid and the development of recipients, i.e., "development effectiveness." This marks a historical turning point at which international aid has been separated from international relations and become an independent research field.

"Development" is a common topic in many fields. China's development has been a focus of anthropology from *Peasant Life in China*, authored by Fei Xiaotong in 1939, and a key area of sociology from the

Z. Qiu, *When Friendship Comes First*, China and Globalization 2.0, https://doi.org/10.1007/978-981-32-9308-3

Qinghe investigations conducted by Yang Kaidao. It can be said that Chinese social anthropology is characterized by the attention to development issues.

A common goal the Chinese government and people have been striving for over the past 100-plus years is to make the country prosperous and the people rich. China's development is also at the core of Chinese social anthropology. Using the case of Development aid for health from China to Uganda (DAHCU) to extend the focus from China's development to the development of international aid and recipients is an academic adventure for us. We try to inquire into the development of international aid by means of evaluation research, and to examine the effectiveness of DAH from the perspective of social anthropology. Whether this adventure will be a success is to be tested by time.

In this adventure, we encountered various difficulties in data collection and theoretical analysis. Sharing what we experienced in the process of this adventure may help the readers to better understand the reefs, and help other researchers to avoid detours.

First, data errors. In the traditional training of anthropology, it is a basic skill to study foreign countries, especially primitive societies. Researchers, who usually grow up in developed societies, should try to understand and interpret the social, economic, and cultural phenomena of primitive societies. To put it in another way, researchers should observe the primitive societies with their academic acuity, and express their observations in a language that the general readers in developed societies can understand.

There are three conversions. To begin with, researchers need to observe the social, economic, and cultural phenomena in the primitive societies from the perspective of developed societies, and find the phenomena that the readers in developed societies may be interested in, thus achieving the conversion of topics. Next, dive deep into the primitive societies, and try to put the phenomena back to the primitive societies from their angle to understand the original logic and significance of the phenomena in the primitive societies, thus achieving the conversion of facts and logic in the primitive societies. Finally, go back to the developed societies, and express the logic of the primitive societies with the logic of the developed societies, so the conversion of logic from the primitive societies to the developed societies is achieved.

From the sociological point of view, any of the three conversions may have "errors," which will affect the credibility and reliability of conclusions. Nonetheless, there seem to be no alternatives for anthropological studies on foreign societies. In sociology, the generality and particularity of the primitive societies' social facts in human society are often emphasized, and researchers are always reminded to be sensitive to "errors" when studying foreign societies.

Second, object languages. Among the three conversions, the second is the biggest source of errors. In order to reduce errors, anthropologists studying the primitive societies are trained to acquire the language of the object of study. Past experience, however, suggests that many studies still need to rely on the insiders. This is because it is difficult for an outsider to truly enter a foreign society, not only in language but also cultural integration, and adaption to customs and living habits. During our research in Uganda, we felt that, not knowing their language, it is difficult to understand local people's logic of life; and without understanding their logic of life, it is difficult to truly understand the meaning of aid to local people. More importantly, we realized that in order to understand the subtle differences in the meaning of aid to different social groups from the local people's logic of life and logic of society, a quick way is to acquire local language and colloquial expressions.

Third, disciplinary perspectives. In social anthropology, it is a matter of course to regard the object of study as the subject of human society with free will. To distinguish between subjects and objects is also an internalized consensus among social anthropologists. In international relations, in contrast, the researchers seem not to do so.

Take "effectiveness" as an example. In international aid from the perspective of international relations, aid effectiveness is a self-evident concept measuring whether aid has achieved the designed effectiveness. But in social anthropology, the first question concerning effectiveness is "whose effectiveness." It is a discipline-specific instinct of social anthropology to distinguish between donors and recipients. The basic idea of social anthropology in observing human society is that every society is differentiated, and every activity has stakeholders. Without doubt, the benefits for different stakeholders vary. Therefore, defining "whose effectiveness" is the basic perspective to understand the effectiveness of international aid. Our research shows that one important reason why controversies over aid effectiveness abound in the international community is that the effectiveness of donors and the effectiveness of recipients are not distinguished. Taking it a step further, we can ask which group of the recipients is the biggest beneficiary.

Fourth, multilateral cooperation. With the development of international aid, aid activities have become more and more professional. Some aid activities have even started from professional activities. In China's agricultural aid and health aid to Africa, for example, agricultural experts and health experts play a core role. Therefore, it is impossible to study international aid without paying attention to professional issues.

Aid planning and implementation, in a large part, is a kind of management activity. For both donors and recipients, official aid usually involves a number of government departments, even in Britain and the US, where management is highly integrated. For this reason, government supports, and knowledge about international politics, international relations, and management science cannot be ignored in international aid research.

Moreover, discussions about aid implementation and effectiveness involve the understanding of groups in human society, the observation and interpretation of procedural fairness, as well as the judgment and prediction of social consequences, and thus entail evaluation research of social sciences, mainly social anthropology. Therefore, in international aid research, it is impossible to ignore the perspectives and approaches of social anthropology and other fields.

In fact, ignoring any of the above will lead to deficiencies in international aid research. Only multilateral cooperation is the right choice.

This book tries to study DAHCU, part of international aid, from the perspective of social anthropology. While we have made every effort to address the problems faced in the process, and ensure our research activities are objective, these problems may have not been necessarily handled in the best way impossible due to various factors.

In the process of research, we have received a lot of support and help, and hereby would like to express our sincere gratitude.

Our thanks first go to the Department of International Cooperation of the Ministry of Health of China for providing primary data, and the Project Funding Supervision and Service Center for supporting our research activities; to the Foreign Aid Department of the Ministry of Commerce for their efforts to facilitate our research; and to the Economic and Commercial Counselor's Office of the Chinese Embassy in Uganda for providing data, accepting our interviews, and supporting our interviews with relevant Ugandan departments and officials. We want to thank Yunnan Provincial Department of Health and Yunnan Provincial Archive for supporting our literature research, and Doctor Dai Zheng, head of the 16th batch of Yunnan's medical teams to Uganda, for his guidance and communication with us.

We are grateful to the Ministry of Health of Uganda for providing us data, and accepting our interviews; and to Jinja Hospital for supporting our field research, and the hospitals' managers, doctors, nurse, as well as patients, for having interviews with us.

We are deeply indebted to these people and institutions. Without their support, there would be no fundamental data for this study.

We also want to thank Ms. Fang Min, President of Fangfang Hotel in Kampala, for her hospitality that makes our stay in Uganda a pleasant one.

The initial members involved in the study are Professor Qiu Zeqi, Professor Zhang Tuohong, Professor Xie Zheng, Dr. Ma Yumin, Master Zhang Huaxin, and Dr. Rehema Bavuma, and those who joined later include Master Zhuang Yu, Professor Xu Qinghong, as well as students of Yunnan University such as Zhang Weiwei, Jia Shaojie, Zhang Wenyue, Xu Chengchuan, Liao Aidi, Sun Xiao, and Zhang Xiaoqian.

At the annual meeting of China Global Healthcare systems in November 2016 and the seminar in December, some experts put forward constructive suggestions on our research, and spoke highly of our project outcomes. During the revision of the book, Professor Liu Peilong made useful comments. Thanks are due to all of them.

Our gratitude also goes to Ding Chaochao who has provided generous support in project management throughout the research process.

The first draft of this book originates from two reports prepared by Qiu Zeqi (*Two-sided four-tiered Embeddedness of Development Aid for Health from China To Uganda: A Literature Review*, and *Evaluation on the Effectiveness of Development Aid for Health from China to Uganda*), and an ethnography co-authored by Qiu Zeqi and Zhuang Yu (*Hosts and Guests: Jinja Hospital and Chinese Medical Teams*). They are part of the China-UK Global Health Support Program—Output 2 (GHSP OP2R1) funded by the UK Department for International Development.

Zhuang Yu and Ma Yumin contributed to the rearrangement of the reports. Zhuang Yu proofread the draft of the book and checked the references. Huang Shiman helped proofread the final version.

Finally, we would like to thank the Social Sciences Academic Press and the editors for helping us to make this book a reality.

Zaojun Temple
Beijing
February 2, 2017

Bibliography

Abbot, George C. 1973. Two Concepts of Foreign Aid. *World Development* 1 (9): 1–10. https://doi.org/10.1016/0305-750x(73)90153-8.
Acht, Martin, Toman Omar Mahmoud, and Rainer Thiele. 2014. Corrupt Governments Receive Less State-to-State Aid: Governance and the Delivery of Foreign Aid Through Non-state Actors. *Journal of Development Economics.* https://doi.org/10.1016/j.jdeveco.2014.11.005.
Adelman, Carol C., and Jeremiah Norris. 2001. Usefulness of Foreign Aid for Health Care in Less-Developed Countries. *The Lancet* 358 (9299): 2174. https://doi.org/10.1016/S0140-6736(01)07212-9.
Afridi, Muhammad Asim, and Bruno Ventelou. 2013. Impact of Health Aid in Developing Countries: The Public vs. The Private Channels. *Economic Modelling* 31: 759–765. https://doi.org/10.1016/j.econmod.2013.01.009.
Agénor, Pierre-Richard, Nihal Bayraktar, and Karim El Aynaoui. 2008. Roads out of Poverty? Assessing the Links Between Aid, Public Investment, Growth, and Poverty Reduction. *Journal of Development Economics* 86 (2): 277–295. https://doi.org/10.1016/j.jdeveco.2007.07.001.
Alden, Chris. 2005. China in Africa. *Survival* 47 (3): 147–164. https://doi.org/10.1080/00396330500248086.
Ali, Abdiweli M., and Hodan Said Isse. 2007. Foreign Aid and Free Trade and Their Effect on Income: A Panel Analysis. *The Journal of Developing Areas* 41 (1): 127–142. https://doi.org/10.2307/40376162.
Allen, Kenneth, and Eva Baguma. 2013. China-Uganda Relations: Closer Is Not Necessarily Better. China Brief 13. The Jamestown Foundation.

Z. Qiu, *When Friendship Comes First*, China and Globalization 2.0, https://doi.org/10.1007/978-981-32-9308-3

Anderson, G. William. 2014. Bridging the Divide: How Can USAID and DoD Integrate Security and Development More Effectively in Africa? *The Fletcher Forum of World Affairs* 38 (1): 101–126.

Angeles, Luis, and Kyriakos C. Neanidis. 2009. Aid Effectiveness: The Role of the Local Elite. *Journal of Development Economics* 90 (1): 120–134. https://doi.org/10.1016/j.jdeveco.2008.05.002.

Anonymous. 2011. Rethinking Aid Policy: Working with Recipient Communities. *Harvard International Review* 32 (4): 78–79.

Arndt, Channing, Sam Jones, and Finn Tarp. 2015. Assessing Foreign Aid's Long Run Contribution to Growth and Development. *World Development* 69: 6–18. https://doi.org/10.1016/j.worlddev.2013.12.016.

Atwood, J. Brian, M. Peter McPherson, and Andrew Natsios. 2008. Arrested Development: Making Foreign Aid a More Effective Tool. *Foreign Affairs* 87 (6): 123–132. https://doi.org/10.2307/20699376.

Ayittey, George B.N. 2003. Aid and Reform in Africa: Lessons from *Ten Case Studies. Journal of Economic Literature* 41 (1): 248–250.

Baccini, Leonardo, and Johannes Urpelainen. 2012. Strategic Side Payments: Preferential Trading Agreements, Economic Reform, and Foreign Aid. *The Journal of Politics* 74 (4): 932–949. https://doi.org/10.1017/S0022381612000485.

Baehr, Peter R. 1980. The Dutch Foreign Policy Elite: A Descriptive Study of Perceptions and Attitudes. *International Studies Quarterly* 24 (2): 223–261. https://doi.org/10.2307/2600201.

Bai, Jianfeng. 2013. Beijing Declaration Issued at China-Africa Ministerial Conference on Health Cooperation and Development. *People's Daily*, August 17, P3.

Balla, Eliana, and Gina Yannitell Reinhardt. 2008. Giving and Receiving Foreign Aid: Does Conflict Count? *World Development* 36 (12): 2566–2585. https://doi.org/10.1016/j.worlddev.2008.03.008.

Bauhr, Monika, Nicholas Charron, and Naghmeh Nasiritousi. 2013. Does Corruption Cause Aid Fatigue? Public Opinion and the Aid-Corruption Paradox1. *International Studies Quarterly* 57 (3): 568–579. https://doi.org/10.1111/isqu.12025.

Bearce, David H., Steven E. Finkel, Anibal S. Perez-Linan, Juan Rodrfguez-Zepeda, and Lena Surzhko-Harned. 2013. Has the New Aid for Trade Agenda Been Export Effective? Evidence on the Impact of Us AfT Allocations 1999–2008. *International Studies Quarterly* 57 (1): 163–170. https://doi.org/10.2307/41804855.

Bello, Walden. 2007. China Eyes Africa: The New Imperialism? *Multinational Monitor* 28 (1): 23–26.

Bendavid, Eran. 2014. Is Health Aid Reaching the Poor? Analysis of Household Data from Aid Recipient Countries. *PLoS ONE* 9 (1): 1–9. https://doi.org/10.1371/journal.pone.0084025.

Bendavid, Eran. 2016. Past and Future Performance: PEPFAR in the Landscape of Foreign Aid for Health. *Current HIV/AIDS Reports*, 1–7. https://doi.org/10.1007/s11904-016-0326-8.

Bhagwati, Jagdish. 2010. Banned Aid: Why International Assistance Does Not Alleviate Poverty. *Foreign Affairs* 89 (1): 120–125. https://doi.org/10.2307/20699788.

Biswas, Aparajita. 2012. Trade Relations Between BRICS and Low Income Countries: The Cases of China and India's Roles in Africa's Development Paradigm. *International Politics Quarterly* 3: 37–48, 184–185.

Blackorby, Charles, Walter Bossert, and David Donaldson. 1999. Foreign Aid and Population Policy: Some Ethical Considerations. *Journal of Development Economics* 59 (2): 203–232. https://doi.org/10.1016/S0304-3878(99)00010-3.

Boone, Peter. 1996. Politics and the Effectiveness of Foreign Aid. *European Economic Review* 40 (2): 289–329. https://doi.org/10.1016/0014-2921(95)00127-1.

Botting, M.J., E.O. Porbeni, M.R. Joffres, B.C. Johnston, R.E. Black, and E.J. Mills. 2010. Water and Sanitation Infrastructure for Health: The Impact of Foreign Aid. *Global Health* 6: 12. https://doi.org/10.1186/1744-8603-6-12.

Bräutigam, Deborah. 1992. Governance, Economy, and Foreign Aid. *Studies in Comparative International Development* 27 (3): 3.

Bräutigam, Deborah. 1998. *Chinese Aid and African Development: Exporting Green Revolution*. New York: St. Martin's Press.

Bräutigam, Deborah. 2006. State-Building and the Origin of 'Good' Institutions. *Conference Papers-American Political Science Association*, 1.

Bräutigam, Deborah. 2009. *The Dragon's Gift: The Real Story of China in Africa*. Oxford: Oxford University Press.

Bräutigam, Deborah. 2010. China, Africa and the Global Aid Architecture. Rochester: Social Science Research Network.

Bräutigam, Deborah. 2011. Aid 'with Chinese Characteristics': Chinese Foreign Aid and Development Finance Meet the OECD—DAC Aid Regime. *Journal of International Development* 23 (5): 752–764. https://doi.org/10.1002/jid.1798.

Bräutigam, Deborah. 2012. Is China a Challenge to the Global Aid Architecture? *Conference Papers-American Political Science Association*, 1–44.

Bräutigam, Deborah, and Stephen Knack. 2004. Foreign Aid, Institutions, and Governance in Sub-Saharan Africa. *Economic Development and Cultural Change* 52 (2): 255–285.

Bräutigam, Deborah, and Xiaoyang . 2009. China's Engagement in African Agriculture: Down to the Countryside. *The China Quarterly* 199: 686–706. https://doi.org/10.1017/s0305741009990166.

Bräutigam, Deborah, and Xiaoyang Tang. 2011. African Shenzhen: China's Special Economic Zones in Africa. *The Journal of Modern African Studies* 49 (1): 27–54. https://doi.org/10.1017/S0022278X10000649.

Bräutigam, Deborah, and Xiaoyang Tang. 2012. Economic Statecraft in China's New Overseas Special Economic Zones: Soft Power, Business or Resource Security? *International Affairs* 88 (4): 799–816. https://doi.org/10.1111/j.1468-2346.2012.01102.x.

Bräutigam, Deborah, and Haisen Zhang. 2013. Green Dreams: Myth and Reality in China's Agricultural Investment in Africa. *Third World Quarterly* 34 (9): 1676–1696. https://doi.org/10.1080/01436597.2013.843846.

Bräutigam, Deborah, and Kevin P. Gallagher. 2014. Bartering Globalization: China's Commodity-Backed Finance in Africa and Latin America. *Global Policy* 5 (3): 346–352. https://doi.org/10.1111/1758-5899.12138.

Brech, Viktor, and Niklas Potrafke. 2014. Donor Ideology and Types of Foreign Aid. *Journal of Comparative Economics* 42 (1): 61–75. https://doi.org/10.1016/j.jce.2013.07.002.

Broadman, Harry G., Gozde Isik, and World Bank. 2007. *Africa's Silk Road: China and India's New Economic Frontier.* Washington, DC: World Bank.

Broughton, Edward I., Martin Muhire, Esther Karamagi, Herbert Kisamba, and Sarah Smith Lunsford. 2016. *The Effectiveness and Efficiency of Implementing the Chronic Care Model for HIV Care in Uganda.* Washington, DC: USAID.

Brown, Stephen, and Jorn Grävingholt. 2016. *The Securitization of Foreign Aid.* New York: Palgrave Macmillan.

Browne, Stephen. 2012. *Aid and Influence: Do Donors Help or Hinder?* Hoboken: Taylor & Francis.

Burhop, Carsten. 2005. Foreign Assistance and Economic Development: A Re-evaluation. *Economics Letters* 86 (1): 57–61. https://doi.org/10.1016/j.econlet.2004.06.007.

Burt, Ronald. 2008. *Structural Hole: The Social Structure of Competition*, trans. Ren Min, Li Lu, and Lin Hong. Shanghai People's Publishing House.

Burton, A. Abrams, and Kenneth A. Lewis. 1993. Human Rights and the Distribution of U. S. Foreign Aid. *Public Choice* 77 (4): 815–821. https://doi.org/10.2307/30027190.

Busse, Matthias, and Steffen Gröning. 2009. Does Foreign Aid Improve Governance? *Economics Letters* 104 (2): 76–78. https://doi.org/10.1016/j.econlet.2009.04.002.

Cao, Li. 2013. From Millennium Development Goals to Busan Declaration: Evolution of International Aid Theory. *Economic Research Guide* 9: 202–204.

Cao, Jinli, and Wei Song. 2012. Effectiveness Evaluation of American Policy on Aid to Africa. *Journal of International Economic Cooperation* 12: 68–72.

Carey, Sabine C. 2007. European Aid: Human Rights Versus Bureaucratic Inertia? *Journal of Peace Research* 44 (4): 447–464. https://doi.org/10.2307/27640540.

Chai, Wei. 2013. Community Relations Management by CNOOC in Uganda. *China WTO Tribune* 8: 56–57.

Chan-Fishel, Michelle, and Roxanne Lawson. 2007. Quid Pro Quo? China's Investment-for-Resource Swaps in Africa. *Development* 50 (3): 63–68. https://doi.org/10.1057/palgrave.development.1100403.

Charmaz, Kathy. 2009. *Constructing Grounded Theory: A Practical Guide Through Qualitative Analysis*, trans. Bian Guoying. Chongqing University Press.

Chen, Yi. 1962. Foreign Minister Chen Yi's Message to Prime Minister Apollo Milton Obote of Uganda on the Decision of the Government of the People's Republic of China to Recognize Uganda's Independence. *State Council Gazette* 11: 219.

Chen, Luqi. 2009. New Development of China's Aid to Africa in the 21st Century. Master's Thesis, China Foreign Affairs University.

Chen, Haibo. 2014. 51 Years of China Medical Teams in Africa. *Guangming Daily*, August 14, P5.

Chen, Meng, and Shilei Zhai. 2013. Analysis of Comments from German Think Tanks on China-Africa Economic and Trade Relations in Recent Years. *Deutschland-Studien* 4: 62–74, 127.

Chen, Shuisheng, and Guigui Xi. 2013. People's Lives or Democracy? Analysis of China's Aid Diplomacy from the Perspective of Aid to Africa. *Fudan International Studies Review* 1: 174–191.

Cheru, Fantu, and Cyril Obi. 2010. *The Rise of China and India in Africa: Challenges, Opportunities and Critical Interventions.* London, New York, Uppsala and Sweden: Zed Books.

Chhotray, Vasudha, and David Hulme. 2009. Contrasting Visions for Aid and Governance in the 21 st Century: The White House Millennium Challenge Account and DFID's Drivers of Change. *World Development* 37 (1): 36–49. https://doi.org/10.1016/j.worlddev.2007.11.004.

Chong, Alberto, Mark Gradstein, and Cecilia Calderon. 2009. Can Foreign Aid Reduce Income Inequality and Poverty? *Public Choice* 140 (1/2): 59–84. https://doi.org/10.2307/40270909.

Christakis, Nicholas A. and James H. Fowler. 2009. *Connected: The Surprising Power of Our Social Networks and How They Shape Our Lives.* New York: Little, Brown & Company.

Clad, James C., and Roger D. Stone. 1992. New Mission for Foreign Aid. *Foreign Affairs* 72 (1): 196–205. https://doi.org/10.2307/20045506.

Cogneau, Denis, and Jean-David Naudet. 2007. Who Deserves Aid? Equality of Opportunity, International Aid, and Poverty Reduction. *World Development* 35 (1): 104–120. https://doi.org/10.1016/j.worlddev.2006.09.006.

Cohen, Michael A. 2013. Giving to Developing Countries: Controversies and Paradoxes of International Aid. *Social Research* 80 (2): 591–606.

Cohen, John M., Merilee S. Grindle, and S. Tjip Walker. 1985. Foreign Aid and Conditions Precedent: Political and Bureaucratic Dimensions. *World Development* 13 (12): 1211–1230. https://doi.org/10.1016/0305-750x(85)90122-6.

Colenbrander, S., C. Birungi, and A.K. Mbonye. 2015. Consensus and Contention in the Priority Setting Process: Examining the Health Sector in Uganda. *Health Policy and Panning* 30 (5): 555–565. https://doi.org/10.1093/heapol/czu030.

Collier, Paul, and David Dollar. 2001. Can the World Cut Poverty in Half? How Policy Reform and Effective Aid Can Meet International Development Goals. *World Development* 29 (11): 1787–1802. https://doi.org/10.1016/s0305-750x(01)00076-6.

Copper, John Franklin. 2016. *China's Foreign Aid and Investment Diplomacy, Volume II: History and Practice in Asia, 1950–Present*. New York: Palgrave Macmillan.

Crawford, Gordon. 2001. *Foreign Aid and Political Reform: A Comparative Analysis of Democracy Assistance and Political Conditionality*. Basingstoke: Palgrave.

Cumming, Gordon. 1995. French Development Assistance to Africa: Towards a New Agenda? *African Affairs* 94 (376): 383.

Davis, Thomas W.D. 2011. Foreign Aid in Australia's Relationship with the South: Institutional Narratives. *Round Table* 100 (415): 389–406. https://doi.org/10.1080/00358533.2011.595254.

De Waal, Alex. 1997. Democratizing the Aid Encounter in Africa. *International Affairs* 73 (4): 623–639.

Demirel-Pegg, Tijen, and James Moskowitz. 2009. Us Aid Allocation: The Nexus of Human Rights, Democracy, and Development. *Journal of Peace Research* 46 (2): 181–198. https://doi.org/10.2307/25654379.

Dent, Christopher M. 2011. *China and Africa Development Relations*. Hoboken: Taylor & Francis.

Department of International Cooperation, Ministry of Health. 2003. Strengthen the Implementation of New Strategy to Reform Health Aid to Africa—40th Anniversary of the Dispatch of Chinese Medical Teams for Foreign Aid. *West Asia & Africa* 5: 15–18.

de Ree, Joppe, and Eleonora Nillesen. 2009. Aiding Violence or Peace? The Impact of Foreign Aid on the Risk of Civil Conflict in Sub-Saharan Africa. *Journal of Development Economics* 88 (2): 301–313. https://doi.org/10.1016/j.jdeveco.2008.03.005.

Diana, Ntono. 2013. Chinese Multinational Enterprises in East Africa and Economic Diversification. Doctoral Dissertation, Jilin University.

Dicklitch, Susan, and Heather Rice. 2004. The Mennonite Central Committee (MCC) and Faith-Based NGO Aid to Africa. *Development in Practice* 14 (5): 660–672. https://doi.org/10.2307/4029894.

Dieleman, Joseph L., Matthew T. Schneider, Annie Haakenstad, Lavanya Singh, Nafis Sadat, Maxwell Birger, Alex Reynolds, Tara Templin, Hannah Hamavid, Abigail Chapin, and Christopher J. L. Murray. 2016. Development Assistance for Health: Past Trends, Associations, and the Future of International Financial Flows for Health. *The Lancet* 387 (10037): 2536–2544. http://dx.doi.org/10.1016/S0140-6736(16)30168-4.

Dietrich, Simone. 2011. The Politics of Public Health Aid: Why Corrupt Governments Have Incentives to Implement Aid Effectively. *World Development* 39 (1): 55–63. http://dx.doi.org/10.1016/j.worlddev.2010.06.011.

Ding, Xuhong, and Daqing Zhang. 2010. Early Chinese Medical Teams in Africa (1963–1978): Among Medicine, Politics and Culture. *Medicine & Philosophy* 15: 76–78.

Dollar, David, and Victoria Levin. 2006. The Increasing Selectivity of Foreign Aid, 1984–2003. *World Development* 34 (12): 2034–2046. https://doi.org/10.1016/j.worlddev.2006.06.002.

Dreher, Axel, Andreas Fuchs, Roland Hodler, Bradley Parks, Paul A. Raschky, and Michael J. Tierney. 2015. *Aid on Demand: African Leaders and the Geography of China's Foreign Assistance.* Rochester: Social Science Research Network.

Du, Ying. 2011. Research on the Relations Between India and East African Countries (1964–2000). Doctoral Dissertation, East China Normal University.

Due, Jean M. 1993. Liberalization and Privatization in Tanzania and Zambia. *World Development* 21 (12): 1981.

Dutta, Nabamita, Peter T. Leeson, and Claudia R. Williamson. 2013. The Amplification Effect: Foreign Aid's Impact on Political Institutions. *Kyklos* 66 (2): 208–228. https://doi.org/10.1111/kykl12018.

Easterly, William. 2006. *The White Man's Burden: Why the West's Efforts to Aid the Rest Have Done So Much Ill and So Little Good.* Oxford: Oxford University Press.

Easterly, William. 2009. Can the West Save Africa? *Journal of Economic Literature* 47 (2): 373–447. https://doi.org/10.2307/27739927.

Easterly, William, and Claudia R. Williamson. 2011. Rhetoric Versus Reality: The Best and Worst of Aid Agency Practices. *World Development* 39 (11): 1930–1949. https://doi.org/10.1016/j.worlddev.2011.07.027.

Economic and Commercial Counsellor's Office, Chinese Embassy in Uganda. 2013. China-Uganda Economic and Trade Cooperation into New Stage. *International Business Daily*, October 22, C03.

Fan, Victoria Y., Karen A. Grepin, Gordon C. Shen, and Lucy Chen. 2014. Tracking the Flow of Health Aid from BRICS Countries. *Bulletin of the World Health Organization* 92 (6): 457–458. https://doi.org/10.1377/hlthaff.2011.1154. PMID: 22174301.

Feeny, Simon, and Ashton de Silva. 2012. Measuring Absorptive Capacity Constraints to Foreign Aid. *Economic Modelling* 29 (3): 725–733. https://doi.org/10.1016/j.econmod.2012.01.013.

Feeny, Simon, and Tim R.L. Fry. 2014. How Sustainable is the Macro-economic Impact of Foreign Aid? *Journal of Policy Modeling* 36 (6): 1066–1081. https://doi.org/10.1016/j.jpolmod.2014.11.001.

Feng, Zheying. 2010. A Comparative Study of Aid to Africa from China and the US in the Early 21st Century. Master's Thesis, China Foreign Affairs University.

Fisher, Jonathan. 2015. 'Does It Work?': Work for Whom? Britain and Political Conditionality Since the Cold War. *World Development* 75: 13–25. https://doi.org/10.1016/j.worlddev.2014.12.005.

Fleck, Robert K., and Christopher Kilby. 2010. Changing Aid Regimes? U.S. Foreign Aid from the Cold War to the War on Terror. *Journal of Development Economics* 91 (2): 185–197. https://doi.org/10.1016/j.jdeveco.2009.09.011.

Francken, Nathalie, Bart Minten, and Johan F.M. Swinnen. 2012. The Political Economy of Relief Aid Allocation: Evidence from Madagascar. *World Development* 40 (3): 486.

Freeman, Charles, and Xiaoqing Boynton Lu. 2011. *China's Emerging Global Health and Foreign Aid Engagement in Africa*. Washington, DC: CSIS.

French, Howard W. 2014. *China's Second Continent: How a Million Migrants are Building a New Empire in Africa*. New York: Vintage Books.

Frenk, Julio, and Steven Hoffman. 2015. *To Save Humanity: What Matters Most for a Healthy Future*. Oxford: Oxford University Press.

Fu, Qingye. 2013. Study on Health Aid from Hunan to Africa (1973–2013). Master's Thesis, Hunan Normal University.

Fu, Ruiwei, and Xiaoqing Lv. 2011. China's Policy on Global Health and Foreign Aid in Africa. Reports of the Center for and International Studies.

Fuchs, Andreas, and Krishna Chaitanya Vadlamannati. 2013. The Needy Donor: An Empirical Analysis of India's Aid Motives. *World Development* 44: 110–128. https://doi.org/10.1016/j.worlddev.2012.12.012.

Fuchs, Andreas, Axel Dreher, and Peter Nunnenkamp. 2014. Determinants of Donor Generosity: A Survey of the Aid Budget Literature. *World Development* 56: 172–199. https://doi.org/10.1016/j.worlddev.2013.09.004.

Furia, Annalisa. 2015. *The Foreign Aid Regime: Gift-Giving, States and Global Dis/Order*. New York: Palgrave Macmillan.

Gadzala, Aleksandra W. 2010. From Formal-to Informal-Sector Employment: Examining the Chinese Presence in Zambia. *Review of African Political Economy* 37 (123): 41–59. https://doi.org/10.2307/27860746.

Gao, Guixian. 2014. China-Africa Agricultural Cooperation: Patterns, Performance and Strategies. Doctoral Dissertation, Huazhong Agricultural University.

Gerhart, Gail M. 1999. Aid to Africa: So Much to Do, So Little Done. *Foreign Affairs* 78 (6): 163.

Ghosh Banerjee, Sudeshna, and Dennis A. Rondinelli. 2003. Does Foreign Aid Promote Privatization? Empirical Evidence from Developing Countries. *World Development* 31 (9): 1527–1548. https://doi.org/10.1016/s0305-750x(03)00107-4.

Giddens, Anthony. 1998. *The Constitution of Society*, trans. Li Kang and Li Meng. DAX Joint Publishing Company.

Golley, Jane, and Ligang Song. 2011. *Rising China: Global Challenges and Opportunities*. Canberra: ANU Press.

Gomez, Simon Peter. 2007. Human Rights and the Allocation of Foreign Aid: A Cross-National Analysis of the Last Years of the Cold War, 1980–1989. *The Social Science Journal* 44 (2): 275–285. https://doi.org/10.1016/j.soscij.2007.03.018.

Gong, Wei. 2014. Analysis of Political Functions of Japan's Development Aid to Africa. *Pacific Journal* 2: 63–75.

Granovetter, Mark. 1985. Economic Action and Social Structure: The Problem of Embeddedness. *American Journal of Sociology* 91 (3): 481–510. https://doi.org/10.2307/2780199.

Grépin, Karen A., Victoria Y. Fan, Gordon C. Shen, and Lucy Chen. 2014. China's Role as a Global Health Donor in Africa: What Can We Learn from Studying Under Reported Resource Flows? *Global Health* 10 (1): 1–11. https://doi.org/10.1186/s12992-014-0084-6.

Grimm, Sven. 2008. Africa-China-Europe Trilateral Co-operation: Is Europe Naive? EDC 2020-Opinion No. 1. European Development Co-operation to 2020.

Grimm, Sven. 2011. Engaging with China in Africa Trilateral Cooperation as an Option? EDC 2020-Policy Brief No. 9. European Development Cooperation to 2020.

Grimm, Sven, John Humphrey, Erik Lundsgaarde, and Sarah-Lea John de Sousa. 2009. Challenges by New Actors in International Development. EDC 2020-Working Paper No. 4, European Development Co-operation to 2020.

Gu, Jing, and Anthony Carty. 2014. China and African Development: Partnership Not Mentoring. *IDS Bulletin* 45: 57–69. https://doi.org/10.1111/1759-5436.12093.

Gui, Xian, Yueji Zhu, and Deyi Zhou. 2014. China-Africa Agricultural Cooperation: Dilemma, Status and Countermeasures. *China Soft Science* 1: 36–42.

Guloba, Madina, Nicholas Kilimani, and Winnie Nabiddo. 2010. *Impact of China-Africa Aid Relations: A Case Study of Uganda*. Kampala: Economic Policy Research Centre (EPRC).

Gulrajani, Nilima. 2011. Transcending the Great Foreign Aid Debate: Managerialism, Radicalism and the Search for Aid Effectiveness. *Third World Quarterly* 32 (2): 199–216. https://doi.org/10.1080/01436597.2011.560465.

Hackenesch, Christine. 2011. European Good Governance Policies Meet China in Africa: Insights from Angola and Ethiopia. EDC 2020-Working Paper No. 10, European Development Co-operation to 2020.

Han, Qide, Lincoln Chen, Tim Evans, and Richard Horton. 2008. China and Global Health. *The Lancet* 372 (9648): 1439–1441. https://doi.org/10.1016/s0140-6736(08)61350-1.

Harneit-Sievers, Axel, Stephen Marks, and Sanusha Naidu. 2010. *Chinese and African Perspectives on China in Africa*. London: Fahamu and Pambazuka.

Hatzipanayotou, Panos, and Michael S. Michael. 1995. Foreign Aid and Public Goods. *Journal of Development Economics* 47 (2): 455–467. https://doi.org/10.1016/0304-3878(95)00020-Q.

He, Xianfeng. 2011. Evolution and Characteristics of China's Aid to Africa. *Reform & Opening* 14: 23–24.

He, Wenping. 2011a. From "Aid Effectiveness" to "Development Effectiveness": Evolution of Aid Concepts and Role of Chinese Experience. *West Asia and Africa* 9: 120–135.

He, Wenping. 2011b. China's Aid to Africa: "Teach Them to Fish". *People's Daily* (Overseas Edition), September 3, P1.

He, Tianhao. 2012. Back to ABCs: Emerging Partnerships Among Africa, Brazil, and China. *Harvard International Review* 34 (1): 30–33.

He, Dazhuo. 2013. "Expensive Aid": Tanzania-China Friendship Textile Company. *China Textile & Apparel* 5: 35.

He, Wenping. 2013. Japan's Aid to Africa: Objectives and Impacts. *Contemporary World* 8: 25–28.

Heckelman, Jac C., and Stephen Knack. 2008. Foreign Aid and Market Liberalizing Reform. *Economica* 75 (299): 524–548. https://doi.org/10.2307/40071816.

Hermano, Vmtor, and Natalia Martm-Cruz. 2013. How to Deliver Foreign Aid? The Case of Projects Governed by the Spanish International Agency. *World Development* 43: 298–314. https://doi.org/10.1016/j.worlddev.2012.10.017.

Hsieh, Chang-Tai. 2000. Bargaining over Reform. *European Economic Review* 44 (9): 1659–1676. https://doi.org/10.1016/s0014-2921(99)00012-4.

https://doi.org/10.1377/hlthaff.2011.1154. PMID: 22174301.

Hu, Mei. 2010. A Comparative Study of China's and the US Strategies for Aid to Africa. *Journal of Hunan University of Arts and Science* 5: 30–34.

Hu, Mei. 2011. 50 Years of China's Aid to Africa and Innovation of International Aid Theory. *Socialism Study* 1: 141–146.

Hu, Mei, and Hingwu Liu. 2009. Ideology First or Livelihood First: A Comparative Study on Western and China's Policies on Aid to Africa after the Cold War. *World Economy and Politics* 10: 17–24.

Hu, Angang, Yuning Gao, Yilong Yan, and Xing Wei. 2014. China's Role in the Rising of the South: Vision for 2030. *IDS Bulletin* 45: 6–21. https://doi.org/10.1111/1759-5436.12089.

Huang, Y. 2010. Pursuing Health as Foreign Policy: The Case of China. *Indiana Journal of Global Legal Studies* 17: 105–146. https://doi.org/10.2979/gls.2010.17.1.105.

Huang, Jianyin. 2012. Opportunities and Challenges of Traditional Chinese Medicine in Africa. *China Medicine Daily*, May 7, P8.

Huang, Zhanhua. 2013. *Ningxia Medical Team in Benin*. Yinchuan: Ningxia People's Publishing House.

Huang, Ling. 2016. Set an Example for China-Africa Agricultural Cooperation: Practice and Exploration of Sichuan-Uganda Agricultural Cooperation. *Sichuan Agriculture and Agricultural Machinery* 2: 6–7.

Huang, Yan. 2016. China Supports Uganda Agricultural Trade Organization. *World Tropical Agriculture Information* 2: 19.

Huang, Meibo, and Jianyan Lang. 2010. China's Aid to Africa and the Challenges. *Journal of International Economic Cooperation* 6: 34–40.

Huang, Meibo, and Qi Xie. 2012. Characteristics and Trends of India's Foreign Aid. *Journal of International Economic Cooperation* 1: 63–68.

Humphrey, John. 2011. Chinese Development Cooperation and the EU. EDC 2020-Policy Brief No. 17. European Development Co-operation to 2020.

Hyden, Goran, and Shlomo Reutlinger. 1992. Foreign Aid in a Period of Democratization: The Case of Politically Autonomous Food Funds. *World Development* 20 (9): 1253–1260. https://doi.org/10.1016/0305-750x(92)90076-8.

International Business Daily. 2010. Aid to Africa: Eight New and Old Initiatives. *International Business Daily*, August 14, B04.

Jakobson, Linda. 2009. China's Diplomacy Toward Africa: Drivers and Constraints. *International Relations of the Asia Pacific* 9 (3): 403–433. https://doi.org/10.1093/irap/lcp008.

Jakupec, Viktor, and Max Kelly (eds.). 2016. *Assessing the Impact of Foreign Aid: Value for Money and Aid for Trade*. Amsterdam: Academic Press.

Jiang, Lei, and Haijun Wang. 2011. Analysis of Differences in Political Strings in Foreign Aid: A Comparative Study Based on Foreign Aid Practices of China and Western Countries. *Pacific Journal* 7: 53–62.

Jiang, Huajie. 2015. Reexamination of the History of China's Medical Teams to Africa (1963–1983): A Discussion on Effectiveness and Sustainability of

International Aid. *Foreign Affairs Review—Journal of China Foreign Affairs University* 4: 61–81.

Jiang, Xiaoxiao, and Chen Zhang. 2013. Investigative Report on Chinese Medical Teams to the Democratic Republic of Congo. *China African Research Review* 2012: 18.

Johnson, Ken Deji. 2010. Reorienting U.S. Aid to Africa-in America's Interest. *American Foreign Policy Interests,* 32 (4), 229–236.

Jones, Sam. 2015. Aid Supplies over Time: Addressing Heterogeneity, Trends, and Dynamics. *World Development* 69: 31–43. https://doi.org/10.1016/j.worlddev.2013.12.014.

Ju, Zhengbo. 2010. Research on Direct Investment of Chinese Enterprises in Africa. Master's Thesis, Yunnan University.

Juliet, Nabyonga Orem, Ssengooba Freddie, and Sam Okuonzi. 2009. Can Donor Aid for Health Be Effective in a Poor Country? Assessment of Prerequisites for Aid Effectiveness in Uganda. *The Pan African Medical Journal* 3 (9): 9.

Kang, Sheng. 2012. India's Strategy for Expanding Economic and Trade Relations with Africa and Its Inspiration for China. *Macroeconomic Research* 12: 98–105.

Kasekende, L.A., and Atingi-Ego, M. 1999. Uganda's Experience with Aid. *Journal of African Economies* 8 (4): 617.

Kenyon, Georgina. 2010. China Offers Billions in Loans to Boost Health Research in Africa. *Nature Medicine* 16 (1): 8. https://doi.org/10.1038/nm0110-8b.

Kersting, Erasmus, and Christopher Kilby. 2014. Aid and Democracy Redux. *European Economic Review* 67: 125–143. https://doi.org/10.1016/j.euroecorev.2014.01.016.

Khan, Haider Ali, and Eiichi Hoshino. 1992. Impact of Foreign Aid on the Fiscal Behavior of LDC Governments. *World Development* 20 (10): 1481–1488. https://doi.org/10.1016/0305-750x(92)90068-7.

Kilby, Christopher. 2011. What Determines the Size of Aid Projects? *World Development* 39 (11): 1981–1994. https://doi.org/10.1016/j.worlddev.2011.07.023.

King, J.R. 1953. Science Versus Administration in Certain U. S. Foreign Aid Efforts. *Science* 117 (3047): 568–569. https://doi.org/10.1126/science.117.3047.568.

King, Kenneth. 2010. China's Cooperation in Education and Training with Kenya: A Different Model? *International Journal of Educational Development* 30 (5): 488–496. https://doi.org/10.1016/j.ijedudev.2010.03.014.

King, Kenneth. 2011. The New Aid Architecture in Ghana: Influencing Policy and Practice? *The European Journal of Development Research* 23 (4): 648–667. https://doi.org/10.1057/ejdr.2011.26.

King, Kenneth. 2013. *China's Aid & Soft Power in Africa: The Case of Education & Training*. Woodbridge, Suffolk: James Currey.

Knack, Stephen. 2004. Does Foreign Aid Promote Democracy? *International Studies Quarterly* 48 (1): 251–266. https://doi.org/10.2307/3693571.

Kobayashi, Takaaki. 2008. *Evolution of China's Aid Policy*, vol. 27. Tokyo: JBIC Institute.

Koch, Svea. 2015. A Typology of Political Conditionality Beyond Aid: Conceptual Horizons Based on Lessons from the European Union. *World Development* 75: 97–108. https://doi.org/10.1016/j.worlddev.2015.01.006.

Kono, Daniel Yuichi, and Gabriella R. Montinola. 2009. Does Foreign Aid Support Autocrats, Democrats, or Both? *The Journal of Politics* 71 (2): 704–718. https://doi.org/10.2307/30218980.

Kosack, Stephen. 2003. Effective Aid: How Democracy Allows Development Aid to Improve the Quality of Life. *World Development* 31 (1): 1–22. https://doi.org/10.1016/s0305-750x(02)00177-8.

Kourtellos, Andros, Chih Ming, and Xiaobo Zhang. 2007. Is the Relationship Between Aid and Economic Growth Nonlinear? *Journal of Macroeconomics* 29 (3): 515–540. https://doi.org/10.1016/j.jmacro.2007.02.07.

Kurlantzick, Joshua. 2007. *Charm Offensive: How China's Soft Power is Transforming the World*. New Haven: Yale University Press.

Lambert, Marie-Laurence. 1996. Foreign Aid and Tuberculosis Control Policy in the Federated States of Micronesia. *The Lancet* 347 (8997): 334–335. https://doi.org/10.1016/S0140-6736(96)90516-4.

Lancaster, Carol. 2007. *Foreign Aid: Diplomacy, Development, Domestic Politics*. Chicago, IL and London: University of Chicago Press.

Lebovic, James H. 2005. Donor Positioning: Development Assistance from the U. S., Japan, France, Germany, and Britain. *Political Research Quarterly* 58 (1): 119–126. https://doi.org/10.2307/3595601.

Lebovic, James H., and Erik Voeten. 2009. The Cost of Shame: International Organizations and Foreign Aid in the Punishing of Human Rights Violators. *Journal of Peace Research* 46 (1): 79–97. https://doi.org/10.2307/27640800.

Lei, Vivian, Steven Tucker, and Filip Vesely. 2007. Foreign Aid and Weakest-Link International Public Goods: An Experimental Study. *European Economic Review* 51 (3): 599–623. https://doi.org/10.1016/j.euroecorev.2006.03.008.

Leonard, David K. 2005. Foreign Aid and Development: Lessons Learnt and Directions for the Future. *The Journal of Modern African Studies* 43 (1): 153–154.

Li, Anshan. 2008a. China's Africa Strategy: National Image and Strategies. *China International Strategic Review* 2008: 14.

Li, Anshan. 2008b. In Defense of China: China's Africa Strategy and National Image. *World Economy and Politics* 4: 6–15.

Li, Anshan. 2009. History, Scale and Impact of Chinese Medical Teams for Foreign Aid. *Foreign Affairs Review—Journal of China Foreign Affairs University* 1: 25–45.

Li, Anshan. 2010. China's Aid to Africa: A Narrative by an American Scholar. *Foreign Affairs Review—Journal of China Foreign Affairs University* 5: 12–19.

Li, Anshan. 2011. *Chinese Medical Cooperation in Africa: With Special Emphasis on the Medical Teams and Anti-Malaria Campaign*. Uppsala: Nordiska Afrikainstitutet. ISBN: 9171066837.

Li, Weitao. 2011. A Comparative Study of China's and EU Aid to Africa. Master's Degree Thesis, Central China Normal University.

Li, Jiali. 2012a. The Origin, Essence and Impact of "New Colonialism" Theory on China's Aid to Africa. Master's Thesis, East China Normal University.

Li, Jiali. 2012b. The Forms and Effectiveness of China-Africa Agricultural Cooperation. *World Agriculture* 12: 8–12.

Li, Wengang. 2013. "Soft Power" in China-Africa Relations. *West Asia and Africa* 5: 130–146.

Li, Xuedong. 2016. Potential and Dilemma of China-Africa Industrial Cooperation: A Case Study of Uganda. *Modern Management Science* 4: 69–71.

Li, Xiaoyun, and Jin Wu. 2009. Practical Experience and Challenges of China's Aid to Africa. *Journal of China Agricultural University* (Social Science Edition) 4: 45–54.

Li, Xiying, and Junying Huang. 2012. Adjustment to Britain's Policy on Aid to Africa. *Journal of International Economic Cooperation* 4: 82–86.

Li, Jihonh, and Jiashun Li. 2016. Ugandan AN Expressway Project Successfully Delivered by China Railway No. 5 Engineering Group. *International Project Contracting & Labor Service* 7: 93.

Liang, Wenjie. 2015. Status Quo and Development Strategy of Guangxi Medical Team to Africa. Master's Thesis, Guangxi Medical University.

Liao, Lan, and Jing Liu. 2012. Research on China's Foreign Aid from the Western Perspective. *Journal of China Agricultural University* (Social Science Edition) 4: 93–101.

Lim, Sijeong, Layna Mosley, and Aseem Prakash. 2015. Revenue Substitution? How Foreign Aid Inflows Moderate the Effect of Bilateral Trade Pressures on Labor Rights. *World Development* 67: 295–309. https://doi.org/10.1016/j.worlddev.2014.10.025.

Liu, Zhongwei. 2012. An Analysis of German Development Aid to Rwanda. *West Asia and Africa* 5: 144–160.

Liu, Guijin. 2013. The US Africa Strategy and Its Inspiration for China. *Party Building* 5: 62–64.

Liu, Jianhao, and Xiaoxiang Quan. 2013. The Health Status of Zanzibar and Service Effectiveness of Chinese Medical Teams to Sangzang. *Jiangsu Health Management* 5: 283–285.

Liu, Xiangbo, Xiaomeng Zhang, and Chi-Chur Chao. 2014. Foreign Aid, Leisure Effort Choice, and Economic Growth. *Economic Modelling* 43: 435–438. https://doi.org/10.1016/j.econmod.2014.09.006.

Liu, Peilong, Yan Guo, Xu Qian, Shenglan Tang, Zhihui Li, and Lincoln Chen. 2014. China's Distinctive Engagement in Global Health. *The Lancet* 384 (9945): 793–804. https://doi.org/10.1016/s0140-6736(14)60725-X.

Lo, Gourmo Abdoul. 2012. Africa and China: New Colonialism or New Strategic Partnership. *Foreign Theoretical Trends* 9: 77–82.

Lof, Matthijs, Tseday Jemaneh Mekasha, and Finn Tarp. 2014. Aid and Income: Another Time-Series Perspective. *World Development*. https://doi.org/10.1016/j.worlddev.2013.12.015.

Lopes Sanches, Leinira. 2009. Aid to Africa: Chinese Modes. Master's Thesis, Jilin University.

Lskavyan, Vahe. 2014. Donor-Recipient Ideological Differences and Economic Aid. *Economics Letters* 123 (3): 345–347. https://doi.org/10.1016/j.econlet.2014.03.016.

Lu, Miaomiao. 2015. An Analysis of Investment and Business Environment of Chinese Enterprises in Uganda. Master's Thesis, China Foreign Affairs University.

Luo, Jianbo. 2007. Improve China's Soft Power in Africa. *Asia & Africa Review* 6: 18–24.

Ma, Jianhua. 1992. Revival of Kibimba Farm in Uganda. *Journal of International Economic Cooperation* 12: 38.

Ma, Yao. 2016. No Political Strings Ever—60 Years of China's Aid to Africa. *World Vision* 12: 22–25.

Martin, George. 2013. China's Soft Power in Africa: A Case Study in Uganda. Master's Thesis, Fudan University.

Martins, Pedro M.G. 2011. Aid Absorption and Spending in Africa: A Panel Cointegration Approach. *The Journal of Development Studies* 47 (12): 1925–1953. https://doi.org/10.1080/00220388.2011.579115.

Matsiko, Charles W. 2010. Positive Practice Environments in Uganda: Enhancing Health Worker and Healthcare System Performance. The Global Health Workforce Alliance.

McCormick, Dorothy. 2008. China & India as Africa's New Donors: The Impact of Aid on Development. *Review of African Political Economy* 35 (115): 73–92. https://doi.org/10.2307/20406478.

McGiffert, Carola. 2009. *Chinese Soft Power and Its Implications for the United States: Competition and Cooperation in the Developing World*. Washington, DC: Center for Strategic and International Studies.

McGrath, Simon. 2010. Beyond Aid Effectiveness: The Development of the South African Further Education and Training College Sector, 1994–2009. *International Journal of Educational Development* 30 (5): 525–534. https://doi.org/10.1016/j.ijedudev.2010.03.011.

Mekasha, Tseday Jemaneh, and Finn Tarp. 2013. Aid and Growth: What Meta-Analysis Reveals. *The Journal of Development Studies* 49 (4): 564–583. https://doi.org/10.1080/00220388.2012.709621.

Men, Jing, and Benjamin Barton. 2011. *China and the European Union in Africa: Partners or Competitors?*. Burlington, VT: Ashgate.

Meredith, Martin. 2001. *The State of Africa*, trans. Ya Ming. World Knowledge Press, 6–7.

Miller, Daniel C. 2014. Explaining Global Patterns of International Aid for Linked Biodiversity Conservation and Development. *World Development* 59: 341–359. https://doi.org/10.1016/j.worlddev.2014.01.004.

Ministry of Health. 2015. *Healthcare Workers Bi-Annual Report.* Kampala: Ministey of Health.

Minoiu, Camelia, and Sanjay G. Reddy. 2010. Development Aid and Economic Growth: A Positive Long-Run Relation. *The Quarterly Review of Economics and Finance* 50 (1): 27–39. https://doi.org/10.1016/j.qref.2009.10.004.

Mishra, Prachi, and David Newhouse. 2009. Does Health Aid Matter? *Journal of Health Economics* 28 (4): 855–872. https://doi.org/10.1016/j.jhealeco.2009.05.004.

Molenaers, Nadia, Sebastian Dellepiane, and Jorg Faust. 2015. Political Conditionality and Foreign Aid. *World Development* 75: 2–12. https://doi.org/10.1016/j.worlddev.2015.04.001.

Moyo, Dambisa. 2009. *Dead Aid: Why Aid Is Not Working and How There Is Another Way for Africa*. London: Allen Lane.

Moyo, Dambisa. 2012. *Winner Take All: China's Race for Resources and What It Means for Us.* London: Allen Lane.

Muchapondwa, Edwin, Daniel Nielson, Bradley Parks, Austin M. Strange, and Michael J. Tierney. 2014. 'Ground-Truthing' Chinese Development Finance in Africa. Wider Working Paper 2014/031, World Institute for Development Economics Research.

Mundy, Karen, Megan Haggerty, Malini Sivasubramaniam, Suzanne Cherry, and Richard Maclure. 2010. Civil Society, Basic Education, and Sector-Wide Aid: Insights from Sub-Saharan Africa. *Development in Practice* 20 (4/5): 484–497. https://doi.org/10.2307/20750147.

Muravchik, Joshua. 1996. Affording Foreign Policy: The Problem Is Not Wallet, But Will. *Foreign Affairs* 75 (2): 8–13. https://doi.org/10.2307/20047484.

Murray, C.J.L., B. Anderson, R. Burstein, K. Leach-Kemon, M. Schneider, A. Tardif, and R. Zhang. 2011. Development Assistance for Health: Trends and Prospects. *The Lancet* 378. https://doi.org/10.1016/s0140-6736(10)62356-2.

Museru, Malimu, Francois Toerien, and Sean Gossel. 2014. The Impact of Aid and Public Investment Volatility on Economic Growth in Sub-Saharan

Africa. *World Development* 57: 138–147. https://doi.org/10.1016/j.worlddev.2013.12.001.

Musolf, Lloyd D. 1963. Overview Overseas: Dilemma for Aid Missions. *Public Administration Review* 23 (4): 219–226. https://doi.org/10.2307/973896.

Mwenda, Andrew M., and Roger Tangri. 2005. Patronage Politics, Donor Reforms, and Regime Consolidation in Uganda. *African Affairs* 104 (416): 449–467. https://doi.org/10.2307/3518724.

Ndikumana, Léonce and Lynda Pickbourn. 2015. The Impact of Foreign Aid Allocation on Access to Social Services in Sub-Saharan Africa: The Case of Water and Sanitation, vol. 400. Working Paper, Political Economy Research Institute, Umass Amherst.

Ni, Guohua, Jing Zhang, Dong Ding, and Fengtian Zheng. 2014. Influence of Personal Traits of Experts Aiding Africa on Their Performance: An Empirical Analysis Based on Cross-Sectional Data of 100 Experts. *World Agriculture* 9: 163–169.

Nielsen, Richard A., Michael G. Findley, Zachary S. Davis, Tara Candland, and Daniel L. Nielson. 2011. Foreign Aid Shocks as a Cause of Violent Armed Conflict. *American Journal of Political Science* 55 (2): 219–232. https://doi.org/10.1111/j.1540-5907.2010.00492.x.

Niu, Changsong. 2014. China's Educational Cooperation with Africa: Toward New Strategic Partnerships. *Asian Education and Development Studies* 3 (1): 31–45. https://doi.org/10.1108/aeds-09-2013-0057.

Niyizonkiza, Deogratias, and Alyssa Yamamoto. 2013. Grassroots Philanthropy: Fighting the Power Asymmetries of Aid in Rural Burundi. *Social Research* 80 (2): 321–336.

Nunnenkamp, Peter, and Hannes Ohler. 2012. Funding, Competition and the Efficiency of NGOs: An Empirical Analysis of Non-charitable Expenditure of Us NGOs Engaged in Foreign Aid. *Kyklos* 65 (1): 81–110. https://doi.org/10.1111/j.1467-6435.201.00528.x.

Obermann, Konrad. 2007. Global Health and Foreign Policy. *The Lancet* 369 (9574): 1688. https://doi.org/10.1016/s0140-6736(07)60769-7.

Odokonyero, Tonny, Alex Ijjo, Robert Marty, Tony Muhumuza, and Godfrey Owot Moses. 2015. Sub-national Perspectives on Aid Effectiveness: Impact of Aid on Health Outcomes in Uganda. Working Paper 18, AidData.

OECD. 1991. *DAC Principles for Evaluation of Development Assistance*. Paris: Development Assistance Committee.

OECD. 2012. *OECD Factbook* 2011: *Economic, Environmental and Social Statistics*. Paris, France and Bristol, UK: OECD.

Ohler, Hannes, Peter Nunnenkamp, and Axel Dreher. 2012. Does Conditionality Work? A Test for an Innovative Us Aid Scheme. *European Economic Review* 56 (1): 138–153. https://doi.org/10.1016/j.euroecorev.2011.05.003.

Okada, Keisuke, and Sovannroeun Samreth. 2012. The Effect of Foreign Aid on Corruption: A Quantile Regression Approach. *Economics Letters* 115 (2): 240–243. https://doi.org/10.1016/j.econlet.2011.12.051.

Okwero, Peter, Ajay Tandon, Susan Sparkes, Julie McLaughlin, and Johannes G. Hoogeveen. 2010. *Fiscal Space for Health in Uganda*, vol. 186. Washington, DC: World Bank.

Otter, Mark. 2003. Domestic Public Support for Foreign Aid: Does It Matter? *Third World Quarterly* 24 (1):115–125. https://doi.org/10.2307/3993633.

Ouattara, B. 2006. Foreign Aid and Government Fiscal Behaviour in Developing Countries: Panel Data Evidence. *Economic Modelling* 23 (3): 506–514. https://doi.org/10.1016/j.econmod.2006.02.001.

Papanek, Gustav F. 1973. Aid, Foreign Private Investment, Savings, and Growth in Less Developed Countries. *Journal of Political Economy* 81 (1): 120–130. https://doi.org/10.2307/1837329.

Parfitt, Tom. 2005. Russia Clamps Down on Foreign Aid Organisations. *The Lancet* 366 (9502): 1993. https://doi.org/10.1016/S0140-6736(05)67798-7.

Paxton, Pamela, and Stephen Knack. 2012. Individual and Country-Level Factors Affecting Support for Foreign Aid. *International Political Science Review/Revue internationale de science politique* 33 (2): 171–192. https://doi.org/10.1177/0192512111406095.

Pfaff, William. 1995. A New Colonialism? Europe Must Go Back into Africa. *Foreign Affairs* 74 (1): 2.

Phelps, Nicholas A., John C.H. Stillwell, and Roseline Wanjiru. 2009. Broken Chain? AGOA and Foreign Direct Investment in the Kenyan Clothing Industry. *World Development* 37 (2): 314.

Polanyi, Karl. 2007. *The Great Transformation*, trans. Yang Liu and Gang Feng. Zhejiang People's Publishing House.

Power, Marcus, Giles Mohan, and May Tan-Mullins. 2012. *China's Resource Diplomacy in Africa: Powering Development?* Houndmills, Basingstoke and New York, NY: Palgrave Macmillan.

Puetz, Detlev. 2006. *Uganda Joint Assistance Strategy: A Review of the Harmonization Process in Five Countries.* Abidjan: African Development Bank Group.

Qiu, Changqing, and Erwei Liu. 2012. An Analysis of India's Economic Diplomacy in Africa from the Perspective of Political Power. *South Asia Studies* 1: 30–44.

Rebol, Max. 2011. Non-interference and Practical Cooperation: An Analysis on China's Soft Power in Africa. Doctoral Dissertation, Fudan University.

Reinsberg, Bernhard. 2014. Foreign Aid Responses to Political Liberalization. *World Development*. https://doi.org/10.1016/j.worlddev.2014.11.006.

Ren, Minghui and Guoping Lu. 2014. China's Global Health Strategy. *The Lancet* 384 (9945):719–721. https://doi.org/10.1016/s0140-6736(14)61317-9.

Resnick, Danielle, and Nicolas Van de Walle. 2013. Democratic Trajectories in Africa: Unravelling the Impact of Foreign Aid. A Study Prepared by the United Nations University World Institute for Development Economics Research (UNU-WIDER).

Rimmer, Douglas. 2000. Aid and Corruption. *African Affairs* 99 (394): 121–128.

Rioux, Jean-Sebastien, and Douglas A. Van Belle. 2005. The Influence of Le Monde Coverage on French Foreign Aid Allocations. *International Studies Quarterly* 49 (3): 481–502. https://doi.org/10.2307/3693604.

Roodman, David. 2012. Doubts About the Evidence That Foreign Aid for Health Is Displaced into Non-health Uses. *The Lancet* 380 (9846): 972–973. https://doi.org/10.1016/s0140-6736(12)61529-3.

Rotberg, Robert I. 2009. *China into Africa: Trade, Aid, and Influence.* Washington, DC: Brookings Institution Press.

Rupp, Stephanie. 2013. China and the European Union in Africa: Partners or Competitors? *African Studies Review* 56: 190–192. https://doi.org/10.1353/arw.2013.0005.

Saghafi, Massoud Mokhtari, and Jeffrey B. Nugent. 1983. Foreign Aid in the Form of Commodity Transfers That Increase the Income Gap Between Rich and Poor Countries: The Chichilnisky Theorems Revisited. *Journal of Development Economics* 13 (1–2): 213–216. https://doi.org/10.1016/0304-3878(83)90061-5.

Sam, Waigolo. 2013. Impact of FDI on Specific Interests of Established and New Firms in Uganda's Business Environment. Master's Thesis, Ningbo University.

Santos-Paulino, Amelia U., and Guanghua Wan. 2010. *The Rise of China and India.* London, UK: Palgrave Macmillan.

Sautman, Barry, and Yan Hairong. 2007. Friends and Interests: China's Distinctive Links with Africa. *African Studies Review* 50 (3): 75–114. https://doi.org/10.2307/27667241.

Schaferhoff, Marco, Sara Fewer, Jessica Kraus, Emil Richter, Lawrence H. Summers, Jesper Sundewall, Gavin Yamey, and Dean T. Jamison. 2015. How Much Donor Financing for Health Is Channelled to Global Versus Country-Specific Aid Functions? *The Lancet* 386 (10011): 2436–2441. https://doi.org/10.1016/s0140-6736(15)61161-8.

Schiere, Richard. 2014. The Impact of China on the Donor Landscape in African Fragile States. *IDS Bulletin* 45: 46–56. https://doi.org/10.111/1759-5436.12092.

Schiere, Richard, Leonce Ndikumana, and Peter Walkenhorst. 2011. *China and Africa: An Emerging Partnership for Development?* ed. R. Schiere, L. Ndikumana and P. Walkenhorst. Abidjan: African Development Bank Group.

Schmidt, Heide-Irene. 2003. Pushed to the Front: The Foreign Assistance Policy of the Federal Republic of Germany, 1958–1971. *Contemporary European History* 12 (4): 473–507. https://doi.org/10.2307/20081179.

Schraeder, Peter J., Steven W. Hook, and Bruce Taylor. 1998. Clarifying the Foreign Aid Puzzle: A Comparison of American, Japanese, French, and Swedish Aid Flows. *World Politics* 50 (2): 294–323. https://doi.org/10.2307/25054039.

Schwalbenberg, Henry M. 1998. Does Foreign Aid Cause the Adoption of Harmful Economic Policies? *Journal of Policy Modeling* 20 (5): 669–675. https://doi.org/10.1016/s0161-8938(97)00111-7.

Scott, James M., and Carie A. Steele. 2011. Sponsoring Democracy: The United States and Democracy Aid to the Developing World, 1988–2001. *International Studies Quarterly* 55 (1): 47–69. https://doi.org/10.2307/23019513.

Sekidde, Serufusa. 2013. A Record of Aid to Uganda. *China Healthcare Workforce* (10): 33–34.

Sen, Amartya. 2006. The Man Without a Plan: Can Foreign Aid Work? *Foreign Affairs* 85 (2):171–177. https://doi.org/10.2307/20031920.

Severino, Jean-Michel, and Olivier Ray. 2009. The End of ODA: Death and Rebirth of a Global Public Policy, vol. 167. Working Paper, Center for Global Development.

Severino, Jean-Michel, and Olivier Ray. 2010. The End of ODA (Ii): The Birth of Hypercollective Action, vol. 218. Working Paper, Center for Global Development.

Shen, Gordon C., and Victoria Y. Fan. 2014. China's Provincial Diplomacy to Africa: Applications to Health Cooperation. *Contemporary Politics* 20: 182–208. https://doi.org/10.1080/13569775.2014.907993.

Shi, Yunyu. 2010. Medicine in China's Foreign Health Aid. *Strait Pharmaceutical Journal* 8: 275–277.

Shu, Yunguo. 2010. China's Aid to Africa: History, Theory and Characteristics. *Journal of Shanghai Normal University* (Philosophy & Social Sciences Edition) 5: 83–89.

Siringi, S. 2003. Africa and China Join Forces to Combat Malaria. *The Lancet* 362. https://doi.org/10.1016/s0140-6736(03)14105-0.

Smith, Clark. 2010. *Ineffectiveness of Official Development Assistance in Ethiopia and Sudan*. Rochester: Social Science Research Network. SSRN-ID2317463.

Smith, Nicholas T. 2010. Africa's Freedom Railway: How a Chinese Development Project Changed Lives and Livelihoods in Tanzania. *African Studies Quarterly* 11 (2/3): 174–176.

Song, Yanmei. 2013. Characteristics of Russian Development Aid: Comparison with the Soviet Union Period. *Russian Studies* 4: 150–171.

Song, Wei. 2014. China in Africa: Innovative Mechanisms to Meet Challenges. *International Business Daily*, April 7, A07.

Stein, Howard. 1994. Theories of Institutions and Economic Reform in Africa. *World Development* 22 (12): 1833–1849. https://doi.org/10.1016/0305-750X(94)90177-5.

Stein, Howard. 2002. Chinese Aid and African Development: Exporting Green Revolution. *Africa: Journal of the International African Institute* 72 (1): 164–166.

Stierman, E., F. Ssengooba, and S. Bennett. 2013. Aid Alignment: A Longer Term Lens on Trends in Development Assistance for Health in Uganda. *Global Health* 9 (1): 7. https://doi.org/10.1186/1744-8603-9-7.

Stiles, Kendall W. 1990. IMF Conditionality: Coercion or Compromise? *World Development* 18 (7): 959–974. https://doi.org/10.1016/0305-750X(90)90079-D.

Stokke, Olav. 1995. *Aid and Political Conditionality.* London: F. Cass, in association with The European Association of Development Research and Training Institutes (EADI).

Strauss, Julia C. 2009. The Past in the Present: Historical and Rhetorical Lineages in China's Relations with Africa. *The China Quarterly* 199: 777–795. https://doi.org/10.1017/s0305741009990208.

Strauss, Julia C., and Martha Saavedra. 2009. *China and Africa: Emerging Patterns in Globalization and Development*, No. 9. Cambridge: Cambridge University Press.

Sumner, Andrew, and Richard Mallett. 2013. *The Future of Foreign Aid: Development Cooperation and the New Geography of Global Poverty.* New York: Palgrave Macmillan.

Sun, Xian. 2013. Research on Medical Aid from Shandong to Africa. Master's Thesis, Shandong University.

Sun, Yun. 2014. Africa in China's Foreign Policy. Washington, DC: Brookings Institution Press.

Szmant, H.H. 1978. Foreign Aid Support of Science and Economic Growth. *Science* 199 (4334): 1173–1182.

Tang, Xioayang. 2013. Evolution and Effect of China's Agricultural Aid to Africa. *World Economy and Politics* 5: 55–69.

Tang, Lixia, Jin Wu, and Xiaoyun Li. 2011. International Aid for Agricultural Development in Africa. *World Agriculture* 7: 51–56.

Tao, Duanfang. 2011. India Follow China's Path in Africa. *World Vision* 12: 22–23.

Taw, Jennifer Morrison. 2011. Distributive Domestic Response. *Review of International Studies* 37 (3): 1357–1382. https://doi.org/10.2307/23025424.

The State Council. 1962. Joint Bulletin of the People's Republic of China and Uganda on the Establishment of Diplomatic Relations. *State Council Gazette* 11: 218.

The State Council. 1965. Joint Communique of China and Uganda. *State Council Gazette* 9: 144–146.

The State Council. 2006. China and Uganda Issued Joint Communique. *People's Daily*, June 25, P3.

Thérien, Jean-Philippe. 2002. Debating Foreign Aid: Right Versus Left. *Third World Quarterly* 23 (3): 449–466. https://doi.org/10.2307/3993536.

Tingley, Dustin. 2010. Donors and Domestic Politics: Political Influences on Foreign Aid Effort. *The Quarterly Review of Economics and Finance* 50 (1): 40–49. https://doi.org/10.1016/j.qref.2009.10.003.

Tull, Denis M. 2006. China's Engagement in Africa: Scope, Significance and Consequences. *The Journal of Modern African Studies* 44 (3): 459–479. https://doi.org/10.2307/3876304.

Uganda, African Development Bank, Australia, Germany, The Netherlands, Norway, Sweden, United Kingdom and The World Bank. 2005. The Uganda Joint Assistance Strategy. Kampala.

Uganda Bureau of Statistics. 2016. *The National Population and Housing Census2014—Main Report*. Kampala, Uganda.

United Nations. 2016. *African Statistical Yearbook 2016*. Scanprint, Denmark.

USAID. 2015a. *Mass Distribution of Long Lasting Insecticidal Nets for Universal Coverage in Uganda Evaluation Report*. Washington, DC: USAID.

USAID. 2015b. Evaluation Toolkit. Washington, DC: USAID.

Van de Maele, Nathalie, David B. Evans, and Tessa Tan-Torres. 2013. Development Assistance for Health in Africa: Are We Telling the Right Story? *Bulletin of the World Health Organization* 91: 483–490. https://doi.org/10.2471/blt.12.115410.

van de Walle, Nicolas. 2010. Us Policy Towards Africa: The Bush Legacy and the Obama Administration. *African Affairs* 109 (434): 1–21. https://doi.org/10.2307/40388444.

Vuving, Alexander. 2009. *How Soft Power Works*. Rochester, NY: Social Science Research Network. SSRN: 1466220.

Walker, Brian W. 1986. The African Environment and the Aid Process. *International Journal* 41 (4): 734–747.

Wang, Xinying. 2009. Adjustment of EU's Policy on Aid to Africa. *Asia & Africa Review* 4: 45–49.

Wang, Xinying. 2011. A Comparative Study of EU and China's Policy on Aid to Africa. *Asia & Africa Review* 1: 50–54.

Wang, Liang. 2012. Research on Rockefeller Foundation's Agricultural Aid to Black Africa (1952–1972). Master's Thesis, East China Normal University.

Wang, Ping. 2012. Review of Japan's Development Aid to Non-Governmental Organizations: From the Perspective of Diplomatic Strategy. *Foreign Affairs Review—Journal of China Foreign Affairs University* 6: 113–126.

Wang, Qingqing. 2012. A Comparative Study of Aid to Africa from China and Japan Since the 21st Century. Master's Thesis, Huazhong Normal University.

Wang, Yuhong. 2012. Cooperation and Development: A Study on China's Aid to Africa. Doctoral Dissertation, Jilin University.

Wang, Xinying. 2013. Achievements and Challenges of China's Aid to Africa. *International Study Reference* 7: 23–28.

Wang, Chao, and Shanggang Liang. 2010. China's Aid to Africa: Improving People's Lives through Practical Work. *Outlook Weekly* 48: 28–30.

Wang, Yanlei, and Wei Lei. 2013. Framework Analysis of the Paris Declaration. *Journal of Beijing Union University* (Humanities and Social Sciences Edition) 2: 125–128.

Wang, Lijuan, and Xinru Jiang. 2014. The Influence and Essential Evaluation of the United States' Aid to Africa. *Pacific Journal* 2: 52–62.

Wang, Xiangcheng, and Tao Sun. 2014. China's Engagement in Global Health Governance: A Critical Analysis of China's Assistance to the Health Sector of Africa. *Journal of Global Health* 4 (1): 010301. https://doi.org/10.7189/jogh.04.010301.

Wang, K., S. Gimbel, E. Malik, S. Hassen, and A. Hagopian. 2012. The Experience of Chinese Physicians in the National Health Diplomacy Programme Deployed to Sudan. *Glob Public Health* 7 (2): 196–211. https://doi.org/10.1080/17441692.2011.594450.

Warmerdam, Ward, and Meine Pieter van Dijk. 2013. Chinese Stateowned Enterprise Investments in Uganda: Findings from a Recent Survey of Chinese Firms in Kampala. *Journal of Chinese Political Science* 18 (3): 281–301. https://doi.org/10.1007/s11366-013-9250-6.

Watson, Helena. 2009. Aid, Aid Everywhere but Still Not a Drop in the Sink. *British Medical Journal* 338 (7688): 239. https://doi.org/10.2307/20511889.

Wei, Xuemei. 2011. China's Aid to Africa and Improvement of China's Soft Power. *Journal of University of International Relations* 1: 31–36.

Wen, Cuiping. 2014. A Comparative Study of Aid to Africa from China and India in the 21st Century. Master's Thesis, China Foreign Affairs University.

Wilson III, Ernest J. 1993. French Support for Structural Adjustment Programs in Africa. *World Development* 21 (3): 331–347. https://doi.org/10.1016/0305-750x(93)90148-3.

Winters, Matthew S. 2010. Accountability, Participation and Foreign Aid Effectiveness. *International Studies Review* 12 (2): 218–243. https://doi.org/10.1111/j.1468-2486.2010.00929.x.

Winters, Matthew S., and Gina Martinez. 2015. The Role of Governance in Determining Foreign Aid Flow Composition. *World Development* 66: 516–531. https://doi.org/10.1016/j.worlddev.2014.09.020.

Woods, Ngaire. 2005. The Shifting Politics of Foreign Aid. *International Affairs (Royal Institute of International Affairs 1944–)* 81 (2): 393–409. https://doi.org/10.2307/3568895.

Woods, Ngaire. 2008. Whose Aid? Whose Influence? China, Emerging Donors and the Silent Revolution in Development Assistance. *International Affairs (Royal Institute of International Affairs 1944–)* 84 (6): 1205–1221. https://doi.org/10.2307/25144989.

Xia, Qingjie, and Yujiang Chen. 2016. Models of Health Aid to Africa in the World and China's Investment in Health Aid to Africa. *International Aid* 2: 18–32.

Xie, Qi, Tian Feng, and Meibo Huang. 2012. Clarify Misunderstandings about China's Foreign Aid. *International Economic Review* 4: 147–157.

Xiao, Yang. 2013. Reputation and Rights: Strategies for Improving China's National Image in North Africa. *Contemporary World* 3: 65–67.

Xie, Qiang. 2012. Aid from China and EU to Africa: Seeking Cooperation in Differences. Master's Thesis, Fudan University.

Xinhua News Agency. 1962. Uganda, a New African Country. *World Knowledge* 21: 2.

Xu, Wenying. 2011. Research on Medical Team from Shanghai to Morocco (1975–1985). Master's Thesis, East China Normal University.

Xu, Guoqing. 2015. An Analysis of New Situation of India-Africa Relations under Modi. *South Asia Studies* 2: 62–80.

Xu, Xiuli, Gubo Qi, and Xiaoyun Li. 2014. Business Borderlands: China's Overseas State Agribusiness. *IDS Bulletin* 45: 114–124. https://doi.org/10.1111/1759-5436.12097.

Xu, Qianlei, Xu Xiangqian, Shiping Xie, Huijun Guo, and Liran Xu. 2016. AIDS Prevention and Treatment with Traditional Chinese Medicine: Practice and Reflection. *Chinese Journal of Traditional Chinese Medicine* 4: 1368–1370.

Yang, Xinjian. 2013. *Forty Years of Dedication: A Collection of Commemorative Essays on the 40th Anniversary of Hebei's Foreign Medical Aid*. Lagos: Academy Press.

Yasutomo, Dennis T. 1989. Why Aid? Japan as an Aid Great Power. *Pacific Affairs* 62 (4): 490–503. https://doi.org/10.2307/2759672.

Yeats, Alexander J. 1982. Development Assistance: Trade Versus Aid and the Relative Performance of Industrial Countries. *World Development* 10 (10): 863–869. https://doi.org/10.1016/0305-750X(82)90061-4.

Yin, Hongwei. 2006. Charm of Chinese Medical Teams to Africa. *South Reviews* 22: 38–41.

Yogo, Urbain Thierry, and Douzounet Mallaye. 2015. Health Aid and Health Improvement in Sub-Saharan Africa: Accounting for the Heterogeneity Between Stable States and Post-conflict States. *Journal of International Development* 27 (7): 1178–1196. https://doi.org/10.1002/jid.3034.

Youde, Jeremy. 2010. China's Health Diplomacy in Africa. *China: An International Journal* 8: 151–163.

Young, Andrew T., and Kathleen M. Sheehan. 2014. Foreign Aid, Institutional Quality, and Growth. *European Journal of Political Economy* 36: 195–208. https://doi.org/10.1016/j.ejpoleco.2014.08.003.

Yu, Weibin. 2014. Research on China's Cultural Soft Power in Non-foreign Policy. Doctoral Dissertation, Wuhan University.

Yuan, Qing. 2013. Chinese Anti-malarial Drugs Are All Reliable. *Xinhua Daily Telegraph*, January 5, P3.

Yuan, Jirong. 2014. Chinese Investment Boosts Uganda's Manufacturing Industry. *People's Daily*, November 23, P21.

Yuan, Jirong, Pengfei Shi, Zimei Fu, Ke Wang, and Hui Cheng. 2013. Chinese Anti-malarial Drugs into Africa Are Not Fake Drugs. *People's Daily*, January 8, P4.

Zafar, Ali. 2007. The Growing Relationship Between China and Sub-Saharan Africa: Macroeconomic, Trade, Investment and Aid Links. *The World Bank Research Observer* 22 (1): 103–130. https://doi.org/10.2307/40282338.

Zalanga, Samuel. 2014. Rural Development in Africa: An International Political Economy Perspective on the Significance of Healthcare in Human Development. *Journal of Third World Studies* 31 (1): 17–50.

Zhang, Yuhui. 2006. Research on China's Foreign Aid. Doctoral Dissertation, Central Party School.

Zhang, Xiangdong. 2007. Western Misunderstanding of China's Africa Policy and Practice. *Peace and Development* 1: 52–54.

Zhang, Chun. 2010. Medical Diplomacy and Cultivation of Soft Power: A Case Study of Chinese Medical Teams to Africa. *Modern International Relations* 3: 49–53.

Zhang, Guangrong. 2011. UK Aid to Africa: Overview, Characteristics and Influencing Factors. *Journal of International Economic Cooperation* 5: 38–42.

Zhang, Haibing. 2012. Development-Oriented Aid: A Study of China's Model of Aid to Africa. *World Economic Research* 12: 78–83.

Zhang, Yuting. 2014. Aid Effectiveness Research within the Framework of the Paris Declaration: A Case Study of Aid to Ethiopia's Education. *Comparative Education Review* 12: 86–91.

Zhang, Zhen. 2016. Teacher Education in Uganda Under Effective Aid Agenda. *Asia-Pacific Education* 4: 270.

Zhang, Yanbing, and Ying Huang. 2012. Differences in Foreign Aid Concepts Between China and the West. *Modern International Relations* 2: 41–47.

Zhang, Xioamin, and Tongquan Sun. 2014. Research one Regulatory System of Britain's Foreign Aid. *Journal of International Economic Cooperation* 5: 50–55.

Zhang, Bin, and Yun Zhang. 2016. The US Foreign Aid and Its Inspiration for China. *World Agriculture* 7: 102–105.

Zhang, Xiaohua, Yi Yang, and Haipeng Guo. 2015. Social Responsibility in Going Global. *Chinese and Foreign Company Culture* 12: 30.

Zheng, Song, and Xiaochen Sun. 2012. International Aid for Education in Uganda: Structure and Effect. *Comparative Education Review* 12: 10–14.

Zhong, Ling, and Xiaoyun Li. 2013. Review of Busan Declaration and Its Latest Progress. *Journal of Guangxi University* (Philosophy and Social Sciences Edition) 2: 95–98.

Zhou, D. 1956. Uganda. *World Knowledge* 10: 23.

Zhou, Haichuan. 2012. Sustainable Development of China-Africa Agricultural Technology Demonstration Centers: Problems and Countermeasures. *China Soft Science* 9: 45–54.

Zhou, Quanfa. 2014. Reflection on Ways towards Sustainable Development of China-Africa Agricultural Technology Demonstration Center. *China Journal of Tropical Agriculture* 10: 101–104.

Zhu, Shan. 1959. Uganda. *World Knowledge* 14: 18–19.

Zhu, Mingzhong. 2005. India and Africa (1947–2004). *South Asia Studies* 1: 20–26.

Ziesemer, Thomas. 2016. The Impact of Development Aid on Education and Health: Survey and New Evidence for Low-Income Countries from Dynamic Models. *Journal of International Development* n/a–n/a. https://doi.org/10.1002/jid.3223.

Zou, Guanyang, Barbara McPake, and Xiaolin Wei. 2014. Chinese Health Foreign Aid and Policy: Beyond Medical Aid. *The Lancet* 383 (9927): 1461–1462. https://doi.org/10.1016/S0140-6736(14)60713-3.

Index

Z. Qiu, *When Friendship Comes First*, China and Globalization 2.0, https://doi.org/10.1007/978-981-32-9308-3

C

CPSIA information can be obtained
at www.ICGtesting.com
Printed in the USA
LVHW041841011219
639064LV00013B/833/P

9 789813 293076